Instant Pot Mini Cookbook

300 Easy and Foolproof Instant Pot Mini Recipes for Your 3-Quart Models

By

Laurel Sanchez

Copyright © 2018 by Laurel Sanchez All rights reserved.

No part of this book may be reproduced in any form You cannot offer this book for free or sell it. You do not have reselling legal rights to this book. This Book may not be recreated in any file format or physical format without having the expressed written approval of author. All Violators will be sued

This declaration is deemed fair and valid by both the American Bar Association and the Committee of Publishers Association and is legally binding throughout the United States

Furthermore, the transmission, duplication or reproduction of any of the following work including specific information will be considered an illegal act irrespective of if it is done electronically or in print. This extends to creating a secondary or tertiary copy of the work or a recorded copy and is only allowed with express written consent from the Publisher. All additional right reserved

Disclaimer: No part of this publication may be reproduced or transmitted in any form or by any means, mechanical or electronic, including photocopying or recording, or by any information storage and retrieval system, or transmitted by email without permission in writing from the publisher.

TABLE OF CONTENTS

Introduction 1
Benefits of Instant Pot 2
Instant Pot Buttons 3
Breakfast Recipes 5

    Strawberry Oatmeal Recipe 5

    Cheesy Mushroom Omelet 5

    Cinnamon Porridge 6

    Breakfast Frittatas 6

    Pistachio Quinoa 7

    Egg and Ham Casserole 7

    Sausage Potato Rice 8

    Sprout Salad 8

    Hard-Boiled Eggs 9

    Banana Buckwheat Porridge 9

    Instant Pot Polenta 9

    Asian Instant Lentils 10

    Bacon Muffins 10

    Sweet Potato Oats 11

    Almond Porridge 11

    Wholesome Peach Oats Breakfast 11

    Quinoa Porridge 12

    Quinoa Salad 12

    Spiced Pilaf 13

    Mango Rice 13

    Mashed Potatoes 14

    Green Been Mushroom Recipe 14

    Carrot Cake Oatmeal Breakfast 15

    Lentil Potato Rice 15

    Asparagus Risotto 16

Sweet Potato Hash Breakfast 16

Quinoa with Peaches 17

Buttery Polenta 17

Pumpkin Cinnamon Oats 18

Cherry Apple Risotto 18

Poultry Recipes 19

Shredded Chicken with Mayo Sauce 19

Greek Style Turkey Recipe 19

Spicy Herbs Wrapped Chicken 20

Steamed Chicken Wings 21

Instant Honey Chicken 21

Sweet Brown Chicken 22

California Style Chicken 22

Tangy and Spicy Honey Chicken 23

Chicken Curry with Zucchinis 23

Chicken Thighs with Rice 24

Chipotle Salsa Chicken 25

Garlic Chicken Thighs 25

BBQ Chicken 26

Lemongrass Coconut Chicken 26

Turkey Stacks 27

Quick Dumplings 27

Garlic Chicken 28

Butter Chicken 28

Instant Chicken Wings 29

Apple Turkey Curry Recipe 29

Chicken in Mushroom Sauce 30

Tasty Cajun Chicken with Rice 31

Cheesy Chicken Bowl 32

Pancetta and Chicken Risotto 32

Turkey Meatballs Recipe 33

Hungarian Style Chicken 33

Chicken and Coca Cola 34

Steamed Chicken Thigh 35

Turkey Meatloaf BBQ 35

Lemon Chicken 36

Buttermilk Chicken Rosemary 37

Spiced Chicken Breats 37

Cornish Hens with Gravy 38

Cranberry Turkey Recipe 38

Potato Chicken 39

Yellow Chicken 39

Tomato Turkey Meal 40

Pasta Chicken 41

Spicy and Sweet Honey Chicken 41

Rosemary Turkey Paprika 42

Special Turkey Breasts 42

BBQ Chicken Sliders 43

Spaghetti Squash with Chicken 43

Chicken Teriyaki 44

Lemon Chicken with Kalamata Olives 45

Beef Recipes 46

Hearty Beef Stew 46

Asian Beef Stew 46

Beef and Pasta 47

Beef Potato Tots 47

Western Beef Recipe 48

Spicy Sliced Beef 48

Cheesy Beef Pie 49

Sour Spice Beef Brisket 49

Peppercorns Beef 50

Spicy Beef Tenderloin 50

Beef Lasagna 51

Beef Stroganoff 51

Red Beef Balls 52

Sweet Beef 52

Beef Curry Stew Recipe 53

Beef Black Pepper 54

French Style Beef Chuck Roast 54

Steamed Ground Beef Vegetables 55

Delightful Red Wine Flank Steak 55

Beef Meatballs 56

Beef Meatloaf 56

Coffee Pulled Beef 57

Cheesy Beef Roll 57

Beef Bulgogi Tender 58

Beef Bourguignon 58

Beef Sirloin Recipe 59

Cheesy Beef Casserole 59

Beef Fritters in Gravy 60

Coconut Spiced Beef 60

Beef Teriyaki 61

Tomato Beef Stew 62

Beef Polenta 62

Sweet Beef Ribs in Sweet Gravy 63

Pork Recipes 64

Lettuce Pork Wraps Recipe 64

Pork Congee 64

Pulled Pork Garlic 65

Pulled Pork BBQ 65

Honey Glazed Pork Roast Recipe 66

Pork in Coconut Gravy 66

Pork Stew with Canola 67

Pork Bites Oregano	67
Rice and Ham Treat	68
Pork Chili Tomato	68
Pork Belly Paprika	69
Pineapple Pork	69
Sweet Pork Tender	70
Classic Sweet Pork Ribs	70
Juicy Pork Chops	71
Saucy Pork Meatballs	71
Green Chili Pork Stew Recipe	72
Pork Fritter	72
Cheesy Pork Bombs	73
Cheesy Pork Macaroni	73
Spicy and Sour Pork Ribs	74
Pork Baby Back Ribs	74
Taco Pork Bowl Recipe	75
Loin Pork with Herbed Butter and Veggies	75
Pork Stew in Sweet Ginger Soy	76
Mustard Pork Chops	76
Lime Ginger Pork	77
Pork Roast Rosemary	77
Garlic Pork Rinds	78
Spicy Pork Ribs	78
Pork Ribs Barbecue	79
Pulled Pork	79
Pork Chops with Cinnamon	80
Mushroom Tomato Pork Meatloaf	80
Pork Sausages and Mushrooms Recipe	81
Tropical Pork Stew	81
Pork and Beef Gumbo Recipe	82
BBQ Pork Ribs Recipe	82

Soups and Stews 83

- Chicken and Radish Soup 83
- Celery Soup 83
- Coconut Squash Soup 84
- Chicken Zucchini Noodles Soup 84
- Black Bean Soup 85
- Thai Style Chicken Soup 85
- Lentils Chicken Soup 86
- Salmon Stew 86
- Carrot Tarragon Soup Recipe 86
- Pork Ribs Soup with Green Collard 87
- Onion Soup 87
- Chicken Noodle Soup 88
- Sweet Potato Stew 88
- Chicken and Vegetable Soup 89
- Beef Soup 89
- Oxtail Soup 90
- Chicken Mushroom Soup 90
- Creamy Cauliflower Soup 91
- Mexican Style Beef Soup 91
- Spicy Beef Soup 92
- Carrot Soup 92
- Tomato Soup 93
- Chicken Corn Soup 93
- Carrot Soup 94
- Salmon Soup with Basil 94
- Cheesy Broccoli Soup 95
- Beef in Turmeric Yellow Soup 95
- Beef Stew 96
- Elbow Pasta Soup 96
- Pork Soup 97

Chicken Soup 97

Delightful Goulash 98

Beef Stew 98

Cabbage Tomato Soup 99

Chicken Lentil Soup 99

Fish and Seafood 100

Mahi Mahi Fillets 100

Sour and Sweet Fish 100

Dijon Lemon Whitefish 100

Ricotta and Tomatoes Shrimps Recipe 101

Tasty Spicy Mussels Mania 101

Simple Swordfish Fra Diavolo 102

Coconut Scallops Curry Recipe 102

Raspberry Sauce Salmon Recipe 103

Steamed Tilapia 103

Broccoli Salmon Meal 104

Sweet Caramel Salmon 104

Fish Boil 105

Asian Salmon 105

Honey Shrimps 106

Shrimp Scampi 106

Mussels Tomatino 107

Steamed Clams 107

Bacon and Clam Chowder 107

Sesame Anchovies 108

Cheesy Crab Quiche 108

Mussel Garlic 109

Lobster Meat with Mayo 109

Sweet Brown Calamari 110

Savory Crab Legs 110

Garlic Lemon Shrimp 111

Rosemary Salmon Recipe 111

White Wine Haddock 112

Mushroom Stuffed Squids 112

Coconut Shrimp Curry 113

Salmon Dinner 113

Braised Cod 113

Salmon Rice 114

Chili Snapper 114

Calamari with Anchovies 115

Thai Style Scallops with Oranges 115

Flavors Cod Recipe 116

Tuna in Red Sauce 116

Masala Shrimps Curry 117

Jalapeno Shrimp 117

Delightful Paella 118

Fried Sea Bass 118

Classic Crab Cakes with Roasted Pepper Sauce 119

Parmesan Tilapia Recipe 119

Salmon with Dill 120

Tasty Tangy Crabs 120

Soy Honey Shrimps 121

Orange Steamed Salmon 121

Scallop Ginger with Maple Syrup 122

Coconut Fish Curry 122

Marinated Shrimps 123

Snacks and Appetizers 124

Eggplant Tomato Spread 124

Bacon Muffins 124

Asparagus Lemon Snack 125

Spicy Potato Appetizer 125

Sweet Brussels 126

Jalapeno Dip 126

Amazing Artichoke Dip with Nachos 127

Instant Asparagus 127

Sweet Honey Carrots 128

Soy Garlic Tofu 128

Simple Garlic Hummus 129

Eggplant and Green beans 129

Vegetable Dishes 130

Tomato Soup Black Pepper 130

Penne Pasta Primavera 130

Mushroom Balls in Coconut Mushroom Gravy 131

Eggplant and Olives Spread 131

Eggplant Tomato Curry Stew 132

Quick Mac and Cheese 132

Cheesy Zucchini Noodles 133

Veg Rigatoni Bolognese 133

Spinach in Cheese Gravy 134

Delightful Quinoa Mixed Vegetable 135

Cabbage with Apple Sauce 135

Lentil Curry Recipe 136

Healthy Black Beans 136

Sweet Potato Chili 137

Chickpea Broccoli 138

Steamed Artichokes Recipe 138

Tasty Baked Ziti 139

Veg Stew Ratatouille 139

Walnut Beets Bowl 140

Zuppa Toscana Recipe 140

Classic Lentil Gumbo 141

Green Beans Stew 141

Cheesy Asparagus Garlic 142

- Green Beans Stir Fry 142
- Quinoa Burrito Bowls Recipe 143
- Quick Peas Risotto 143
- Mushroom Soup Recipe 144
- butternut Squash and Mushroom Meal 144
- Garbanzo Beans and Potato 145
- Glazed Cinnamon Honey Carrots 145
- Spinach and Fusilli Pasta 146
- Mushroom Risotto 146
- Buttery Green Beans Recipe 147
- Carrots with Dill 147
- Cauliflower Florets 148
- Brussels sprouts Tender 148
- Mushroom and Navy Bean 149
- Tuscan Pasta Recipe 149
- Spicy Cabbage Wedges 150
- Tomato Eggplant and Cheese Lasagna 150

Desserts 151

- Tasty Tapioca Pudding 151
- Honey Yogurt Panna Cotta 151
- Plain Banana Bread Recipe 152
- Chocolate Ramekins 152
- Pumpkin Pie 153
- Delightful Brownies 153
- Pumpkin Cake 154
- Mix Berry Cheesecake 154
- New Cheese-cake 155
- Nutty Chocolate Fudge Balls 155
- Raisin Apples 156
- Fruit Bowl 156
- Oreo Crust Cheese-cake 157

Wine Pears 157

Introduction

Instant pot is a trend in the market for a new style of cooking. It makes your life more convenient and easier. People usually do not have enough time to cook nowadays, which is why they prefer quick cooking, and here is where the help of instant pot comes in! It helps you make food in just a few minutes, without putting in extra effort. Anyone who cooks with an instant pot will surely not get tired!

All the recipes are easy to make with the simple ingredients found in your kitchen all the time. Pick the best recipes you like and start cooking with Instant pot now. You will be amazed at how simple it is to use. The machine plays with you, but you need to make sure to handle it with care. It gives you healthy food with all the nutrients your body requires. You can cook a week's food and keep it stored in your fridge with the help of this machine.

Instant pot makes life easier by giving quick results to its users. Any recipe can be cooked in the instant pot. If you do not have enough time in the morning, then all you need is a quick recipe for breakfast with the instant pot. Learn the recipes now, so you do not have an empty stomach when you leave for work or school.

You can cook in instant pot the whole day and you still won't be able to get enough of this awesome innovation. It is designed beautifully and creates less hassle for people who do not have enough time to cook.

The recipes are short and easy to understand. Anyone can make the recipes with the instant pot. You just need to know the right measurements, and you will have a great recipe ready for you. You do not have to deal with fire or flames on the stoves; instant pot has made life easier for the people now. Once you know how to cook with instant pot, you will want to cook with it every time. There are a variety of recipes found in this book to try, so get started now, without wasting any time!

Once you get your hands on instant pot, you will be so pleased that you will want to cook every dish in this pot. This is an amazing product for working people who cannot take the time to cook food. If you are worried that the taste will change if you cook in this pot, do not be concerned about that. You simply have to add all the ingredients in the pot and it will give you great results within few minutes.

Benefits of Instant Pot

1. Saves Energy: No more excessive gas or electricity bills when you welcome the instant pot into your household. Compared to other household appliances that do the same job as the Instant Pot, you can find yourself saving up to 70% on energy bills. Being innately pressurized, moisture is retained in foods and any water that you put in will stay, thus cutting water needs for cooking

2. Fast Cooking: Cooking under a pressurized appliance will make sure the cooking conditions are stable. Because of this, the times needed to fully cook your meal have been cut down significantly. Soon enough, you'll have more time than you know how to deal with

3. Preserves Nutrients in Cooking: Since the ingredients aren't cooked in too much excess water, coupled with the pressurized conditions, very little in the way of nutrients is lost in the process of cooking or via evaporation. Also, with little air exposure, food is not as easily oxidized

4. Safety: Today's pressure cookers are worked with the client's security on a fundamental level. It might have been awful and regularly detonated in the prior days when our mom used them yet present day variations are substantially more secure to use with their implicit layers and wellbeing highlights which can without much of a stretch return any risk

5. Delayed Cooking: The feature of delayed cooking helps the food to stay warm and moist when in the pot. Everyone loves to serve hot and delicious food and thus, the instant pot has the delayed cooking feature which keeps the food warm until it gets served. No need to reheat the food and burn more energy

6. Smart Built-In Features and Programming: If you watch the pictures of the instant pot, you will find up to 14 in-built features which are advanced in every aspect as well as completely exceptional! These smart features allow you to cook different foods at different temperatures. This maintains the texture, taste and nutritional value of the food.

Prepare yogurt, slow cook your rice, steam your foods, warm your food, sauté vegetables or prepare your delicious soups and so much more with a click of a single button!

7. Makes Your Meals Taste Better: There are definitely no two routes about this. The pressure cooker cooks your sustenance at higher temperatures route past what can be accomplished by most ordinary cookers. This empowers it to draw out more flavors from the sustenance. Improving it taste a considerable measure.

8. Easy Cleaning and Maintenance: When you get any cooking appliance, maintenance is your first concern. The appliances can get irremovable stains and can also get scratches with the usage of dishwashers! In case of instant pot, you don't have to worry about the maintenance. Just wash it with a gel and wiper or you can also use your dishwasher. It supports quick and easy cleaning

Instant Pot Buttons

You've probably noticed that your instant pot has a ton of buttons. It seems like a lot, but there are various uses for this. This section will go over the buttons you use the most.

Manual / Pressure Buttons: This is probably going to be the buttons you use most on the Instant Pot. It will allow you to pressure cook and manually select the time you want – rather than the preset buttons (such as Soup/Stew or Meat buttons). You can adjust the pressure, temperature and time by selecting the "+/- "buttons

Sauté: this is the one that you can use to brown your food, but along with that, you can use it to help cook and thicken stews and soups. You should use this with the lid off, and you can adjust it to more or less to a simmer.

Keep Warm Button: When pressure cooking is done, the Instant Pot will beep and automatically go into the "Keep Warm" function. It will display an "L" in front of a number to indicate how long it's been warm – e.g. "L0:30" for 30 minutes. It's a great feature to keep food warm for up to 99 hours, 50 minutes. It's perfect for pot lucks

Cancel Button: At any time, you can cancel cooking and return to standby mode by pressing the "Keep Warm" / "Cancel" button. This is a great option if you selected the wrong time for pressure cooking and need to stop to make adjustments to the pressure or time

There are specific buttons as well that are important to know about when using the instant pot, and they are listed as follows:

Meat/Stew: Make your favorite stew or meat dish in the Instant Pot. Adjust the settings depending on the texture you want. For instance, the "More" setting is better for fall-off-the-bone cooking

It will default to a High Pressure for 35 minutes. You can adjust for "More" to High Pressure for 45 minutes or "Less" for High Pressure for 20 minutes

Soup: As the name implies, the "Soup" button is used to make soups, broth or stock in the instant pot. Its preset in such a way that the Instant Pot controls the pressure and temperature at the same time so that the liquid doesn't boil heavily. By default, the time is set to 30 minutes cook time. You can adjust this based on the recipe instruction. You can also change the pressure to either low or high.

Bean/Chili: Use for black beans, kidney beans, or whatever beans you can think of. It's so much much faster (and tastier) in it. By default the "Bean / Chili" button, is set to 30 minutes on High Pressure. You can adjust for "More" to get 40 minutes on High Pressure or "Less" for 25 minutes on High Pressure.

Rice: this cooks on low pressure automatically. This is great for cooking rice, and you can adjust based on the water.

Multigrain: The "Multigrain" button is best for cooking brown and wild rice, which typically takes longer than normal white rice to cook. By default, the "Normal" setting is set to 40 mins pressure cooking time. "Less" setting is 20 mins of pressure cooking time, while "More" is set to 45 minutes of warm water soaking & 60 minutes pressure cooking.

Poultry: When you use this setting, it is important for you to know that it is only to be used for small portions of poultry because it will only cook on high pressure for 15 minutes. You can adjust the timer.

Porridge: The "Porridge" button is used for making rice porridge and other grains (not necessarily white or brown rice). It is set to cook on High Pressure for 20 minutes by default, which is best for rice porridge. You can adjust this to "More" for 30 minutes on High Pressure or "Less" for High Pressure for 15 minutes.

When the timer down to zero, do not use the QPR (quick release) method. Because it has a high starch content. Using will only amount to you splattering the porridge through the steam release valve. So use the NPR for this purpose.

Steam: this will cook it on high pressure for 10 minutes. In this function, you should have the steamer basket there, and it will be at full power the entire time, which means you don't want the food to be directed at the bottom. Often, once it reaches the highest pressure, it'll cycle the pressure again.

Yogurt: this is used for making yogurt in separate jars.

Slow cook: This is one great features that allow you to use your Instant Pot electric pressure cooker like a slower cooker. Just add all the recipe ingredients as you normally would to a slow cooker into you instant pot and close the lid. Press the "Slow Cook" button, adjust the time, and that's all. By default, the time is set to 4-hours slow cook time. You can make changes to this by using the "+/- "adjust buttons.

Timer: this is for delayed cooking. To use this, choose a function, make adjustments, and then adjust with the plus and minus buttons.

All of these specific functions can be changed with the plus and minus buttons, changing the default cooking time, so it cooks the food effectively.

You should try to consider ones that typically have the manual setting so that you can adjust the time. When you're ready, you can move to more specific ones, allowing you to create more food.

Breakfast Recipes

Strawberry Oatmeal Recipe

(Prep + Cooking Time: 25 minutes | Serves: 3)

Ingredients:
- 1 ½ cup fresh and sliced strawberries
- 1 cup steel cut oats
- 1 tablespoon butter
- 4 tablespoon chia seeds
- 3 tablespoon brown sugar
- 1/4 cup cream
- 4 cup water
- 1/4 teaspoon salt

Directions:
1. Add butter into the instant pot and set the pot on sauté mode.
2. Once butter is melted then add oats and stir constantly for 3 minutes.
3. Add water, brown sugar, cream; and salt. Stir well.
4. Seal pot with lid and select *HIGH* pressure for 10 minutes.
5. Allow releasing pressure naturally then Open the lid; Add chia seeds and strawberries. Stir well.

Nutrition Facts: Calories: 246, Fat: 10.3g, Carbs: 37.4g, Protein: 6.3g

Cheesy Mushroom Omelet

(Prep + Cooking Time: 15 minutes | Serves: 4)

Ingredients:
- 1 ½ cup sliced mushrooms
- 5 lightly beaten eggs
- 2 tablespoon Minced chives
- 1/2 cup coconut milk
- 2 tablespoon Butter
- 1/2 tablespoon cheddar cheese
- 1 chopped bell pepper
- 1 chopped onion

Directions:
1. Add butter into the instant pot and set the pot on sauté mode, In a bowl; add eggs and beat until well combined.
2. Add remaining ingredients and mix well. Pour egg mixture into the instant pot and cook for 2 minutes.
3. Seal pot with lid and select *HIGH* pressure for 8 minutes.
4. Release pressure using quick release method than open the lid. Serve hot and enjoy.

Nutrition Facts: Calories: 229, Fat: 18.9g, Carbs: 7.8g, Protein: 9.4g

Cinnamon Porridge

(Prep + Cooking Time: 28 minutes | Serves: 2)

Ingredients:
- 1 (1¼-pound) whole squash
- 2 medium apples; cored and chopped roughly
- 1/2 teaspoon ground cinnamon
- ⅛ teaspoon ground ginger
- ⅛ teaspoon ground cloves
- 1/2 cup chicken broth
- 2 tablespoons maple syrup
- 2 tablespoons gelatin
- Pinch of salt

Directions:
1. Switch on the pot after placing it on a clean and dry platform.
2. Open the pot lid and place the squash, apples, broth and spices in the cooking pot area. Give the ingredients a little stir. Close the pot by closing the top lid. Also, ensure to seal the valve.
3. Press *Manual* cooking function and set cooking time to 8 minutes. It will start cooking after a few minutes. Let the pot mix cook under pressure until the timer reads zero.
4. Press *Cancel* cooking function and press *Natural release* setting. It will take 8-10 minutes for natural pressure release.
5. Open the pot. Cool down the mixture and then transfer the squash onto a cutting board. Cut the squash in half lengthwise and discard the seeds.
6. In a blender, add the squash, apple mixture from the pot, maple syrup, gelatin and salt. Blend on a pulse mode until smooth. Serve warm.

Nutrition Facts:
Calories: 312; Fat: 0.8g; Carbohydrates: 44g; Fiber: 9g; Protein 13.5g

Breakfast Frittatas

(Prep + Cooking Time: 15 minutes | Serves: 3)

Ingredients:
- 1 chopped scallion
- 1 chopped zucchini
- 4 tablespoon shredded cheddar cheese
- 2 cooked bacon slices
- 1/4 teaspoon lemon pepper seasoning
- 3 eggs
- 1/4 cup almond milk
- Pepper and Salt to taste

Directions:
1. Pour water into the instant pot (approximately 1 cup) and then place trivet into the pot.
2. Add all ingredients into the bowl and whisk well to combine.
3. Pour mixture into the silicone molds and place on top of the trivet, Seal pot with lid and select *HIGH* pressure for 5 minutes.
4. Release pressure using quick release method than open the lid. Serve immediately and enjoy.

Nutrition Facts:
Calories: 228, Fat: 17.7g, Carbs: 4.5g, Protein: 13.9g

Pistachio Quinoa

(Prep + Cooking Time: 11 minutes | Serves: 2)

Ingredients:
- 3/4 cup white quinoa
- 1/8 cup pistachios; chopped
- 3 tablespoons blueberries
- 1/8 cup raisins
- 1/2 cup apple juice
- 1/2 cup plain yogurt
- 1/2 cup apples; grated
- 1/2 tablespoon honey
- 3/4 cup water
- 1 small cinnamon stick

Directions:
1. Rinse the quinoa and strain gently using a fine mesh strainer.
2. Switch on the pot after placing it on a clean and dry platform. Open the pot lid and place the water, quinoa and cinnamon stick in the cooking pot area.
3. Close the pot by closing the top lid. Also, ensure to seal the valve.
4. Press *Manual* cooking function and set cooking time to 1 minutes. It will start cooking after a few minutes. Let the pot mix cook under pressure until the timer reads zero.
5. Press *Cancel* cooking function and press *Natural release* setting. It will take 8-10 minutes for natural pressure release.
6. Open the pot. Spoon the quinoa into a bowl and remove the cinnamon stick.
7. Mix in the apple, apple juice, raisins and honey. Refrigerate for at least 1 hour or overnight.
8. Add the yogurt and stir well. Top with the pistachio and blueberries. Serve warm!

Nutrition Facts: Calories: 418; Fat: 6.5g; Carbohydrates: 44.5g; Fiber: 7g; Protein 14g

Egg and Ham Casserole

(Prep + Cooking Time: 30 minutes | Serves: 6)

Ingredients:
- 2 cup Cheddar cheese; shredded
- 1/2 diced onion
- 4 red potatoes
- 1 cup whole milk
- 1 teaspoon pepper
- 10 eggs
- 1 cup ham; chopped
- 1 teaspoon salt

Directions:
1. Spray the inside of the Mini Instant Pot with cooking spray. For the insert, you can use a glass bowl which fits into the mini pot.
2. Pour the milk and eggs inside the insert or bowl and continue to whisk them until they blend perfectly. Gradually, put the potatoes, onions, ham, salt, pepper and cheese with the eggs.
3. Mix everything till to ensure they are coated with egg mixture. Now you need to cover the bowl with a foil.
4. Place the steam rack inside the Mini Instant Pot and add 2 cups of water. Now you need to put the foil-covered bowl on the rack.
5. Close the lid of the pot and push the Manual button. Set the timer at 25 minutes.
6. Once the cooking is done, you have to do a quick release and remove the lid immediately, so that pressure releases fast.
7. Now take out the casserole and serve it with your favorite toppings.
8. The choice of toppings can range from avocado, salsa, cheese tomatoes, pepper; and salt.
9. Enjoy the freshly cooked casserole this hearty breakfast will definitely kick-start your day.

Nutrition Facts: Calories: 205, Fat: 14.3g, Carbs: 5.1g, Protein: 12g

Sausage Potato Rice

(Prep + Cooking Time: 18 minutes | Serves: 3)

Ingredients:
- 2 lean sausages; thinly sliced
- 4 slices ginger
- 5 small yellow potatoes; peeled
- 1 ½ tablespoon green onion; finely chopped
- 1/6 teaspoon black pepper; ground
- 1 ½ tablespoon olive oil
- 2 cups long grain rice
- 1 tablespoon green onion; finely chopped
- 1/4 teaspoon chicken broth mix
- 3 cups water
- 1 teaspoon salt

Directions:
1. Place your Instant Pot on a flat kitchen surface', plug it and turn it on.
2. To start making the recipe, press *Sauté* button. Add the oil, onions and ginger; cook for 2 minutes to soften the ingredients.
3. Now add the sausages and cook for 1-2 minutes. Add the potatoes and continue cooking for another 2 minutes. Then after, mix in the rice and stir to combine.
4. Add the remaining ingredients and carefully close its lid and firmly lock it. Then after, seal the valve too.
5. To start making the recipe, press *Rice* button. Now you have to set cooking time', set the timer for 4 minutes. Allow the pot to cook the mixture until the timer goes off.
6. Turn off the pot and press *Cancel.* Allow the built up pressure to vent out naturally', it will take 8-10 minutes to completely release inside pressure.
7. Open its lid and transfer the cooked mixture into serving container/containers. Garnish with green onion and serve.

Nutrition Facts:
Calories: 377; Fat: 12g; Carbohydrates: 55.6g; Fiber: 4g; Protein 13.7g

Sprout Salad

(Prep + Cooking Time: 15 minutes | Serves: 3)

Ingredients:
- 1–pound Brussels sprouts
- 2 tablespoon Pomegranate seeds
- 1 cup crumbled feta cheese
- 2 tablespoon Melted butter
- 1/4 cup chopped cashew nuts

Directions:
1. Pour a cup water into your instant pot and place trivet into the pot.
2. Place Brussels sprouts on a trivet. Seal pot with lid and select *HIGH* pressure for 3 minutes.
3. Release pressure using quick release method than open the lid.
4. Transfer Brussels sprouts in a bowl and drizzle with melted butter, add remaining ingredients and toss well.

Nutrition Facts:
Calories: 379, Fat: 24.8g, Carbs: 20.2g, Protein: 14.8g

Hard-Boiled Eggs

(Prep + Cooking Time: 6 minutes | Serves: 2)

Ingredients:
- 1 ½ cup water
- 6 eggs

Directions:
1. Pour the water into the pot. Place eggs in the steamer basket and set the basket over the water.
2. Close the lid and set the cook time for 5 minutes on High pressure.
3. After the pressure naturally releases, place the eggs in cold water. Peel when cool enough to handle.

Nutrition Facts:
Calories: 470; Fat: 13.22 g; Carbohydrates: 81.95 g; Fiber: 10.1 g; Protein: 13.04 g

Banana Buckwheat Porridge

(Prep + Cooking Time: 8 minutes | Serves: 2)

Ingredients:
- 1 cup buckwheat groats; rinsed
- 2 tablespoons brown sugar; plus more for serving
- 3 cups milk; plus more for serving
- 1 teaspoon ground cinnamon
- 1 ripe banana; sliced

Directions:
1. Pour the groats, milk, banana, cinnamon and sugar into the Instant Pot.
2. Close the lid and set to 6 minutes on *HIGH* pressure. Serve porridge with additional milk and brown sugar.

Nutrition Facts: Calories: 409; Fat: 12.7 g; Carbohydrates: 62.26 g; Fiber: 4.5 g; Protein: 15.08 g

Instant Pot Polenta

(Prep + Cooking Time: 15 minutes | Serves: 2)

Ingredients:
- 1 bunch green onions
- 2 tablespoons cilantro
- 1/2 teaspoon cumin
- 1 cup broth
- 1/2 teaspoon oregano
- 1 ½ teaspoon chili powder
- 1 cup boiling water
- 1/2 cup cornmeal
- 1 teaspoon garlic; minced
- Pinch of cayenne
- 1/4 teaspoon paprika

Directions:
1. Switch on the pot after placing it on a clean and dry platform. Press *Sauté* cooking function. Open the lid; add some cooking oil, garlic and onions in the pot; cook for 2-3 minutes to cook well and soften.
2. Mix in the broth, cilantro, cornmeal, spices and boiling water. Close the pot by closing the top lid. Also, ensure to seal the valve.
3. Press *Manual* cooking function and set cooking time to 5 minutes. It will start cooking after a few minutes. Let the pot mix cook under pressure until the timer reads zero.
4. Press *Cancel* cooking function and press *Natural release* setting.
5. It will take 8-10 minutes for natural pressure release. Open the pot and serve warm.

Nutrition Facts: Calories: 98; Fat: 1.5g; Carbohydrates: 6g; Fiber: 3g; Protein 4g

Asian Instant Lentils

(Prep + Cooking Time: 55 minutes | Serves: 3)

Ingredients:
- 1 cup whole and split lentils, soaked for 12-14 hours and drained
- 1 teaspoon Garam masala
- 2 tablespoons ghee or butter
- 1 ½ inch ginger; minced
- 6 garlic cloves; minced
- 2 tablespoons avocado oil
- 3 cups water
- 1 large onion; chopped
- 1 tablespoon cumin seeds
- 1 teaspoon turmeric
- 2 tomatoes; chopped
- 1 teaspoon cayenne
- 1 bay leaf
- Cilantro leaves (optional)
- 1/2 teaspoon black pepper
- Salt to taste

Directions:
1. Place your Instant Pot on a flat kitchen surface', plug it and turn it on.
2. To start making the recipe, press *Sauté* button. Add the oil and seeds', cook for 1 minutes', now add the onions and bay leaf; continue cooking for 8-10 minutes to soften the ingredients.
3. Add the spices, ginger, garlic and combine well; add the tomatoes and sauté for 5 more minutes.
4. Add lentils and water and mix the ingredients', carefully close its lid and firmly lock it. Then after, seal the valve too.
5. To start making the recipe, press *Bean/chili* button. Now you have to set cooking time', set the timer for 30 minutes. Allow the pot to cook the mixture until the timer goes off.
6. Turn off the pot and press *Cancel.* Allow the built up pressure to vent out naturally', it will take 8-10 minutes to completely release inside pressure.
7. Open its lid and transfer the cooked mixture into serving container/containers. Add ghee, stir, then garnish with cilantro and serve warm!

Nutrition Facts: Calories 210; Fat: 14g; Carbohydrates: 15g; Fiber: 5.7g; Protein 6.9g

Bacon Muffins

(Prep + Cooking Time: 13 minutes | Serves: 2)

Ingredients:
- 2 crumbled bacon slices
- 1 medium diced onion
- 2 eggs
- 1/4 teaspoon lemon pepper seasoning
- Shredded cheese as needed

Directions:
1. In two silicon molds, separate the cheese, onion and bacon.
2. Beat one of the eggs and pour it into one of the molds. Repeat the process with the other egg.
3. Switch on the pot after placing it on a clean and dry platform.
4. Pour 1 ½ cup water into the pot. Arrange the trivet inside it*, arrange the molds over the trivet.
5. Close the pot by closing the top lid. Also, ensure to seal the valve.
6. Press *Manual* cooking function and set cooking time to 8 minutes. It will start cooking after a few minutes. Let the pot mix cook under pressure until the timer reads zero.
7. Press *Cancel* cooking function and press *Quick release* setting. Open the pot and serve warm.

Nutrition Facts: Calories: 112; Fat: 8g; Carbohydrates: 1g; Fiber: 0g; Protein 9g

Sweet Potato Oats

***(Prep + Cooking Time:** 25 minutes | **Serves:** 2)*

Ingredients:
- 1/2 cup steel cut oats
- 1/4 teaspoon cardamom
- 1/2 teaspoon cinnamon
- 1/2 teaspoon vanilla extract
- 1/4 cup almond milk
- 1/8 teaspoon ginger
- 1 ⅓ cup water
- 2 tablespoon raisins
- 1 cup chopped sweet potato
- Salt to taste

Directions:
1. Add oats, spices, water, raisins; and sweet potato into the instant pot and stir well.
2. Seal pot with lid and select low pressure and set the timer for 15 minutes.
3. Release pressure using the quick release method than open the lid.
4. Add sweet potato chunks and stir to blend, Add a pinch of salt and almond milk and stir well.

Nutrition Facts:
Calories: 270, Fat: 8.7g, Carbs: 44.2g, Protein: 5.7g

Almond Porridge

***(Prep + Cooking Time:** 25 minutes | **Serves:** 3)*

Ingredients:
- 1/2 cup almond flour
- 1 tablespoon flax meal
- 1 tablespoon heavy cream
- 2 teaspoon butter
- 1 ½ tablespoon blueberries
- 1 eggs
- 1 tablespoon sugar
- 1 cup water

Directions:
1. Add butter into the instant pot and set the pot on sauté mode.
2. Add water, ground flax meal, almond flour; and salt into the instant pot and stir well and cook for 2–3 minutes.
3. Add beaten egg and stir constantly, Seal pot with lid and select *HIGH* pressure for 10 minutes.
4. Release pressure using quick release method than Open the lid; Stir in blueberries and serve.

Nutrition Facts:
Calories: 195, Fat: 16g, Carbs: 9.6g, Protein: 6.5g

Wholesome Peach Oats Breakfast

***(Prep + Cooking Time:** 15 minutes | **Serves:** 2)*

Ingredients:
- 2 medium size peaches; diced
- 1 cup coconut milk
- 2 cups water
- 1 cup oats

Directions:
1. Take your Instant Pot and place it on a clean kitchen platform. Turn it on after plugging it into a power socket.
2. Open the lid from the top and put it aside; start adding the mentioned ingredients inside.
3. Thoroughly mix them. Close the lid and lock. Ensure that you have sealed the valve to avoid leakage.

4. Press *Manual* mode and set timer for 10 minutes. It will take a few minutes for the pot to build inside pressure and start cooking.
5. After the timer reads zero, press *Cancel* and naturally release pressure.
6. It takes about 8-10 minutes to naturally release pressure. Carefully remove the lid. Sweeten as desired and serve warm!

Nutrition Facts:
Calories 189; Fat: 6.5g; Carbohydrates: 32g; Fiber: 9.5g; Protein 15g

Quinoa Porridge

(Prep + Cooking Time: 20 minutes | Serves: 3)

Ingredients:
- 1 tablespoon coconut oil
- 1 cup coconut milk
- 3 tablespoon maple syrup
- 1 cup rinsed quinoa
- 1 teaspoon vanilla extract
- 1 cup water

Directions:
1. Add all ingredients into the instant pot and stir well to combine.
2. Seal pressure cooker with lid and select *HIGH* pressure for 2 minutes.
3. Allow releasing pressure naturally for 10 minutes then release using quick release method, Stir well and serve with your choice of topping.

Nutrition Facts:
Calories: 488, Fat: 27.1g, Carbs: 54.4g, Protein: 9.8g

Quinoa Salad

(Prep + Cooking Time: 12minutes | Serves: 2)

Ingredients:
- 1 cup quinoa
- 1/2 teaspoon black pepper
- 2 tablespoons apple cider vinegar
- 1/2 avocado; diced
- 1 fresh tomato; diced
- 1/4 cup fresh cilantro; chopped
- 1 cup water
- 2 tablespoons olive oil
- 1/2 teaspoon salt

Directions:
1. Combine quinoa and water in a pot. Close lid and set cooking time for 1 minute on *HIGH* pressure.
2. While steam is releasing, make salad dressing. Whisk together oil, vinegar, salt and pepper.
3. When quinoa is ready, toss with dressing, avocado, tomato and cilantro. Serve warm or chilled.

Nutrition Facts:
Calories: 529; Fat: 26.18 g; Carbohydrates: 61.91 g; Fiber: 10.3 g; Protein: 13.67 g

Spiced Pilaf

***(Prep + Cooking Time:** 15 minutes | **Serves:** 2)*

Ingredients:
- 1 stick cinnamon
- 1 cup millet; decorticated
- 2 teaspoons whole cumin
- 1 ½ cups water
- 1 tablespoon oil
- 1 bay leaf
- 2 pods cardamom
- 1 large onion; sliced
- Salt to taste

Directions:
1. Take your Instant Pot and place it on a clean kitchen platform. Turn it on after plugging it into a power socket.
2. Put the pot on *Sauté* mode. In the pot; add the oil and whole spices; cook until the cumin crackles.
3. Add the onions and cook for 2-3 minutes. Turn off the pot and add the millet; cook for a few more minutes until the millet is well coated.
4. Pour water and salt. Close the lid and lock. Ensure that you have sealed the valve to avoid leakage.
5. Press *Manual* mode and set timer for 1 minutes. It will take a few minutes for the pot to build inside pressure and start cooking.
6. After the timer reads zero, press *Cancel* and naturally release pressure.
7. It takes about 8-10 minutes to naturally release pressure. Carefully remove the lid; fluff with the fork and serve warm!

Nutrition Facts:
Calories 315; Fat: 7g; Carbohydrates: 18.5g; Fiber: 0g; Protein 3g

Mango Rice

***(Prep + Cooking Time:** 15 minutes | **Serves:** 3)*

Ingredients:
- 1 cup mango chunks
- 1/3 cup coconut milk; lightly sweetened
- 1 cup white jasmine rice; uncooked
- 1 ¼ cup coconut milk; lightly sweetened
- 2 tablespoon brown sugar
- Black sesame seeds as needed

Directions:
1. Place your Instant Pot on a flat kitchen surface', plug it and turn it on.
2. Open the lid and one by one add the rice, mango and coconut milk (1 ¼ cup) in the pot. Carefully close its lid and firmly lock it. Then after, seal the valve too.
3. To start making the recipe, press *Manual* button. Now you have to set cooking time', set the timer for 4 minutes. Allow the pot to cook the mixture until the timer goes off.
4. Turn off the pot and press *Cancel.* Allow the built up pressure to vent out naturally', it will take 8-10 minutes to completely release inside pressure.
5. Open its lid and transfer the cooked mixture into serving container/containers.
6. Mix the coconut milk (1/3 cup) once done and mix well. Top with brown sugar alongside some sesame seeds. Serve warm!

Nutrition Facts:
Calories: 261; Fat: 6g; Carbohydrates: 38.4g; Fiber: 3.2g; Protein 4g

Mashed Potatoes

(Prep + Cooking Time: 15 minutes | Serves: 4)

Ingredients:
- 3 cubed potatoes
- 2 tablespoon chopped parsley
- 1/4 cup grated parmesan cheese
- 1/8 teaspoon black pepper
- 1/2 cup milk
- 3 tablespoon butter
- 1 cup water
- 1 teaspoon salt

Directions:
1. Add potatoes, salt; and 1 cup water into the instant pot. Stir well.
2. Seal pot with lid and select *HIGH* pressure for 3 minutes, Release pressure using quick release method than open the lid.
3. Drain potatoes well and place in a large bowl.
4. Add butter into the potatoes and mash potatoes using the masher until smooth and creamy.
5. Add milk and pepper and stir well to combine, Garnish with parmesan cheese and parsley.

Nutrition Facts:
Calories: 352, Fat: 18.4g, Carbs: 26.7g, Protein: 15.8g

Green Been Mushroom Recipe

(Prep + Cooking Time: 25 minutes | Serves: 3)

Ingredients:
- 16-ounce green beans
- 1/2 cup green onions to garnish; chopped
- 1 cup chicken broth
- 2 tablespoons butter
- 12-ounce sliced mushroom
- 1 cup heavy cream
- 1 small onion; chopped

Directions:
1. Place your Instant Pot on a flat kitchen surface', plug it and turn it on.
2. To start making the recipe, press *Sauté* button. Add the oil, mushrooms and onion', cook for 2-3 minutes to soften the ingredients.
3. Add the broth, beans and heavy cream. Carefully close its lid and firmly lock it. Then after, seal the valve too.
4. To start making the recipe, press *Manual* button. Now you have to set cooking time', set the timer for 15 minutes. Allow the pot to cook the mixture until the timer goes off.
5. Turn off the pot and press *Cancel.* Allow the built up pressure to vent out naturally', it will take 8-10 minutes to completely release inside pressure.
6. Open its lid and add 1-2 tablespoons of cornstarch to make it thicker. Top with the green onions and serve.

Nutrition Facts:
Calories: 353; Fat: 34g; Carbohydrates: 17g; Fiber: 3g; Protein 9.4g

Carrot Cake Oatmeal Breakfast

(Prep + Cooking Time: *20 minutes* | **Serves:** *2)*

Ingredients:
- 1 cup steel-cut oats
- 2 cups milk; plus more for serving
- 2 cups water
- 2 carrots; grated
- 1/2 teaspoon nutmeg
- 1/2 cup raisins
- 1/4 cup brown sugar
- 1 teaspoon ground cinnamon
- 1 tablespoon butter

Directions:
1. Set Instant Pot to *Sauté*. Melt butter in the pot and add oats. Toast until oats are lightly browned and smell nutty.
2. Pour milk, water, carrots, sugar, cinnamon, nutmeg and raisins into the pot.
3. Close lid and set cook time to 10 minutes on *HIGH* pressure. Serve with additional milk.

Nutrition Facts:
Calories: 451; Fat: 17.4 g; Carbohydrates: 77.05 g; Fiber: 9.8 g; Protein: 16.57 g

Lentil Potato Rice

(Prep + Cooking Time: *20 minutes* | **Serves:** *2)*

Ingredients:
- 1 small potato; cut into small pieces
- 1/2 cup split green lentils; rinsed
- 1/2 cup carrots; peeled and diced
- 1/2 of a small onion; chopped
- 1/2 tablespoon ginger paste
- 1/2 cup fresh green peas; shelled
- 1 tablespoon olive oil
- 1/4 teaspoon red chili powder
- 1/2 cup white rice; rinsed
- 1/4 teaspoon ground turmeric
- 1 tablespoon fresh cilantro; chopped
- 1/2 teaspoon cumin seeds
- 3 cups water
- 1 tomato; chopped finely
- Salt as per taste preference

Directions:
1. Switch on the pot after placing it on a clean and dry platform. Press *Sauté* cooking function.
2. Open the lid; add the oil and cumin seeds and cook for 30 seconds.
3. Add the onions and ginger and cook for about 2 minutes. Add the vegetables and spices and cook for 2 minutes.
4. Mix in other ingredients and stir well. Do not add the cilantro. Close the pot by closing the top lid. Also, ensure to seal the valve.
5. Press *Manual* cooking function and set cooking time to 5 minutes. It will start cooking after a few minutes. Let the pot mix cook under pressure until the timer reads zero.
6. Press *Cancel* cooking function and press *Natural release* setting. It will take 8-10 minutes for natural pressure release. Open the instant pot; top with the cilantro and serve warm.

Nutrition Facts:
Calories 358; Fat: 16g; Carbohydrates: 55.5g; Fiber: 11g; Protein 20g

Asparagus Risotto

(Prep + Cooking Time: 20 minutes | Serves: 2)

Ingredients:
- 1 small onion; chopped
- 1/4 cup parmesan; grated
- 1 ⅓ cup vegetable stock
- 1 tablespoon olive oil
- 1 tablespoon thyme
- 2 tablespoons orange juice
- 1/2-pound asparagus; diced
- 1/2 cup risotto rice
- 2 garlic cloves; chopped

Directions:
1. Switch on the pot after placing it on a clean and dry platform. Press *Sauté* cooking function.
2. Open the lid; add the oil and onions in the pot; cook for 2 minutes to cook well and soften.
3. Mix the rice and the garlic; cook until the garlic becomes fragrant. Mix in the stock and the orange juice. Close the pot by closing the top lid. Also, ensure to seal the valve.
4. Press *Manual* cooking function and set cooking time to 7 minutes. It will start cooking after a few minutes. Let the pot mix cook under pressure until the timer reads zero.
5. Press *Cancel* cooking function and press *Quick release* setting.
6. Open the pot and mix the thyme and asparagus. Do not cover, let it sit for 5-8 more minutes for asparagus to soften. Place in a serving bowl and top with the cheese. Serve warm!

Nutrition Facts:
Calories: 436; Fat: 15g; Carbohydrates: 44.5g; Fiber: 4g; Protein 24g

Sweet Potato Hash Breakfast

(Prep + Cooking Time: 20 minutes | Serves: 2)

Ingredients:
- 1 cup bell pepper; chopped
- 1/2 teaspoon pepper
- 1 medium potato; diced
- 1 teaspoon cumin
- 1 clove minced garlic
- 1 teaspoon paprika
- 1 tablespoon oil
- 1 medium sweet potato; diced
- 1/4 cup water
- Pinch of cayenne
- 1/2 teaspoon salt

Directions:
1. In a bowl, toss all the potatoes and pepper in the spices and oil. Switch on your instant pot after placing it on a clean and dry kitchen platform.
2. Add them to the bottom of the pot and add a half cup of water. Close the pot by closing the top lid. Also, ensure to seal the valve.
3. Press *Manual* cooking function and set cooking time to 10 minutes. It will start cooking after a few minutes. Let the pot mix cook under pressure until the timer reads zero.
4. Turn off and press *Cancel* cooking function. Quick release pressure. Open the pot and cook the mixture on sauté mode to brown the potatoes a little more. Serve warm!

Nutrition Facts:
Calories: 256; Fat: –12g; Carbohydrates: 21.5g; Fiber: 7g; Protein 4g

Quinoa with Peaches

*(**Prep + Cooking Time:** 15 minutes | **Serves:** 3)*

Ingredients:
- 1/2 teaspoon vanilla extract
- 1 cup peaches
- 3/4 cup half and half
- 1 cup quinoa
- 1 cup milk
- 1/2 cup water
- 1 tablespoon cinnamon
- 1 tablespoon butter

Directions:
1. Add butter into the instant pot and set the pot on sauté mode.
2. Once butter is melted then add quinoa and stir for 2 minutes.
3. Add milk and water and stir well. Add vanilla and cinnamon and stir, Seal pot with lid and select *HIGH* pressure for 4 minutes.
4. Release pressure using quick release method than Open the lid; Stir in half and half and peaches.

Nutrition Facts:
Calories: 389, Fat: 16.1g, Carbs: 49.6g, Protein: 13.1g

Buttery Polenta

*(**Prep + Cooking Time:** 13 minutes | **Serves:** 2)*

Ingredients:
- 3 tablespoons milk
- 3 tablespoons butter
- 1/2 cup polenta
- 1/2 teaspoon salt
- 2 cup milk

Directions:
1. Switch on the pot after placing it on a clean and dry platform. Press *Sauté* cooking function.
2. Open the lid; add the milk and boil it. Mix in the polenta with the salt. Close the pot by closing the top lid. Also, ensure to seal the valve.
3. Press *Manual* cooking function and set cooking time to 8 minutes. It will start cooking after a few minutes. Let the pot mix cook under pressure until the timer reads zero.
4. Press *Cancel* cooking function and press *Quick release* setting. Open the instant pot; mix 3 tablespoons of milk and butter. Serve warm.

Nutrition Facts:
Calories 102; Fat: 1.6g; Carbohydrates: 6.3; Fiber: 3.3g; Protein 5g

Pumpkin Cinnamon Oats

(Prep + Cooking Time: 20 minutes | Serves: 4)

Ingredients:
- 1/4 cup pumpkin
- 14-ounce can coconut milk
- 1 cup steel cut oats
- 1/4 teaspoon cinnamon
- 1 tablespoon brown sugar
- 1 ¼ cup water
- 2 tablespoon maple syrup
- 1 teaspoon vanilla
- 1/2 teaspoon salt

Directions:
1. Add oats, vanilla, water, coconut milk; and salt into the instant pot and stir well.
2. Seal pot with lid and select high for 10 minutes, Release pressure using quick release method than open the lid.
3. Add cinnamon, brown sugar, maple syrup; and pumpkin and stir well.

Nutrition Facts:
Calories: 316, Fat: 22.6g, Carbs: 27g, Protein: 4.9g

Cherry Apple Risotto

(Prep + Cooking Time: 23 minutes | Serves: 2)

Ingredients:
- 3/4 cup risotto rice
- 1/2 cup apple juice
- 1 large apple; peeled, cored and diced
- 3/4 teaspoon cinnamon
- 1/4 cup dried cherries
- 1 tablespoon butter
- 1 ½ cups milk
- 1/4 cup brown sugar

Directions:
1. Switch on the pot after placing it on a clean and dry platform. Press *Sauté* cooking function.
2. Open the lid; add the butter and rice in the pot; cook for 4 minutes to cook well and turn opaque.
3. Mix in the apples, spices and brown sugar, stirring well to combine. Pour in the milk and juice and stir.
4. Close the pot by closing the top lid. Also, ensure to seal the valve. Press *Manual* cooking function and set cooking time to 6 minutes.
5. It will start cooking after a few minutes. Let the pot mix cook under pressure until the timer reads zero. Press *Cancel* cooking function and press *Quick release* setting.
6. Open and add the dried cherries and stir well. Transfer the mix into bowls and serve with a splash of milk, sliced almonds and a sprinkle of brown sugar.

Nutrition Facts:
Calories: 556; Fat: 7g; Carbohydrates: 18.5g; Fiber: 8g; Protein 10g

Poultry Recipes

Shredded Chicken with Mayo Sauce

*(**Prep + Cooking Time:** 17 minutes | **Serves:** 2)*

Ingredients:

- 1/2 lb. boneless chicken breast
- 1/2 teaspoon cumin
- 1/4 teaspoon garlic powder
- 1/2 teaspoon grated orange zest
- 1/4 cup orange juice
- 2 tablespoons chicken broth
- 3 teaspoons minced' garlic
- 2 tablespoons chopped' onion
- 1 bay leaf
- 2 tablespoons mayonnaise
- 1 tablespoon tomato chili sauce
- 1/4 teaspoon chili powder
- 1/4 teaspoon oregano
- 1/4 teaspoon salt
- 1/4 teaspoon pepper
- 1/4 teaspoon salt

Directions:

1. Place boneless chicken breast in the inner pot of an Instant Pot then add cumin, chili powder, oregano, salt, pepper, grated orange zest, minced' garlic, chopped' onion and bay leaf
2. Pour chicken broth and orange juice over the chicken then close the Instant Pot with the lid. Seal the Instant Pot properly and close the steam valve
3. Select *Chicken* setting on the Instant Pot and cook the chicken on high. Set the time to 12 minutes.
4. Meanwhile, combine mayonnaise with tomato chili sauce, salt and garlic powder. Stir until incorporated then set aside
5. Once the chicken is done, naturally release the Instant Pot and open the lid
6. Take the chicken out of the Instant Pot then place on a flat surface. Leave the liquid in the Instant Pot
7. Using a fork shred the chicken then place in the Instant Pot. Stir the shredded chicken until completely coated with the liquid
8. Transfer the shredded chicken together with the liquid to a serving dish then drizzle mayonnaise mixture on top

Nutrition Facts:
Calories: 352; Net Carbs: 7g; Total Fat: 24.7g; Protein: 26.1g; Carbs: 7.8g;

Greek Style Turkey Recipe

*(**Prep + Cooking Time:** 10 minutes | **Serves:** 3)*

Ingredients:

- 1 sliced turkey breast
- 1/2 minced Poblano pepper
- 1/2 teaspoon chili flakes
- 3 tablespoon sliced olives
- 1/2 cup diced tomatoes
- 1/2 cup crumbled feta cheese
- 2 tablespoon lemon juice
- 1 cup water
- 2 tablespoons olive oil
- 3 minced garlic cloves
- Rosemary
- Basil
- Chopped parsley
- Salt and pepper to taste

Directions:
1. Take a large bowl and put the olive oil, Poblano pepper, garlic, lemon juice, salt, chili flakes, rosemary, basil and pepper in it.
2. Mix all the Ingredients well then immerse the turkey in the mixture to marinate, Let it simmer in the marinade,
3. Cover the bowl with a plastic wrap and put it in a refrigerator for 3 hours,
4. Add water to the instant pot and place a trivet in it, Now place the turkey pieces on the trivet. Pour the marinade generously over the turkey.
5. Secure the cooker lid. Select the *Manual* function and set *HIGH* pressure for 50 minutes,
6. Release all the steam after the beep and remove the lid.
7. Top each piece with a tomato slice, sliced olives and cheese then grill them for 10 minutes in an oven. Garnish with fresh parsley and serve.

Nutrition Facts:
Calories: 932, Fat: 32.2g, Carbs: 15.7g, Protein: 84.7g

Spicy Herbs Wrapped Chicken

(Prep + Cooking Time: 22 minutes | Serves: 2)

Ingredients:
- 1/2 lb. bone-in chicken
- 1/2 teaspoon turmeric
- 1 lemon grass
- 1 bay leaf
- 1/4 cup diced' red tomatoes
- 1/2 cup water
- 2 cloves garlic
- 2 shallots
- 2 red chilies
- 1/2 teaspoon cayenne pepper
- 1/4 teaspoon salt

Directions:
1. Place the garlic, shallots, red chilies, cayenne pepper, salt and turmeric in a food processor. Process until smooth
2. Transfer the smooth spice mixture to a bowl then add diced' red tomatoes to the bowl. Mix until just combined
3. Cut the chicken into medium pieces then rub with the spice mixture. Place the seasoned chicken on a sheet of aluminum foil then place lemon grass and bay leaf on top
4. Wrap the chicken with the aluminum foil then set aside
5. Pour water into the Instant Pot and place a trivet in it.
6. Place the wrapped chicken on the trivet then cover the Instant Pot properly. Close the steam valve
7. Select *Manual* setting on the Instant Pot and cook the chicken on high for 12 minutes.
8. Once it is done; naturally release the Instant Pot then open the lid.
9. Take the wrapped chicken out of the Instant Pot and let it sit for a few minutes or until warm
10. Unwrap the steamed chicken then transfer to a serving dish. Serve and enjoy with a bowl of warm white rice

Nutrition Facts:
Calories: 276; Net Carbs: 6.8 g; Total Fat: 17.4g; Protein: 21.4g; Carbs: 8g

Steamed Chicken Wings

(Prep + Cooking Time: 16 minutes | Serves: 2)

Ingredients:
- 1/2 lb. chicken wings
- 1/2 teaspoon brown sugar
- 1/2 teaspoon honey
- 1/2 teaspoon maple syrup
- 1/2 teaspoon Tabasco
- 1/4 teaspoon ketchup
- 1/4 teaspoon BBQ sauce
- 3/4 cup chicken broth
- 1/4 cup hot sauce
- 2 tablespoons butter
- 1/2 teaspoon molasses
- 1/4 teaspoon salt
- 1/4 teaspoon pepper

Directions:
1. Rub the chicken wings with salt and pepper then set aside. Place a trivet in an Instant Pot then pour chicken broth into the Instant Pot
2. Arrange the seasoned chicken wings on the trivet then cover the Instant Pot with the lid. Seal it properly.
3. Select *Manual* setting on the Instant Pot and cook the chicken on high for 8 minutes
4. Once it is done; quick release the Instant Pot then take the cooked chicken out of the Instant Pot. Remove the trivet.
5. Place the chicken wings on a plate then set aside. Add hot sauce, butter, molasses, brown sugar, honey, maple syrup, Tabasco, ketchup and BBQ sauce to the Instant Pot then stir well
6. Select *Sauté* menu on the Instant Pot then cook the sauce for approximately 2-3 minutes
7. Return the chicken wings back to the Instant Pot then stir until the chicken wings are coated with the sauce.
8. Transfer the chicken wings together with the sauce to a serving dish then serve

Nutrition Facts:
Calories: 338; Net Carbs: 5.8g; Total Fat: 24.4g; Protein: 23.1g; Carbs: 6g;

Instant Honey Chicken

(Prep + Cooking Time: 35 minutes | Serves: 3)

Ingredients:
- 2-pounds boneless chicken thighs; fresh or frozen
- 1/4 cup ghee
- 1/4 cup honey
- 3 tablespoons tamari
- 3 tablespoons ketchup
- 2 teaspoons garlic powder
- 1 ½ teaspoons sea salt
- 1/2 teaspoon black pepper

Directions:
1. Place your instant pot on a flat kitchen surface', plug it and turn it on. Open the lid and one by one add the mentioned ingredients in the pot. Carefully close its lid and firmly lock it. Then after, seal the valve too.
2. To start making the recipe, press *Manual* button. Now you have to set cooking time', set the timer for 18 minutes for fresh chicken and 40 minutes if you are using frozen chicken. Allow the pot to cook the mixture until the timer goes off.
3. Turn off the pot and press *Cancel.* Allow the built up pressure to vent out naturally', it will take 8-10 minutes to completely release inside pressure.

4. Open its lid and transfer the cooked mixture into serving container/containers. Serve warm with vegetables and rice.

Nutrition Facts:
Calories 544; Fat: 22g; Carbohydrates: 48.2g; Fiber: –4g; Protein 36.2g

Sweet Brown Chicken

(Prep + Cooking Time: 5 hours | Serves: 2)

Ingredients:
- 1/2 lb. chicken wings
- 1¼ teaspoons brown sugar
- 1/2 cup water
- 1 teaspoon minced' garlic
- 1/4 teaspoon salt
- 1/4 teaspoon pepper

Directions:
1. Rub the chicken wings with minced' garlic, salt and pepper then place in the inner pot of an Instant Pot.
2. Pour water into the Instant Pot and sprinkle brown sugar over the chicken
3. Cover the Instant Pot with the lid and seal it properly. Select *Slow Cooker* setting on the Instant Pot and set the time to 5 hours. Adjust the temperature on low and ensure that the pressure valve is in the *Venting* position
4. Once the chicken is done, naturally release the Instant Pot then open the lid. Transfer the cooked chicken to a serving dish then serve. Enjoy!

Nutrition Facts:
Calories: 276; Net Carbs: 6.5g; Total Fat: 18g; Protein: 21.1g; Carbs: 6.5g;

California Style Chicken

(Prep + Cooking Time: 25 minutes | Serves: 3)

Ingredients:
- 3 chicken breast halves; boneless and skinless
- 1/2 lemon; thinly sliced
- 1/2 cup white wine
- 1/4 cup parsley; chopped
- 2 tablespoons olive oil
- 1 cup chicken broth
- 1 teaspoon rosemary
- 2 garlic cloves; peeled and sliced
- Salt and Pepper to taste

Directions:
1. Add oil to Instant Pot and press "Sauté" button (*Normal* preset), wait till you see Hot on the display.
2. Add chicken breasts, cook for 6-7 minutes both sides with the lid open until all sides are browned.
3. Season the chicken with rosemary and add garlic. Press *Cancel* button.
4. Mix wine, broth and parsley in a bowl. Add the mixture to the pot.
5. Close the lid and turn the vent to *Sealed*. Press *Pressure Cook* (Manual) button, use *+* or *-* button to set the timer for 8 minutes. Use *Pressure level* button to set Pressure to *HIGH*.
6. Once the timer is up; press *Cancel* button and turn the steam release handle to "Venting" position for quick release, until the float valve drops down. Open the lid; Put lemon slices on top before serving.

Nutrition Facts: Calories: 192 g; Total Fat: 27.7 g; Total Carbohydrate: 1.9 g; Protein: 14.4

Tangy and Spicy Honey Chicken

***(Prep + Cooking Time:** 20 minutes | **Serves:** 4)*

Ingredients:
- 4 chicken breasts
- 3 tablespoon honey
- 1/4 cup soy sauce
- 1 teaspoon Worcestershire sauce
- 1/2 sliced onion
- 1 tablespoon sriracha sauce
- 2 green onions
- 1 tablespoon sesame seeds
- 2 tablespoon cornstarch
- 1 tablespoon brown sugar
- 1 tablespoon minced garlic
- 1 ½ tablespoon minced ginger

Directions:
1. Before you start cooking, you should cut the chicken breasts into bite-size chunks.
2. The onions should be diced into chunks as well.
3. The chicken and onions should be put inside the Mini Instant Pot pressure cooker.
4. Now take a bowl and mix all the other ingredients except the cornstarch. Pour the mixture on the chicken and cover it with the marinade.
5. Close the lid of the steam valve and set it to Manual cooking in High Pressure for 4 minutes.
6. Once the cooking time is over; you need to do a quick release of the steam by carefully lifting the lid.
7. Take another bowl and add the hot sauce along with the cornstarch and whisk it quickly before putting it inside the pot.
8. Now turn on the Sauté function of the Instant Pot, switch on the normal mode; and allow everything to bubble for a few minutes.
9. Allow the chicken to sit for a few minutes; the sauce will thicken by now.
10. The spicy honey chicken is ready to be served with plain rice.
11. This is a good quick fix if you are really hungry and do not want to go for an elaborate cooking process.

Nutrition Facts:
Calories: 155, Fat: 2g, Carbs: 15g, Protein: 17g

Chicken Curry with Zucchinis

***(Prep + Cooking Time:** 18 minutes | **Serves:** 2)*

Ingredients:
- 1/2 lb. boneless chicken breast
- 1/4 cup chopped' zucchinis
- 2 tablespoons chopped' onion
- 2 teaspoons minced' garlic
- 1 teaspoon curry powder
- 1/4 teaspoon brown sugar
- 1/2 cup water
- 1/4 cup pineapple chunks
- 1/4 teaspoon turmeric
- 1/4 teaspoon ginger
- 1/4 teaspoon salt
- 1/4 teaspoon pepper

Directions:
1. Cut the boneless chicken breast into cubes then place in a bowl. Rub the chicken with minced' garlic, curry powder, turmeric, ginger, salt, pepper and brown sugar then place in the inner pot of an Instant Pot
2. Sprinkle chopped' onion and pineapple chunks over the chicken then pour water into the Instant Pot

3. Cover the Instant Pot with the lid then seal it properly. Close the steam valve
4. Select *Manual* setting on the Instant Pot then cook the chicken on high. Set the time to 10 minutes.
5. Once it is done; naturally release the Instant Pot then open the lid
6. Add chopped' zucchinis to the Instant Pot and stir until just wilted. Transfer the chicken curry to a serving dish then serve with a bowl of brown rice

Nutrition Facts:
Calories: 243; Net Carbs: 5.3g; Total Fat: 8.7g; Protein: 33.6g; Carbs: 6.5g;

Chicken Thighs with Rice

(Prep + Cooking Time: 18 minutes | Serves: 2)

Ingredients:
- 2 skinless chicken thighs
- 3/4 cup long-grain white rice
- 1/2 diced small onion
- 1 tablespoon Jamaican jerk seasoning
- 2 teaspoons olive oil
- 1 minced garlic clove
- 1 cup chicken broth

Directions:
1. Begin with rinsing the rice; you will know that the rice is rinsed properly when the water runs clear. Drain the rice and keep it aside.
2. Turn the Sauté function in the Mini Instant Pot. Once the display reads Hot, you can add the olive oil.
3. Start by stirring the onions, cook it for a few minutes and stir them from time to time. You know that the onions are done once they turn translucent.
4. Keep on adding the other ingredients such as garlic; keep stirring for about 20 seconds, Pour the jerk seasoning as well; continue to stir.
5. Now add the chicken broth. Bring the concoction to simmer and then add the rice. Ensure that all the ingredients are fully submerged in the chicken broth.
6. Place the chicken thighs on the broth mixture; they will shrink when they are cooked. Let the thighs sink in the broth as well.
7. Secure the lid on the pot and lock it. Switch the Steam Release knob to Sealing position.
8. Press Pressure or the Manual mode and then choose 7 minutes.
9. Once the cooking is done, you should allow the pot to sit for about 5 minutes.
10. You can now turn the Steam Release knob to Venting position. The remaining steam will be released.
11. Once the pin in the lid drops, you can safely open the lid and simply remove the chicken thighs.
12. You can either serve the thighs with some rice in a bowl or shred the chicken and mix it with the rice. Give one last stir and the rice is ready to be served.
13. This is one of the guilt-free fuss-free meals which you can enjoy at both lunch and dinner.

Nutrition Facts:
Calories: 283, Fat: 2.5g, Carbs: 47g, Protein: 22g

Chipotle Salsa Chicken

(Prep + Cooking Time: 4 hours | Serves: 2)

Ingredients:
- 1/2 lb. chicken thighs
- 1 teaspoon avocado oil
- 1/4 cup chipotle salsa
- 1/4 teaspoon salt
- 1/4 teaspoon pepper

Directions:
1. Brush the inner pot of an Instant Pot with avocado oil. Rub the chicken thighs with salt and pepper then place in the Instant Pot
2. Top the chicken thighs with chipotle salsa then cover the Instant Pot properly
3. Select *Slow Cooker* setting on the Instant Pot and set the time to 4 hours. Adjust the temperature on high and ensure that the pressure valve is in the *Venting* position
4. Once the Instant Pot beeps naturally release the Instant Pot and open the lid. Transfer the cooked chicken to a serving dish

Nutrition Facts:
Calories: 239; Net Carbs: 4.1g; Total Fat: 8.7g; Protein: 32.9g; Carbs: 4.3g;

Garlic Chicken Thighs

(Prep + Cooking Time: 35 minutes | Serves: 2)

Ingredients:
- 4 chicken thighs
- 3/4 cup ketchup
- 3/4 cup soy sauce
- 1/2 cup water or chicken stock
- 1 teaspoon fresh basil; chopped
- 1/2 teaspoon garlic cloves; minced
- 1 teaspoon chili garlic sauce
- 1 tablespoon arrowroot starch; dissolved in 2 tablespoons of water

Directions:
1. Add oil to Instant Pot and press *Sauté* button (*Normal* preset), wait till you see Hot on the display.
2. Add chicken thighs, cook for 6-7 minutes both sides with the lid open until all sides are browned. Press *Cancel* button.
3. Add soy sauce, chili sauce, garlic, water or stock and organic ketchup to the pot. Stir the ingredients and close the lid, turn the vent to *Sealed*.
4. Press *Pressure Cook* (Manual) button, use *+* or *-* button to set the timer for 10 minutes. Use *Pressure level* button to set Pressure to *HIGH*.
5. Once the timer is up; press *Cancel* button and turn the steam release handle to "Venting" position for quick release, until the float valve drops down.
6. Open the lid; Transfer the meat to a plate. Add arrowroot starch mixture to the pot. Press "Sauté" button, adjust to *Less* preset and stir until the sauce thickens. Pour the sauce over the meat before serving.

Nutrition Facts:
Calories: 532 g; Total Fat: 55.4 g; Total Carbohydrate: 15.2 g; Protein: 30.2

BBQ Chicken

(Prep + Cooking Time: 20 minutes | Serves: 2)

Ingredients:
- 2-pounds. chicken wings
- 1/2 cup barbecue sauce
- 1-cup water
- 1/2 cup chopped onion
- 2 ½ tablespoons raw honey
- 1/2 teaspoon pepper
- 1/4 teaspoon salt

Directions:
1. In a bowl, mix the barbecue sauce with water, raw honey, salt and pepper. Switch on the pot after placing it on a clean and dry platform.
2. Open the pot lid and place the chicken and sauce in the cooking pot area. Give the ingredients a little stir. Close the pot by closing the top lid. Also, ensure to seal the valve.
3. Press *Manual* cooking function and set cooking time to 10 minutes. It will start cooking after a few minutes. Let the pot mix cook under pressure until the timer reads zero.
4. Press *Cancel* cooking function and press *Quick release* setting.
5. Open the pot, preheat a pan over medium heat; add the chicken mix to the pan. Bring to simmer and stir until the barbecue sauce is thickened. Serve warm!

Nutrition Facts:
Calories 334; Fat: 10g; Carbohydrates: 45g; Fiber: 1.5g; Protein 10.5g

Lemongrass Coconut Chicken

(Prep + Cooking Time: 20 minutes | Serves: 2)

Ingredients:
- 4 chicken drumsticks
- 1 teaspoon ginger
- 1/2 teaspoon coconut oil
- 3/4 cup coconut milk
- 2 teaspoons minced garlic
- 3 teaspoons fish sauce
- 1/4 teaspoon pepper
- 1 tablespoon lemon juice
- 1/4 cup chopped onion
- 1 lemongrass

Directions:
1. Chop the lemongrass and add in a blender. Add the garlic, ginger, fish sauce, pepper and lemon juice; combine well.
2. Add the coconut milk. Blend until smooth and incorporated. Switch on the pot after placing it on a clean and dry platform. Press *Sauté* cooking function.
3. Open the lid; add the oil and onions in the pot; cook for 2 minutes to cook well and soften.
4. Add the drumsticks to the pot; top with the coconut mixture over the chicken. Close the pot by closing the top lid. Also, ensure to seal the valve.
5. Press *Manual* cooking function and set cooking time to 10 minutes. It will start cooking after a few minutes. Let the pot mix cook under pressure until the timer reads zero.
6. Press *Cancel* cooking function and press *Natural release* setting.
7. It will take 8-10 minutes for natural pressure release. Open the pot and serve warm.

Nutrition Facts:
Calories: 342; Fat: 28.5g; Carbohydrates: 9.5g; Fiber: 2.5g; Protein 13g

Turkey Stacks

(Prep + Cooking Time: 35 minutes | Serves: 4)

Ingredients:
- 1-pound ground turkey
- 1 sliced tomato
- 4 slices turkey bacon
- 4 lettuce leaves
- 1/4 teaspoon cayenne pepper
- 1 teaspoon Herbs de Provence
- 1 tablespoon olive oil
- 4 slices Swiss cheese
- 4 eggs
- Salt and pepper to taste

Directions:
1. Put the ground turkey, cayenne pepper, salt, herbs de Provence and pepper into a bowl and mix all the Ingredients well.
2. Make 4 burger patties using this mixture. To the instant pot, add olive oil and select the *Sauté* function. Carefully place the turkey patties in the pot.
3. Cook them from both sides until they turn golden brown, Remove the patties from the pot and put them aside,
4. Add 1 cup of water to the pot and place the trivet in it.
5. Place the fried patties on the trivet and cover each one with a cheese slice, Place the turkey bacon strips on the trivet too.
6. Secure the lid and select *Manual* function, setting at *HIGH* pressure for 5 minutes,
7. When it beeps; release the steam completely and remove the lid. To serve; take the lettuce leaves and stack them up with a tomato slice, a turkey patty, bacon and fried egg on top.

Nutrition Facts: Calories: 720, Fat: 18.9g, Carbs: 1.7g, Protein: 122.3g

Quick Dumplings

(Prep + Cooking Time: 20 minutes | Serves: 4)

Ingredients:
- 1 ½-pound cubed chicken breast
- 16-ounce refrigerated biscuits
- 1 teaspoon olive oil
- 1 cup frozen peas
- 2 teaspoon oregano
- 1 teaspoon onion powder
- 1 teaspoon basil
- 1 cup water
- 2 cup chicken broth
- 2 minced garlic cloves
- 1 cup chopped carrots
- 1/2 teaspoon salt
- 1/2 teaspoon pepper

Directions:
1. Press the biscuits to flatten them then cut them into 2-inch strips with a sharp knife,
2. Put the olive oil, onion powder, oregano, chicken, garlic, salt, pepper and basil into the pot and mix them well.
3. Select the *Sauté* function on your pressure cooker and allow it to cook until the chicken turns brown.
4. Cancel the *Sauté* function when the cooking is finished.
5. Add the water, peas, carrots and chicken broth to the pot. Add the biscuits then stir well.
6. Cover with the lid and lock it, Select the *Manual* function and set the timer for 5 minutes,
7. When it beeps; use the *Natural Release* for 10 minutes to vent all steam.
8. Press *Cancel* to turn the cooker off then remove the lid. Serve the cooked chicken in a bowl.

Nutrition Facts: Calories: 610, Fat: 12.1g, Carbs: 13.6g, Protein: 100.5g

Garlic Chicken

(Prep + Cooking Time: 18 minutes | Serves: 2)

Ingredients:
- 3/4-pound chopped boneless chicken
- 1-cup low sodium chicken broth
- 2 tablespoons minced garlic
- 1 ½ teaspoons olive oil
- 1 bay leaf
- 1 tablespoon chopped rosemary
- 2 tablespoons chopped celery
- 1/2 cup chopped onion
- 1/4 teaspoon thyme
- 1/2 teaspoon salt
- 1/2 teaspoon pepper

Directions:
1. Switch on the pot after placing it on a clean and dry platform. Press *Sauté* cooking function.
2. Open the lid; add the oil, garlic and onions in the pot; cook for 2 minutes to cook well and turn lightly golden.
3. Add chicken cubes to the pot. Mix the salt, pepper, bay leaf, chopped rosemary and thyme. Close the pot by closing the top lid. Also, ensure to seal the valve.
4. Press *Manual* cooking function and set cooking time to 10 minutes. It will start cooking after a few minutes. Let the pot mix cook under pressure until the timer reads zero.
5. Press *Cancel* cooking function and press *Natural release* setting.
6. It will take 8-10 minutes for natural pressure release. Open the instant pot; topped with some celery and serve warm.

Nutrition Facts:
Calories: 176; Fat: 8g; Carbohydrates: 7.5g; Fiber: 2g; Protein 17g

Butter Chicken

(Prep + Cooking Time: 35 minutes | Serves: 6)

Ingredients:
- 2–pound skinless chicken breasts
- 1 teaspoon ground turmeric
- 1 teaspoon ground coriander
- 1 can diced tomatoes
- 1 chopped onion
- 1/2 cup coconut milk
- 1 tablespoon Garam masala
- 4 tablespoon Unsalted butter
- 3 chopped garlic cloves
- 1 chopped fresh ginger
- 1 teaspoon kosher salt

Directions:
1. Turn on the Sauté function in the Pressure Cooker in the Mini Instant Pot and melt the butter first. Use 2 tablespoons of butter.
2. Start adding the garlic, onion; and gingers along with the spices and sauté them by stirring them occasionally.
3. The onions will start to brown in about 4 minutes. Now you can add the spices like the garam masala, salt; and turmeric and cook them until they become fragrant.
4. Now add the tomatoes; their juices will start to come out. Combine the tomatoes with the other ingredients. It is time to add the chicken breasts; cover the breasts with the sauce.
5. Seal the pressure cooker but please ensure that the vent is closed properly.
6. The cooker should be set to Manual mode in high temperature. The cooking time should be set for 10 minutes.
7. The pressure cooker will take about 10-12 minutes to come to the pressure mode.

8. The cooking time should not be more than 10 minutes. The cooker will release all the pressure in another 10 minutes.
9. Transfer the chicken breasts to a cutting board and let them cool down.
10. In the sauce, add the rest of the butter along with either coconut milk or heavy cream and transfer the sauce to make a fine puree. If required, you can reserve some of the additional sauce for later use.
11. The chicken should be cut into 1–inch pieces, returned to the sauce; and a gentle stir is required for the final touch.
12. You can serve this delicious dish with basmati rice; a healthier option can be brown rice, cauliflower rice, or quinoa.
13. Whatever is your preference, this finger–licking dish will definitely win the hearts of your guests.

Nutrition Facts:
Calories: 537, Fat: 29.3g, Carbs: 14.5g, Protein: 54.2g

Instant Chicken Wings

*(**Prep + Cooking Time:** 30 minutes | **Serves:** 2)*

Ingredients:
- 1-pound. chicken wings
- 2 teaspoons minced garlic
- 2 tablespoons chopped onion
- 1 ½ tablespoons low sodium soy sauce
- 1/2 tablespoon rice wine
- 1/2 tablespoon sesame oil
- 1/2 teaspoon ginger
- 1 cup your choice of cola

Directions:
1. Switch on the pot after placing it on a clean and dry platform. Press *Sauté* cooking function.
2. Open the lid; add the oil, garlic and onions in the pot; cook for 2 minutes to cook well and soften.
3. Add the chicken wings and sauté until brown. Mix in the cola, soy sauce and rice wine then stir well. Close the pot by closing the top lid. Also, ensure to seal the valve.
4. Press *Manual* cooking function and set cooking time to 20 minutes. It will start cooking after a few minutes. Let the pot mix cook under pressure until the timer reads zero.
5. Press *Cancel* cooking function and press *Natural release* setting.
6. It will take 8-10 minutes for natural pressure release. Open the pot and serve warm.

Nutrition Facts:
Calories: 228; Fat: 8.5g; Carbohydrates: 32g; Fiber: 0.5g; Protein 5.5g

Apple Turkey Curry Recipe

*(**Prep + Cooking Time:** 30 minutes | **Serves:** 3)*

Ingredients:
- 1 pound. cooked turkey breasts; chopped
- 1 apple; cored and finely sliced
- 1/2 cup full fat yogurt
- 1 teaspoon Curry powder
- 2 garlic cloves; minced
- 2 tablespoons lemon juice
- 1 cup water
- 2 tablespoons olive oil
- 1 cup onion; sliced
- Salt and Pepper to taste

Directions:
1. Add oil to Instant Pot and press "Sauté" button (*Normal* preset), wait till you see Hot on the display.
2. Add onion, sauté until golden brown. Add garlic, sauté for 20 more seconds. Add Curry powder.
3. Add apple, turkey, water, salt and pepper. Mix well. Close the lid and turn the vent to "Sealed". Press *Pressure Cook* (Manual) button, use *+* or *-* button to set the timer for 12 minutes. Use *Pressure level* button to set Pressure to *HIGH*.
4. Once the timer is up; press *Cancel* button and turn the steam release handle to "Venting" position for quick release, until the float valve drops down. Open the lid; Add yogurt, sprinkle with lemon juice and mix well.
5. Press "Sauté" button and adjust to *Less* preset, cook for 5 minutes stirring well.

Nutrition Facts:
Calories: 320 g; Total Fat: 28 g; Total Carbohydrate: 5 g; Protein: 18

Chicken in Mushroom Sauce

(Prep + Cooking Time: 25 minutes | Serves: 4)

Ingredients:
- 8-ounce sliced cremini mushrooms
- 1 whole chicken
- 1/2 teaspoon black pepper
- 1 cup low-sodium chicken broth
- 2 tablespoons all-purpose flour
- 2 teaspoons kosher salt
- 1 sliced yellow onion
- 1 teaspoon paprika
- 2 tablespoons avocado oil
- 1 chopped garlic clove
- 1/2 teaspoon dried oregano
- 1/2 teaspoon dried thyme
- 1 tablespoon tomato paste

Directions:
1. Take a dry chicken towel and pat the chicken dry. You need to tuck the wings of the chicken under so that they remain flat.
2. As for the drumsticks, you can tie them with kitchen string. Spread the seasoning of salt, pepper; and paprika on the chicken.
3. Turn on the Sauté function of the Mini Instant Pot. Let the oil heat for about 2 minutes.
4. The center of the Pot should be coated well with oil. Use tongs to place the chicken inside the pot with the breast-side up.
5. The chicken should be seared without any interruptions; the chicken will turn brown in 5 minutes. Do not worry if some of the chicken skin sticks to the bottom of the pan.
6. You can now flip the chicken to the breast side and sear it for 5 minutes or until it turns brown. Take the chicken out on the plate and keep it aside.
7. In the Mini Pot, add the mushrooms, onions; and garlic and sauté them until the onion is soft and the mushrooms have wilted completely.
8. Pour the tomato paste along with oregano and thyme and sauté for another 2 minutes until you have a flavorful concoction.
9. You can now add the broth and stir it with a wooden spoon. If there are brown bits at the bottom of the pot, you can easily scrape it with the wooden spoon.
10. Put the trivet in the Instant Pot just on the top of mushrooms and onions. Use the tongs to place the chicken breast-side up on the trivet.
11. Safely place the lid and set the Pressure Release to Sealing position.
12. Select the Poultry button and set the cooking time for 20 minutes at *HIGH* pressure.

13. You need to do a quick release by moving the Pressure Release to Venting position. Use heat-resistant mittens to take out the chicken with the trivet.
14. Put the chicken on the carving board. Strain the liquid through a fine-mesh strainer in a fat-separator bowl. Keep the onions and mushrooms by the side.
15. The liquid minus the fat should be poured back into the Instant Pot; discard the remaining fat. Scoop the fat with a ladle and discard.
16. Select the Sauté function in the Mini Instant Pot and let the sauce boil until it thickens. It will be done within a minute.
17. Taste the sauce and adjust the salt as required, Carve the chicken and arrange it on a platter.
18. Pour the sauce generously on the top and you are ready for a nice cozy meal with your entire family.

Nutrition Facts:
Calories: 370, Fat: 21g, Carbs: 1.4g, Protein: 50.3g

Tasty Cajun Chicken with Rice

*(**Prep + Cooking Time:** 30 minutes | **Serves:** 5)*

Ingredients:
- 1-pound chicken breast
- 1.5 cup white rice
- 1.75 cup chicken broth
- 1 tablespoon olive oil
- 1 tablespoon Cajun seasoning
- 1 diced bell pepper
- 1 tablespoon tomato paste
- 1 minced garlic clove
- 1 diced onion

Directions:
1. You should start by rinsing the rice; you will know that the rice is ready when the water runs clear. It will help you to remove the starch from the rice which might get stuck at the bottom of the Mini Instant Pot.
2. To make the chicken breasts thinner, you should cut them in half lengthwise. Take the Cajun seasoning and spread it lavishly on both sides.
3. Turn on the Sauté function of the Mini Instant Pot and soften both the onion and garlic.
4. If there are brown bits stuck at the bottom, deglaze with a few spoons of water. Remember if anything remains stuck at the bottom, it will prevent the Mini Pot from pressurizing properly.
5. Add the rice, bell peppers; and tomato paste along with 1 teaspoon of Cajun seasoning.
6. The Cajun seasoning is optional and should be only added if you want more heat and more paste. Stir everything until the ingredients are mixed well.
7. Now you can pour the chicken broth over the rice and arrange the chicken breasts on the top.
8. Close the lid of the Mini Instant Pot and turn the valve to Sealing position. Cook everything in *HIGH* pressure on Manual mode for 7-8 minutes.
9. Naturally release pressure for 5 minutes; the remaining pressure can be released by turning the *Venting* mode.
10. Carefully open the lid once the pin drops. Shred the chicken and combine it with rice. Put more salt or pepper if required.
11. Serve it in a bowl with a generous topping of freshly chopped cilantro and just a hint of lime.

Nutrition Facts:
Calories: 473, Fat: 7.4g, Carbs: 64.9g, Protein: 33.4g

Cheesy Chicken Bowl

(Prep + Cooking Time: 19 minutes | Serves: 2)

Ingredients:
- 1½ teaspoons olive oil
- 1/2 teaspoon cumin
- 1/2 cup chicken broth
- 1/2 lb. boneless chicken breast
- 3 tablespoons chopped' onion
- 1 teaspoon minced' garlic
- 1½ teaspoons chili powder
- 1/2 cup salsa
- 1/4 cup grated cheddar cheese
- 1/4 teaspoon pepper
- 1/4 teaspoon salt

Directions:
1. Pour olive oil into the inner pot of an Instant Pot then select *Sauté* menu. Stir in chopped' onion and minced' garlic then sauté until wilted and aromatic. Press the *Cancel* button
2. Cut the boneless chicken breast into small cubes then add to the Instant Pot
3. Season with chili powder, cumin, salt and pepper then pour chicken broth and salsa over the chicken. Stir well.
4. Close the Instant Pot with the lid then seal it properly. Close the steam valve.
5. Select *Manual* setting and cook the chicken on high. Set the time to 12 minutes
6. Once it is done; quick release the Instant Pot then open the lid
7. Sprinkle grated cheddar cheese over the chicken then stir quickly. Serve the cheesy chicken over two bowls of brown rice then enjoy immediately

Nutrition Facts:
Calories: 241; Net Carbs: 5.6g; Total Fat: 10.6g; Protein: 31.4g; Carbs: 7.8g;

Pancetta and Chicken Risotto

(Prep + Cooking Time: 30 minutes | Serves: 2)

Ingredients:
- 3/4-pound. chicken meat, diced
- 2 to 3 slices pancetta; diced
- 3/4 cup risotto or Arborio rice
- 1 teaspoon fresh thyme
- 1 tablespoon lemon zest
- 1 tablespoon unsalted butter
- 1 tablespoon olive oil
- 2 tablespoon parmesan; grated
- 2 garlic cloves; chopped
- 1/2 onion; chopped
- 1/3 cup white wine
- 3 ½ cups chicken stock
- Salt and Pepper to taste

Directions:
1. Add oil and butter to Instant Pot and press "Sauté" button (*Normal* preset), wait till you see Hot on the display.
2. Add onion, cook for 1 to 2 minutes. Add pancetta, chicken and garlic. Cook for another 2 to 3 minutes.
3. Add rice and mix well, rice should be covered with oil-butter mixture. Add wine and scrape the sides of the pot. Cook for 2 to 3 minutes stirring constantly. Press *Cancel* button.
4. Add chicken stock, thyme, lemon zest, salt and pepper. Close the lid and turn the vent to *Sealed*. Press *Pressure Cook* (Manual) button, use *+* or *-* button to set the timer for 6 minutes. Use *Pressure level* button to set Pressure to *HIGH*.

5. Once the timer is up; press *Cancel* button and allow the pressure to be released naturally; until the float valve drops down.
6. Open the lid; Add parmesan cheese to the pot and stir well until it melts. Serve topped with extra parmesan and lemon zest.

Nutrition Facts:
Calories: 586 g; Total Fat: 22.5 g; Total Carbohydrate: 23.6 g; Protein: 45

Turkey Meatballs Recipe

(Prep + Cooking Time: 25 minutes | Serves: 6)

Ingredients:
- 1.3–pound ground turkey breast
- 1/4 cup grated Parmigiano–Reggiano cheese
- 2 ½ cup marinara sauce
- 1/4 cup chopped parsley.
- 1/4 Panko breadcrumbs
- 1 chopped onion
- 1 crushed garlic clove
- Salt and Pepper to taste

Directions:
1. Put all the ingredients; except the marinara sauce, into a large bowl.
2. Mix the Ingredients well with the ground turkey.
3. Use this mixture to make 30 turkey meatballs about 2 inches in diameter.
4. Add the marinara sauce to the instant pot and select the *Sauté* function.
5. Bring it to the boil then add the turkey meatballs,
6. Cover with the lid and lock, Select *Manual* settings to *HIGH* pressure and 20 minutes on the timer.
7. After it beeps sound, use the *Natural Release* to vent the steam. Remove the lid and serve with fresh herbs sprinkled on top.

Nutrition Facts:
Calories: 545, Carbs: 3.2g, Protein: 66.7g, Fat: 24.1g

Hungarian Style Chicken

(Prep + Cooking Time: 40 minutes | Serves: 2)

Ingredients:
- 2 chicken leg quarters; bone-in
- 1 medium tomato; skin removed & coarsely chopped
- 1 cup chicken broth
- 1 small onion; well diced
- 1 tablespoon oil
- 2 teaspoons hot paprika
- 1/2 cup sour cream
- 1 teaspoon salt

Directions:
1. Add oil to Instant Pot and press "Sauté" button (*Normal* preset), wait till you see Hot on the display.
2. Add chicken and brown it for 4 to 5 minutes until golden brown. Add broth, onions and paprika to the Instant Pot.
3. Put tomatoes on top of chicken and sprinkle it with salt. Make sure NOT to stir. Close the lid and turn the vent to *Sealed*. Press *Pressure Cook* (Manual) button, use *+* or *-* button to set the timer for 10 minutes. Use *Pressure level* button to set Pressure to *HIGH*.
4. Once the timer is up; press *Cancel* button and allow the pressure to be released naturally; until the float valve drops down.

5. Open the lid; Take out chicken from Instant Pot and let it cool. Press *Sauté* button and adjust to *Less* preset, sauté for 15 minutes until the leftover liquid thickens.
6. Take 1/4 cup cooking juice out of Instant Pot and add to the sour cream and stir until evenly mixed.
7. Put cream mixture and chicken back into Instant Pot and simmer for few minutes. Serve chicken with sauce on top with noodles on the side.

Nutrition Facts:
Calories: 260 g; Total Fat: 29 g; Total Carbohydrate: 5.9 g; Protein: 16.3

Chicken and Coca Cola

(Prep + Cooking Time: 15 minutes | Serves: 2)

Ingredients:
- 1/2 lb. boneless chicken breast
- 2 tablespoons chopped' onion
- 3/4 tablespoon Worcestershire sauce
- 1/4 teaspoon chili powder
- 1/4 teaspoon oregano
- 1/4 teaspoon garlic powder
- 1 tablespoon chopped' scallions
- 1/4 cup ketchup
- 1/4 cup Coca cola
- 1/4 teaspoon salt
- 1/4 teaspoon pepper

Directions:
1. Pour ketchup, Coca cola and Worcestershire sauce into the inner pot of an Instant Pot. Mix until incorporated
2. Season with chopped' onion, chili powder, salt, pepper, oregano, garlic powder and chopped' scallions then stir well
3. Cut the boneless chicken breast into medium pieces then place in the Instant Pot. Make sure that the chicken is completely submerged in the Coca cola mixture
4. Cover the Instant Pot with the lid and seal it properly. Close the steam valve
5. Select *Manual* setting on the Instant Pot and cook the chicken with Coca cola on high. Set the time to 10 minutes.
6. Once the chicken is done, naturally release the Instant Pot then open the lid
7. Take the chicken out of the Instant Pot and place on a serving dish
8. Now, select *Sauté* menu on the Instant Pot and cook the sauce for about 3 minutes or until the sauce is thickened. Press the *Cancel* button. Drizzle the sauce over the cooked chicken then serve warm

Nutrition Facts:
Calories: 149; Net Carbs: 6.2g; Total Fat: 1.7g; Protein: 26.6g; Carbs: 6.8g;

Steamed Chicken Thigh

(Prep + Cooking Time: 21 minutes | Serves: 2)

Ingredients:
- 1/2 lb. chicken thighs
- 1/4 teaspoon cumin
- 1/4 teaspoon dried basil
- 1/2 cup water
- 1/2 teaspoon garlic powder
- 1/2 teaspoon onion powder
- 1/2 teaspoon chili powder
- 1 tablespoon olive oil
- 1/4 teaspoon salt
- 1/4 teaspoon pepper

Directions:
1. Rub the chicken thighs with olive oil, salt and pepper then set aside.
2. Select *Sauté* menu on the Instant Pot then place the seasoned chicken thighs in the inner pot of an Instant Pot
3. Sauté the chicken for about 2 minutes each side then press the *Cancel* button. Remove the chicken from the Instant Pot
4. Combine garlic powder with onion powder, chili powder, cumin and dried basil then coat the chicken thighs with the spice mixture
5. Place a trivet in the Instant Pot then pour water into it. Put the seasoned chicken thighs on the trivet then cover the Instant Pot with the lid and seal it properly. Close the steam valve
6. Select *Manual* setting on the Instant Pot and cook the chicken on high for 15 minutes
7. Once it is done; naturally release the Instant Pot and open the lid. Take the chicken out of the Instant Pot then arrange on a serving dish

Nutrition Facts:
Calories: 293; Net Carbs: 1.2g; Total Fat: 22.5g; Protein: 20.3g; Carbs: 1.6g;

Turkey Meatloaf BBQ

(Prep + Cooking Time: 15 minutes | Serves: 2)

Ingredients:
- 1/2 lb. ground turkey
- 2 tablespoons diced' onion
- 3 tablespoons water
- 1/4 teaspoon mustard
- 1/2 teaspoon Worcestershire sauce
- 1/2 teaspoon paprika
- 1 tablespoon breadcrumbs
- 1 egg
- 1 teaspoon brown sugar
- 1 teaspoon ketchup
- 2 tablespoons red wine vinegar
- 1/4 teaspoon hot pepper sauce
- 1/4 teaspoon salt
- 1/2 teaspoon pepper

Directions:
1. Combine ground turkey with diced' onion, breadcrumbs and egg then mix well
2. Place the turkey mixture on a sheet of aluminum foil then shape into a log. Wrap the log with aluminum then set aside.
3. Pour water into an Instant Pot then place a trivet in it. Put the turkey log on the trivet then cover and seal the Instant Pot properly. Close the steam valve
4. Select *Manual* setting on the Instant Pot and cook the turkey log on high for 15 minutes

5. In the meantime, place Worcestershire sauce, brown sugar, ketchup, red wine vinegar, water, mustard, paprika, salt, pepper and hot pepper sauce in a blender then blend until smooth and incorporated. Set aside.
6. Once the turkey log is done, naturally release the Instant Pot and open the lid
7. Remove the wrapped turkey log from the Instant Pot and place on a flat surface. Let it cool.
8. Unwrap the turkey log and cut into slices. Drizzle the sauce mixture over the turkey then serve

Nutrition Facts:
Calories: 149; Net Carbs: 6.2g; Total Fat: 1.7g; Protein: 26.6g; Carbs: 6.8g;

Lemon Chicken

(Prep + Cooking Time: 18 minutes | Serves: 2)

Ingredients:
- 1/2 lb. chicken thighs
- 2 tablespoons lemon juice
- 1/2 teaspoon grated lemon zest
- 3 tablespoons chicken broth
- 1/2 teaspoon red chili flakes
- 1 tablespoon butter
- 1/4 cup chopped' onion
- 1 teaspoon garlic powder
- 1/2 teaspoon smoked paprika
- 2 teaspoons minced' garlic
- 3/4 tablespoon Italian seasoning
- 1/4 teaspoon salt
- 1/4 teaspoon pepper

Directions:
1. Cut the chicken thighs into medium pieces then set aside. Place butter into the inner pot of the Instant Pot then press the *Sauté* button
2. Once the butter is melted, stir in chopped' chicken thighs then sauté for 2-3 minutes each side or until brown. Press the *Cancel* button
3. Remove the sautéed chicken from the Instant Pot then set aside
4. Press the *Sauté* button again then stir in chopped' onion and minced' garlic. Sauté until wilted and aromatic then press the *Cancel* button.
5. Return the chicken back to the Instant Pot then season with salt, pepper, garlic powder, smoked paprika, red chili flakes, Italian seasoning, lemon juice and grated lemon zest
6. Close the Instant Pot with the lid then seal it properly. Close the steam valve
7. Select *Manual* setting on the Instant Pot then cook the chicken on high. Set the time to 10 minutes.
8. Once it is done; naturally release the Instant Pot then open the lid. Transfer the cooked chicken to a serving dish then serve

Nutrition Facts:
Calories: 336; Net Carbs: 4.8g; Total Fat: 24.7g; Protein: 21.6g; Carbs: 5.8g;

Buttermilk Chicken Rosemary

(Prep + Cooking Time: 6 hours | Serves: 2)

Ingredients:
- 1/2 lb. chicken drumsticks
- 1/2 teaspoon onion powder
- 1/2 teaspoon garlic powder
- 1/2 cup buttermilk
- 1 teaspoon chopped' rosemary
- 1/4 teaspoon salt
- 1/4 teaspoon pepper

Directions:
1. Combine buttermilk with onion powder, garlic powder, salt, pepper and rosemary then stir well. Place the chicken drumsticks in a zipper-lock plastic bag then pour the buttermilk mixture into the bag
2. Shake the plastic bag to ensure that the chicken drumsticks are completely coated with the buttermilk mixture
3. Marinate the chicken for at least 4 hours or overnight is better. Store in the fridge to keep them fresh.
4. On the next day, remove the chicken out of the fridge and thaw at room temperature
5. Transfer the chicken to an Instant Pot together with the liquid then cover and seal the Instant Pot properly.
6. Select *Slow Cooker* setting on the Instant Pot and set the time to 6 hours. Adjust the temperature on low and ensure that the pressure valve is in the *Venting* position
7. Once the chicken is done, naturally release the Instant Pot then open the lid. Transfer the cooked chicken to a serving dish then serve. Enjoy!

Nutrition Facts:
Calories: 242; Net Carbs: 4.1g; Total Fat: 14.7g; Protein: 23.3g; Carbs: 4.5g;

Spiced Chicken Breats

(Prep + Cooking Time: 30 minutes | Serves: 3)

Ingredients:
- 3 chicken breasts; boneless and skinless
- 1/8 teaspoon black pepper
- 1/8 teaspoon oregano; dried
- 1/8 teaspoon dried basil
- 1 tablespoon olive oil
- 1 cup water
- 1/4 teaspoon garlic powder
- 1/2 teaspoon salt

Directions:
1. In a mixing bowl of medium size, combine the garlic powder, salt, black pepper, oregano and basil. Rinse the chicken, pat dry and season one side with the ½ portion of the prepared mix. Place your Instant Pot on a flat kitchen surface', plug it and turn it on.
2. To start making the recipe, press *Sauté* button. Add the oil and chicken, seasoned side down and then season the second side as well using remaining seasoning mix; cook for 3-4 minutes per side to soften the ingredients.
3. Then remove from the pot. Pour the water into the pot. Arrange the trivet in the pot and add the chicken over the trivet. Carefully close its lid and firmly lock it. Then after, seal the valve too.
4. To start making the recipe, press *Manual* button. Now you have to set cooking time', set the timer for 5 minutes. Allow the pot to cook the mixture until the timer goes off.

5. Turn off the pot and press *Cancel.* Allow the built up pressure to vent out naturally', it will take 8-10 minutes to completely release inside pressure. Open its lid and transfer the cooked mixture into serving container/containers. Serve warm!

Nutrition Facts:
Calories 324; Fat: 9.3g; Carbohydrates: 19.5g; Fiber: 2g; Protein 42.3g

Cornish Hens with Gravy

(Prep + Cooking Time: 30 minutes | Serves: 2)

Ingredients:
- 2 small Cornish hens
- 1/2 teaspoon rosemary
- 1 cup chicken stock
- 1/2 teaspoon black pepper
- 1 teaspoon thyme
- 2 tablespoons flour
- 2 tablespoons water
- 1 teaspoon salt

Directions:
1. Rub the Cornish hens with salt, pepper, thyme and rosemary. Place into Instant Pot and add the stock.
2. Close lid and set cooking time for 20 minutes. Use quick release to remove steam. Open the lid and transfer hen to a serving dish.
3. Set Instant Pot to *Sauté* and bring the stock to a boil. Stir together flour and water in a small bowl.
4. Pour into boiling stock, stirring constantly and cook until thickened. Serve gravy with the hen.

Nutrition Facts:
Calories: 316; Fat: 8.34 g; Carbohydrates: 7.12 g; Fiber: 0.5 g; Protein: 49.6 g

Cranberry Turkey Recipe

(Prep + Cooking Time: 50 minutes | Serves: 2)

Ingredients:
- 1 pound. turkey thighs or legs
- 1 cup apple cider
- 2 tablespoons water
- 1/2 tablespoon dried parsley flakes
- 1 teaspoon dried thyme
- 1 teaspoon ground cinnamon
- 1 small lemon; chopped, seeds removed
- 1 tablespoon arrowroot starch; dissolved in 1 tablespoon of water
- 1/2 cup cranberries; fresh or frozen
- 1 tablespoon olive oil
- 1/4 cup raisins
- 2 garlic cloves; minced
- 1 teaspoon sea salt

Directions:
1. Press "Sauté" button on the pressure cooker (*Normal* preset) and wait till you see Hot on the display. Add oil, garlic and raisins to the pot, sauté for 2 to 3 minutes with the lid open.
2. Add the meat into the skillet; put lemon and 1 cup of cranberries on top of the turkey. Press *Cancel* button.
3. Mix apple cider, ground cinnamon, thyme, parsley flakes and sea salt in a bowl. Add the mixture to the pot. Close the lid and turn the vent to *Sealed*. Press *Meat/Stew* button and adjust to *Normal* preset.
4. Once the timer is up; press "Cancel" button and allow the pressure to be released naturally; until the float valve drops down.

5. Open the lid; Preheat the oven broiler. Transfer the cooked turkey to a casserole. Broil in the oven for 5 minutes.
6. Press "Sauté" button on the pressure cooker and adjust to *Less* preset. Add the remaining cranberries to the sauce.
7. Add the mixture of arrowroot flour and water. Stir the sauce and allow to simmer until it thickens a bit.
8. Serve the browned turkey pieces with the cranberry sauce and steamed veggies on the side.

Nutrition Facts:
Calories: 287 g; Total Fat: 23.7 g; Total Carbohydrate: 19 g; Protein: 21.7

Potato Chicken

*(**Prep + Cooking Time:** 30 minutes | **Serves:** 2)*

Ingredients:
- 1-pound. chopped chicken
- 1-pound potatoes; peeled and make wedges
- 1 tablespoon Italian seasoning
- 2 tablespoons lemon juice
- 1/2 cup low sodium chicken broth
- 1 ½ tablespoons Dijon mustard
- 1 teaspoon lemon zest
- 1/2 teaspoon salt
- 1/2 teaspoon pepper

Directions:
1. Season the chicken with pepper and salt. Switch on the pot after placing it on a clean and dry platform.
2. Open the pot lid and place the above-mentioned ingredients in the cooking pot area. Give the ingredients a little stir.
3. Close the pot by closing the top lid. Also, ensure to seal the valve. Press *Manual* cooking function and set cooking time to 15 minutes.
4. It will start cooking after a few minutes. Let the pot mix cook under pressure until the timer reads zero.
5. Press *Cancel* cooking function and press *Natural release* setting.
6. It will take 8-10 minutes for natural pressure release. Open the pot and serve warm.

Nutrition Facts:
Calories: 256; Fat: 3.5g; Carbohydrates: 34.5g; Fiber: 6g; Protein 18.5g

Yellow Chicken

*(**Prep + Cooking Time:** 17 minutes | **Serves:** 2)*

Ingredients:
- 1/2 lb. boneless chicken breast
- 2 tablespoons minced' onion
- 2 teaspoons minced' garlic
- 1½ teaspoons ginger
- 3/4 teaspoon turmeric
- 3/4 teaspoon smoked paprika
- 1/2 teaspoon cumin
- 1/2 cup diced' tomatoes
- 1/2 cup tomato chili sauce
- 1/4 cup chicken broth
- 2 tablespoons coconut milk
- 1 tablespoon olive oil
- 1/4 teaspoon cayenne pepper
- 1/4 teaspoon salt
- 1/4 teaspoon pepper

Directions:
1. Cut the boneless chicken breast into small cubes then set aside
2. Prepare the Instant Pot then pour olive oil into the inner pot of the Instant Pot. Press *Sauté* button and wait until the oil is hot.
3. Now, stir in minced' garlic and onion then sauté until wilted and aromatic
4. After that; add chicken cubes to the Instant Pot then sauté until wilted and no longer pink. Press the *Cancel* button
5. Season the chicken with ginger, turmeric, smoked paprika, cumin, cayenne pepper, salt and pepper then add diced' tomatoes and tomatoes paste to the Instant Pot
6. Pour chicken broth over the chicken then stir well. Put the lid on the Instant Pot then seal it properly. Close the steam valve
7. Select *Manual* menu then cook the chicken on high for 10 minutes
8. Once it is done; quick release the Instant Pot then open the lid
9. Pour coconut milk over the chicken then stir well. Select *Sauté* setting again then cook the chicken on high for another 3 minutes
10. Once it is done; naturally release the Instant Pot then transfer the cooked chicken together with the gravy to a serving dish. Serve and enjoy with a bowl of warm rice

Nutrition Facts:
Calories: 251; Net Carbs: 6.1g; Total Fat: 13.4g; Protein: 27.4g; Carbs: 8.3g;

Tomato Turkey Meal

(Prep + Cooking Time: 30 minutes | Serves: 2)

Ingredients:
- 2-pounds ground turkey breast
- 1 15-ounce can of diced tomatoes
- 2 cloves garlic; chopped
- 1 red onion; sliced
- 1 cup chicken stock
- 1 tablespoon butter
- 1 red bell pepper; chopped
- 1 green bell pepper; chopped

Directions:
1. Switch on the pot after placing it on a clean and dry platform. Press *Sauté* cooking function.
2. Open the lid; add the butter and meat in the pot; cook for 5 minutes to cook well and soften.
3. Add the tomatoes with their juices, garlic, onion, peppers and stock. Close the pot by closing the top lid. Also, ensure to seal the valve.
4. Press *Manual* cooking function and set cooking time to 15 minutes. It will start cooking after a few minutes. Let the pot mix cook under pressure until the timer reads zero.
5. Press *Cancel* cooking function and press *Quick release* setting. Open the pot and serve warm.

Nutrition Facts:
Calories: 506; Fat: 19.5g; Carbohydrates: 12g; Fiber: 2.5g; Protein 62.5g

Pasta Chicken

*(**Prep + Cooking Time:** 20 minutes | **Serves:** 2)*

Ingredients:
- 2 tablespoons chopped parsley
- Cooked pasta of your choice
- 1 bay leaf
- 1/2 cup chopped onion
- 1 ½ cup diced chicken
- 1/2 teaspoon olive oil
- 1/2 cup diced tomatoes
- 1/2 cup diced red bell pepper
- 1/2 teaspoon oregano
- 1/4 teaspoon salt
- 1/2 teaspoon pepper

Directions:
1. Switch on the pot after placing it on a clean and dry platform. Press *Sauté* cooking function.
2. Open the lid; add the oil and onions in the pot; cook for 2 minutes to cook well and soften.
3. Add the chicken, bell pepper and diced tomatoes. Mix the salt, pepper, oregano and bay leaf. Close the pot by closing the top lid. Also, ensure to seal the valve.
4. Press *Manual* cooking function and set cooking time to 10 minutes. It will start cooking after a few minutes. Let the pot mix cook under pressure until the timer reads zero.
5. Press *Cancel* cooking function and press *Natural release* setting.
6. It will take 8-10 minutes for natural pressure release. Open the instant pot; top with some parsley and serve with cooked pasta!

Nutrition Facts:
Calories: 102; Fat: 2.5g; Carbohydrates: 4g; Fiber: 1g; Protein 15.5g

Spicy and Sweet Honey Chicken

*(**Prep + Cooking Time:** 21 minutes | **Serves:** 2)*

Ingredients:
- 1/2 lb. boneless chicken breast
- 3/4 tablespoon soy sauce
- 1/2 teaspoon Worcestershire sauce
- 1½ tablespoons chopped' onion
- 1/2 teaspoon red chili flakes
- 1/2 teaspoon sesame seeds
- 1/2 teaspoon brown sugar
- 1/2 tablespoon raw honey
- 1/2 teaspoon minced' garlic
- 1/2 teaspoon cayenne pepper

Directions:
1. Cut boneless chicken breast into small or medium cubes then place in the inner pot of an Instant Pot
2. Sprinkle brown sugar, cayenne pepper, red chili flakes and onion over the chicken then drizzle raw honey, soy sauce and Worcestershire sauce on top
3. Cover the Instant Pot with the lid and seal it properly. Close the steam valve
4. Select *Manual* setting and cook the chicken on high for 12 minutes. Once it is done; quick release the Instant Pot then open the lid.
5. Transfer the cooked chicken to a serving dish together with the liquid then sprinkle sesame seeds on top. Serve and enjoy warm with brown rice

Nutrition Facts:
Calories: 147; Net Carbs: 7g; Total Fat: 2g; Protein: 25.5g; Carbs: 7.6g

Rosemary Turkey Paprika

(Prep + Cooking Time: 22 minutes | Serves: 2)

Ingredients:
- 1 lb. bone-in turkey breast
- 3/4 cup water
- 1/4 cup chopped' onion
- 1½ teaspoons olive oil
- 1/2 teaspoon paprika
- 2 teaspoons rosemary
- 1/4 teaspoon salt
- 1/4 teaspoon pepper

Directions:
1. Combine olive oil with paprika, rosemary, salt and pepper then rub the turkey with the spices. Pour water into an Instant Pot and place a trivet in it
2. Arrange the turkey breast on the trivet then cover the Instant Pot properly
3. Select *Manual* setting on the Instant Pot and cook the turkey on high. Set the time to 25 minutes
4. Once it is done; naturally release the Instant Pot then open the lid. Transfer the cooked turkey to a serving dish then sprinkle chopped' onion on top

Nutrition Facts:
Calories: 274; Net Carbs: 1.5g; Total Fat: 15.3g; Protein: 30.4g; Carbs: 2.6g;

Special Turkey Breasts

(Prep + Cooking Time: 25 minutes | Serves: 2)

Ingredients:
- 2 boneless turkey breasts; halved
- 1 teaspoon Dijon mustard
- 1 teaspoon fresh sage; chopped
- 1 teaspoon fresh thyme; chopped
- 1 teaspoon fresh rosemary; chopped
- 2 tablespoons lemon juice
- 2 garlic cloves; minced
- 1/2 orange; juiced
- 1 orange; sliced
- 1 cup chicken broth
- 2 tablespoons oil
- Salt and Pepper to taste

Directions:
1. Mix 1 tablespoon oil, mustard, garlic, sage, thyme and rosemary. Rub the turkey with this mixture, season with salt and pepper.
2. Add 1 tablespoon oil to the Instant pot; press "Sauté" button (*Normal* preset), wait till you see Hot on the display. Add turkey breast to the pot and cook for 3-4 minutes on each side. Press *Cancel* button.
3. Mix orange juice, lemon juice and broth in a bowl. Pour the mixture to the Instant pot over turkey. Add orange slices. Close the lid and turn the vent to *Sealed*.
4. Press *Pressure Cook* (Manual) button, use *+* or *-* button to set the timer for 6 minutes. Use *Pressure level* button to set Pressure to *HIGH*.
5. Once the timer is up; press *Cancel* button and turn the steam release handle to *Venting* position for quick release, until the float valve drops down. Open the lid and serve.

Nutrition Facts:
Calories: 225 g; Total Fat: 8.8 g; Total Carbohydrate: 4.1 g; Protein: 36.7

BBQ Chicken Sliders

(Prep + Cooking Time: 26 minutes | Serves: 2)

Ingredients:

- 4–pound boneless chicken breasts
- 1/2 teaspoon garlic powder
- 2 tablespoon Dijon mustard
- 1 cup mayonnaise
- 2 tablespoon apple cider vinegar
- 1 teaspoon kosher salt
- 1/2 teaspoon onion powder
- 1/2 teaspoon black pepper
- 1 ½ cup barbecue sauce
- 3 cup coleslaw mix
- 12 sliders
- 1 teaspoon celery salt

Directions:

1. Take a large bowl and mix the chicken along with the seasonings in the pressure cooker of Mini Instant Pot. Do not add the barbecue sauce in the beginning.
2. Lock the lid carefully, close the pressure cooker; and set the cooking time for 15 minutes in Manual mode.
3. The display panel should read High Pressure. If the chicken is frozen, it needs to be thawed for about 20 minutes.
4. Once you are done with cooking, you should turn the pressure valve to *Venting* and do a quick pressure release.
5. Be careful about one thing: turn the vent away from the body so that there are no burns.
6. After removing the chicken with the tongs, you should transfer it to a cutting board. Use forks to shred the chicken. Return to the pot once shredded.
7. Now you need to change the setting to either *Sauté* or *Simmer* and add the barbecue sauce.
8. Stir the chicken until it is warm again, or simply allow the chicken to simmer in the sauce so that you have a flavorful chicken.
9. Put the coleslaw veggies into a bowl, take another small bowl and start whisking the apple cider vinegar, Dijon mustard, mayonnaise, black pepper; and celery salt.
10. Taste the mixture; if required, you can add some black pepper and kosher salt.
11. Toss the veggies in this dressing and use it on the sliders.
12. Cut the slider buns into half; add the shredded chicken and top it with coleslaw and put the top bun.
13. You can serve it with barbecue baked beans or southern–style potato salad.

Nutrition Facts:
Calories: 403, Fat: 20g, Carbs: 19g, Protein: 35g

Spaghetti Squash with Chicken

(Prep + Cooking Time: 35 minutes | Serves: 3)

Ingredients:

- 1-pound. chicken; cooked and chopped into cubes
- 1 spaghetti squash; split in half and seeded
- 7-ounce mozzarella cheese
- 1/2 cup marinara sauce
- 2 cups water

Directions:

1. Pour water into Instant Pot. Place a trivet into the Instant Pot.
2. Put squash halves on the trivet. Close the lid and turn the vent to *Sealed*.

3. Press *Pressure Cook* (Manual) button, use *+* or *-* button to set the timer for 20 minutes. Use *Pressure level* button to set Pressure to *HIGH*.
4. Once the timer is up; press *Cancel* button and turn the steam release handle to *Venting* position for quick release, until the float valve drops down.
5. Open the lid; Take out spaghetti squash and shred with a fork. Pour marinara sauce over spaghetti squash and stir until evenly mixed.
6. Put chicken cubes over spaghetti squash. Top with mozzarella cheese and serve.

Nutrition Facts:
Calories: 300 g; Total Fat: 25.3 g; Total Carbohydrate: 4 g; Protein: 14

Chicken Teriyaki

(Prep + Cooking Time: 18 minutes | Serves: 2)

Ingredients:
- 1/2 lb. boneless chicken breast
- 1 teaspoon minced' garlic
- 1/2 tablespoon honey
- 1 teaspoon mirin
- 3/4 tablespoon olive oil
- 1/4 teaspoon ginger
- 2 tablespoons sliced carrots
- 1/2 cup water
- 1 tablespoon soy sauce
- 2 tablespoons apple cider vinegar
- 1/4 teaspoon salt
- 1/4 teaspoon pepper

Directions:
1. Combine soy sauce with apple cider vinegar, honey and mirin in a bowl then stir until incorporated. Set aside. Cut the boneless chicken breast into medium cubes then set aside
2. Pour olive oil into the inner pot of an Instant Pot then select *Sauté* menu
3. Cut the boneless chicken breast into cubes then stir into the Instant Pot
4. Add minced' garlic to the Instant Pot then sauté until aromatic and the chicken is no longer pink. Press the *Cancel* button.
5. Pour half of the sauce mixture and water over the chicken then season with salt, pepper and ginger.
6. Select *Manual* setting and cook the chicken on high for 10 minutes
7. Once it is done; quick release the Instant Pot and open the lid
8. Pour the remaining sauce over the chicken then add chopped' carrot to the Instant Pot
9. Select *Sauté* menu on the Instant Pot then cook the chicken uncovered for 3 minutes. Once it is done; transfer the chicken teriyaki together with the gravy to a serving dish

Nutrition Facts:
Calories: 201; Net Carbs: 6.7g; Total Fat: 8.3g; Protein: 25.2g; Carbs: 7g

Lemon Chicken with Kalamata Olives

(Prep + Cooking Time: 5 hours | Serves: 2)

Ingredients:
- 1/2 lb. chopped' chicken
- 1/4 teaspoon thyme
- 1 teaspoon avocado oil
- 1 teaspoon minced' garlic
- 2 teaspoons diced' red pepper
- 1/2 cup Kalamata olives
- 2 tablespoons chopped' onions
- 1/4 cup chicken broth
- 1 tablespoon red wine vinegar
- 1 tablespoon lemon juice
- 1/4 teaspoon oregano
- 1/4 teaspoon salt
- 1/4 teaspoon pepper

Directions:
1. Rub the chicken with salt and pepper then set aside. Pour avocado oil into the inner pot of an Instant Pot then select *Sauté* menu
2. Stir in minced' garlic then sauté until aromatic and lightly golden brown
3. Now, add chopped' chicken to the Instant Pot then sauté for 2 minutes each side. Press the *Cancel* button.
4. After that; combine chicken broth with red wine vinegar and lemon juice then mix well
5. Drizzle the chicken broth mixture over the chicken then sprinkle diced' red pepper, Kalamata olives, chopped' onion, oregano and thyme on top
6. Cover the Instant Pot with the lid and seal it properly. Select *Slow Cooker* setting on the Instant Pot and set the time to 5 hours. Adjust the temperature on high and ensure that the pressure valve is in the *Venting* position
7. Once the Instant Pot beeps, naturally release the Instant Pot. Open the Instant Pot and transfer the cooked chicken to a serving dish

Nutrition Facts:
Calories: 271; Net Carbs: 3.9g; Total Fat: 4.5g; Protein: 20g; Carbs: 4.5g;

Beef Recipes

Hearty Beef Stew

(Prep + Cooking Time: 55 minutes | Serves: 2)

Ingredients:
- 1-pound chuck beef
- 2 carrots; sliced
- 1 celery stalk; sliced
- 1 teaspoon thyme
- 1/2 teaspoon rosemary
- 1/2 teaspoon black pepper
- 2 tablespoons butter
- 1 onion; chopped
- 2 tablespoons flour
- 1 tablespoon tomato paste
- 2 cups beef broth
- 1/2-pound potatoes; chopped
- 1 teaspoon salt

Directions:
1. Season the beef with salt and pepper. Melt the butter in the Instant Pot on *Sauté* mode. Brown beef in butter. Remove to a plate.
2. Add onion, carrots and celery to the pot. Cook until onion is translucent, then add thyme and rosemary and toast 30 seconds. Add flour and stir until everything is well-coated.
3. Add tomato paste, then beef broth and scrape off anything stuck to the bottom of the pot. Add potatoes and replace beef in pot.
4. Close lid and set cooking time to 35 minutes on *HIGH* pressure. Season to taste with salt and pepper.

Nutrition Facts:
Calories: 570; Fat: 25.33 g; Carbohydrates: 33.68 g; Fiber: 4.5 g; Protein: 53.64 g

Asian Beef Stew

(Prep + Cooking Time: 40 minutes | Serves: 3)

Ingredients:
- 1-pound. lean beef; cut into cubes
- 1 jalapeno pepper; chopped
- 1 tablespoons flour
- 1/2 teaspoon black pepper
- 1/2 teaspoon five spice powder
- 2 cups beef broth
- 1 cinnamon stick
- 2 cardamom pods
- 2 anise star pods
- 2 cloves garlic; crushed and minced
- 1 teaspoon fresh lemongrass; chopped
- 1/2 cup poblano pepper; diced
- 2 cups tomatoes; chopped
- 2 tablespoons rice vinegar
- 1/2 tablespoon soy sauce
- 1 tablespoon honey
- 2 tablespoons olive oil
- 1/2 cup red onion; chopped
- 1/2 cup carrots; chopped
- 2 tablespoons tomato paste
- 1/2 cup acorn squash; cubed

Directions:
1. Mix flour, pepper and five spice powder in a bowl. Dip the meat into the flour mixture, coating generously.
2. Add garlic, lemongrass, rice vinegar, soy sauce and honey. Mix well and refrigerate for at least 30 minutes.

3. Add oil to Instant Pot and press "Sauté" button (*Normal* preset), wait till you see Hot on the display.
4. Add beef, onions and carrots. Sauté until meat is lightly browned, for about 3-5 minutes. Add poblano and jalapeno peppers, cook for another 1 to 2 minutes.
5. Add tomatoes, tomato paste, squash, cinnamon stick, cardamom and anise star. Cook stirring until well blended, for about 3-5 minutes. Press *Cancel* button.
6. Add beef broth, close the lid and turn the vent to *Sealed*. Press *Pressure Cook* (Manual) button, use *+* or *-* button to set the timer for 20 minutes. Use *Pressure level* button to set Pressure to *HIGH*.
7. Once the timer is up; press *Cancel* button and turn the steam release handle to *Venting* position for quick release, until the float valve drops down. Open the lid; Serve with rice on the side.

Nutrition Facts: Calories: 447 g; Total Fat: 15.5 g; Total Carbohydrate: 29 g; Protein: 47.8

Beef and Pasta

(Prep + Cooking Time: 15 minutes | Serves: 2)

Ingredients:
- 1/4-pound ground beef
- 1/4-pound ground pork
- 6 ounces' ruffles pasta
- 4 ounces' ricotta cheese
- 4 ounces' mozzarella cheese
- 1 cup pasta sauce
- 1 cup water
- Cooking oil

Directions:
1. Switch on the pot after placing it on a clean and dry platform. Press *Sauté* cooking function.
2. Open the lid; add the oil, pork and beef in the pot; cook for 3-4 minutes to cook well and evenly browned.
3. Mix the water, pasta and sauce. Close the pot by closing the top lid. Also, ensure to seal the valve.
4. Press *Manual* cooking function and set cooking time to 5 minutes. It will start cooking after a few minutes. Let the pot mix cook under pressure until the timer reads zero.
5. Press *Cancel* cooking function and press *Quick release* setting. Open the pot, mix the cheese and serve warm.

Nutrition Facts:
Calories: 588; Fat: 24g; Carbohydrates: 52.5g; Fiber: 4.5g; Protein 61g

Beef Potato Tots

(Prep + Cooking Time: 15 minutes | Serves: 4)

Ingredients:
- 3/4–pound lean ground beef
- 8–ounce cream chicken soup
- 16–ounce frozen potato rounds
- 2 tablespoon oil
- 1/4 chopped onion.

Directions:
1. Set instant pot to *Sauté* mode and heat the oil, Stir in the beef and onion. Sauté for 5 minutes,
2. Add the cream of chicken soup and place the potato tater tots on top.
3. Secure the lid and cook for 25 minutes at medium pressure on the *Manual* setting.
4. *Natural release* for 5 minutes then remove the lid. Serve warm.

Nutrition Facts: Calories: 1100, Fat: 63.4g, Carbs: 92.7g, Protein: 35.2g

Western Beef Recipe

*(**Prep + Cooking Time:** 20 minutes | **Serves:** 3)*

Ingredients:
- 1/2-pound ground beef
- 1/2-pound uncooked macaroni
- 1 tablespoon olive oil
- 1 cup shredded mozzarella cheese
- 1 onion; diced
- 2 cloves garlic; minced
- 1 can whole tomatoes in their juice; crushed
- 1/2 cup beef stock
- 1 tablespoon Worcestershire sauce
- 1/2 teaspoon salt
- 1/2 teaspoon black pepper

Directions:
1. Heat olive oil in Instant Pot on *Sauté* mode. Brown beef and drain excess fat, then add onions and garlic.
2. Pour in tomatoes, stock, Worcestershire, salt and pepper. Stir in pasta and half of the cheese.
3. Close lid and set cooking time to 8 minutes on *HIGH* pressure. Use quick release to remove steam.
4. Sprinkle the remaining cheese over the pasta and close lid until the cheese is melted. Serve.

Nutrition Facts:
Calories: 495; Fat: 19.89 g; Carbohydrates: 48.74 g; Fiber: 3.3 g; Protein: 29.07 g

Spicy Sliced Beef

*(**Prep + Cooking Time:** 30 minutes | **Serves:** 2)*

Ingredients:
- 1/2 lb. beef tenderloin
- 1 tablespoon minced' garlic
- 2 kaffir lime leaves
- 1/4 cup water
- 1 tablespoon vegetable oil
- 2 tablespoons lemon juice
- 1/4 teaspoon salt
- 2 tablespoons red chili pepper

Directions:
1. Cut the beef into thin slices then place in the inner pot of an Instant Pot
2. Add salt, lemon juice, red chili pepper, minced' garlic and lime leaves to the Instant Pot then pour water over the beef. Cover the Instant Pot with the lid and seal it properly. Close the steam valve
3. Select *Manual* setting on the Instant Pot and cook the beef on high for 20 minutes
4. Once it is done; naturally release the Instant Pot and open the lid. Discard the gravy but let the beef stay in the Instant Pot.
5. Now, drizzle vegetable oil over the beef and select *Sauté* setting again
6. Stir the beef is completely coated with oil and looked shiny. Transfer the beef to a serving dish and serve.

Nutrition Facts:
Calories: 268; Net Carbs: 5.5g; Total Fat: 15.1g; Protein: 25.6g; Carbs: 6.3g;

Cheesy Beef Pie

(Prep + Cooking Time: 20 minutes | Serves: 2)

Ingredients:
- 1/4 lb. ground beef
- 1 tablespoon sesame oil
- 1/4 cup cheddar cubes
- 2 tablespoons cornstarch
- 2 teaspoons garlic powder
- 2 eggs
- 1/2 teaspoon pepper

Directions:
1. Combine the entire ingredients in a bowl then mix well. Transfer the mixture in a disposable aluminum pan then spread evenly
2. Pour water into the Instant Pot and place a trivet in it. Place the disposable aluminum pan on the trivet then cover and seal the Instant Pot properly
3. Select *Steam* setting on the Instant Pot and cook the beef on high for 15 minutes.
4. Once it is done; naturally release the Instant Pot then open the lid
5. Take the disposable aluminum pan out of the Instant Pot and let it cool for a few minutes. Serve with tomato chili sauce

Nutrition Facts:
Calories: 368; Net Carbs: 3.4g; Total Fat: 30.7g; Protein: 19.2g; Carbs: 3.8g;

Sour Spice Beef Brisket

(Prep + Cooking Time: 30 minutes | Serves: 2)

Ingredients:
- 1/2 lb. beef brisket
- 1/2 teaspoon ginger
- 1½ teaspoons red chilies
- 1 teaspoon vegetable oil
- 2 tablespoons sliced shallots
- 2 teaspoons minced' garlic
- 3 tablespoons tamarind water
- 1/4 cup diced' tomatoes
- 1 bay leaf
- 1/4 cup water
- 1/4 teaspoon salt

Directions:
1. Cut the beef brisket into slices then rub with tamarind water. Pour vegetable oil into the inner pot of an Instant Pot then select *Sauté* setting.
2. Stir in minced' garlic and sliced shallots then sauté until wilted and aromatic
3. Add beef brisket to the Instant Pot and season with bay leaf, diced' tomatoes, ginger, red chilies and salt. Sauté until aromatic then press the *Cancel* button
4. Pour water into the Instant Pot then cover and seal it properly. Close the steam valve
5. Select *Manual* setting and cook the beef for 15 minutes. Once it is done; naturally release the Instant Pot and open the lid.
6. Select *Sauté* setting again and cook the beef uncovered for about 3 minutes or until the liquid reduces into a half
7. Transfer the beef and the gravy to a serving dish then serve immediately with a bowl of brown rice. If you like, you can sprinkle sesame seeds and red chili flakes on top for garnish

Nutrition Facts:
Calories: 350; Net Carbs: 3.9g; Total Fat: 27.4g; Protein: 21.7g; Carbs: 4.5g;

Peppercorns Beef

(Prep + Cooking Time: 2 hours | Serves: 2)

Ingredients:
- 2-pound corned beef; flat cut
- 1 cup low-sodium chicken broth
- 1 teaspoon dried thyme
- 4 whole peppercorns
- 2 large bay leaves
- 1/2 quartered onion
- 1/2 cup water

Directions:
1. Put the pork in your instant pot.
2. Add all the remaining Ingredients and secure the lid.
3. Cook for 90 minutes at *HIGH* pressure on *Manual* function, Natural release the steam and remove the lid. Serve hot.

Nutrition Facts:
Calories: 797, Fat: 56.8g, Carbs: 4.9g, Protein: 62g

Spicy Beef Tenderloin

(Prep + Cooking Time: 25 minutes | Serves: 2)

Ingredients:
- 1/2 lb. beef tenderloin
- 1 lemon grass
- 1 tablespoon red chili flakes
- 1 teaspoon cayenne
- 2 shallots
- 2 cloves garlic
- 1/2 teaspoon turmeric
- 1/4 teaspoon ginger
- 1 teaspoon tamarind water
- 4 tablespoons coconut milk
- 2 tablespoons water
- 1/4 teaspoon salt

Directions:
1. Place red chili flakes, cayenne, shallots, garlic, turmeric, ginger, tamarind water and salt in a food processor. Process until smooth
2. Cut the beef tenderloin into slices then place in the inner pot of an Instant Pot.
3. Add the spice mixture to the Instant Pot then pour coconut milk and water over the beef. Stir well
4. Cover the Instant Pot with the lid then seal it properly. Close the steam valve
5. Select *Pressure cook* setting on the Instant Pot then cook the beef on high. Set the time to 20 minutes.
6. Once it is done; naturally release the Instant Pot then open the lid. Transfer the cooked beef and the gravy to a serving dish then serve warm

Nutrition Facts:
Calories: 278; Net Carbs: 6.6g; Total Fat: 15.5g; Protein: 26.8g; Carbs: 8.1g;

Beef Lasagna

*(**Prep + Cooking Time:** 50 minutes | **Serves:** 2)*

Ingredients:
- 15-ounce marinara sauce or Italian sauce
- 1/2-pound. ground beef
- 1 cup Mozzarella cheese
- 6 uncooked lasagna noodles
- 1 tablespoon olive oil
- 1 cup Ricotta cheese
- 2 cups water
- 1/2 onion; chopped
- 2 garlic cloves; minced
- Salt and Pepper to taste

Directions:
1. Add oil to Instant Pot and press "Sauté" button (*Normal* preset), wait till you see Hot on the display. Add onion and garlic, cook for 2 minutes. Add beef, salt and pepper, cook for 3-4 minutes.
2. Transfer Instant pot content to a plate. Insert a trivet into the Instant pot.
3. Prepare a spring form pan that will fit into the Instant Pot. Put lasagna pieces on the bottom of the pan. Add 1/3 part of sauce on top, 1/3 meat, Mozzarella and Ricotta cheese.
4. Add another layer of pasta, sauce, meat and cheese mixture. Repeat with the rest of ingredients. Add water to the Instant pot. Put the spring form pan on a trivet.
5. Close the lid and turn the vent to *Sealed*. Press *Pressure Cook* (Manual) button, use *+* or *-* button to set the timer for 20 minutes. Use *Pressure level* button to set Pressure to *HIGH*.
6. Once the timer is up; press *Cancel* button and allow the pressure to be released naturally; until the float valve drops down, Open the lid.
7. Optional; Preheat the oven broiler and put lasagna into the oven for 5-6 minutes until cheese becomes slightly brown.

Nutrition Facts:
Calories: 712 g; Total Fat: 19.1 g; Total Carbohydrate: 36.1 g; Protein: 56.7

Beef Stroganoff

*(**Prep + Cooking Time:** 35 minutes | **Serves:** 2)*

Ingredients:
- 6-ounce portabello mushrooms
- 1/2-pound. beef stew meat; chopped
- 2 garlic cloves; chopped
- 1 tablespoon fresh parsley; chopped
- 1/4 teaspoon cayenne
- 2 tablespoons dry sherry
- 1 teaspoon Worcestershire sauce
- 1 cup beef broth
- 3 tablespoons sour cream
- 2 sprigs fresh thyme
- 1 tablespoon oil
- 1 tablespoon flour
- 1/2 onion; diced
- Salt and Pepper to taste

Directions:
1. Add oil to Instant Pot and press "Sauté" button (*Normal* preset), wait till you see Hot on the display.
2. Season beef with salt and pepper. Add to the Instant pot and cook for 3-4 minutes. Transfer beef to a plate.
3. Add mushrooms, garlic, thyme and onion, cook for 3 more minutes. Add flour and cook for 1 more minute.

4. Add sherry, broth and meat. Close the lid and turn the vent to *Sealed*. Press *Pressure Cook* (Manual) button, use *+* or *-* button to set the timer for 12 minutes. Use *Pressure level* button to set Pressure to *HIGH*.
5. Once the timer is up; press *Cancel* button and turn the steam release handle to *Venting* position for quick release, until the float valve drops down.
6. Open the lid; press "Sauté" button, adjust to *Less*. Stir in sour cream and parsley, add more salt if needed, cook for 2 to 3 minutes. Serve topped with more parsley leaves on top of noodles.

Nutrition Facts:
Calories: 416 g; Total Fat: 20.4 g; Total Carbohydrate: 9.9 g; Protein: 39.9

Red Beef Balls

(Prep + Cooking Time: 20 minutes | Serves: 2)

Ingredients:
- 1/2 lb. ground beef
- 1/2 cup water
- 1 teaspoon sliced shallots
- 2 tablespoons red chili flakes
- 1 bay leaf
- 1/2 tablespoon flour
- 1 egg white
- 1/2 teaspoon brown sugar
- 1 teaspoon minced' garlic
- 1/4 teaspoon salt

Directions:
1. Combine ground beef with flour and egg white then mix well. Shape the beef mixture into small ball forms then set aside
2. Pour vegetable oil into the inner pot of an Instant Pot then select *Sauté* setting
3. Stir in minced' garlic, sliced shallots and red chili flakes then sauté until aromatic. Press the *Cancel* button.
4. Put beef balls in the Instant Pot then carefully pour water over the beef balls. Add bay leaf, brown sugar and salt then cover and seal the Instant Pot properly
5. Select *Manual* setting on the Instant Pot and cook the beef balls on high for 15 minutes
6. Once it is done; naturally release the Instant Pot and open the lid. Carefully transfer the beef balls to a serving dish and serve

Nutrition Facts:
Calories: 381; Net Carbs: 6.5g; Total Fat: 29.4g; Protein: 21g; Carbs: 7.3g;

Sweet Beef

(Prep + Cooking Time: 23 minutes | Serves: 2)

Ingredients:
- 3/4 lb. beef sirloin
- 1/4 teaspoon sugar
- 1/4 cup beef broth
- 1½ teaspoons fish sauce
- 1½ teaspoons vegetable oil
- 1½ teaspoons soy sauce
- 1½ teaspoons black pepper
- 1/4 cup chopped' onions
- 2 tablespoons diced' red paprika
- 2 tablespoons diced' green paprika
- 1 teaspoon cornstarch
- 1 tablespoon water
- 1 teaspoon minced' garlic
- 1/4 teaspoon pepper
- 1/4 teaspoon salt

Directions:
1. Cut the beef into thin slices then rub with salt and pepper. Set aside. Pour vegetable oil into the inner pot of an Instant Pot then select *Sauté* menu
2. Stir in chopped' onion and minced' garlic then sauté until aromatic and lightly golden brown.
3. Add sliced beef to the Instant Pot then sauté until wilted and the beef is no longer pink. Press the *Cancel* button
4. Sprinkle diced' red pepper and green pepper over the beef then season with fish sauce, soy sauce, black pepper and sugar
5. Pour beef broth into the Instant Pot then cover with the lid.
6. Seal the Instant Pot properly and close the steam valve. Select *Manual* setting on the Instant Pot and cook the beef on high for 15 minutes
7. Once it is done; quick release the Instant Pot and open the lid
8. Stir in cornstarch and water mixture then stir well
9. Select *Sauté* setting again then cook the beef for another 3 minutes. Transfer the beef and the gravy to a serving dish then serve immediately

Nutrition Facts:
Calories: 270; Net Carbs: 6.8g; Total Fat: 10.5g; Protein: 37g; Carbs: 10.2g;

Beef Curry Stew Recipe

*(**Prep + Cooking Time:** 60 minutes | **Serves:** 3)*

Ingredients:
- 1/2 pound. beef stew chunks; chopped into small cubes
- 1 small onion; chopped
- 1 cup carrots; chopped
- 1 zucchini; chopped
- 1/2 cup coconut milk
- 1 teaspoon ginger; chopped
- 1 teaspoon turmeric powder
- 1 cup beef broth
- 1 teaspoon garlic power
- 2 tablespoons oil
- Salt and Pepper to taste

Directions:
1. Add oil to Instant Pot and press "Sauté" button (*Normal* preset), wait till you see Hot on the display.
2. Add beef and cook for 3-5 minutes until brown. Transfer beef to a plate.
3. Add onion, carrot, zucchinis and ginger to the pot. Sauté for 2 to 3 minutes, add more oil if needed. Add 2 tablespoons broth and deglaze the pot. Press *Cancel* button.
4. Add remaining broth, beef, turmeric powder, salt, black pepper and garlic power. Stir well, close the lid and turn the vent to *Sealed*. Press *Meat/Stew* button and adjust to *More* preset.
5. Once the timer is up; press *Cancel* button and turn the steam release handle to *Venting* position for quick release, until the float valve drops down.
6. Open the lid; Add coconut milk and stir with a wooden spoon until evenly mixed.
7. Press "Sauté" button, adjust to *Less* and stir for 2 to 3 minutes. Turn off Instant pot and serve.

Nutrition Facts:
Calories: 180 g; Total Fat: 35 g; Total Carbohydrate: 6 g; Protein: 20

Beef Black Pepper

(Prep + Cooking Time: 26 minutes | Serves: 2)

Ingredients:
- 1/2 lb. beef tenderloin
- 1/4 teaspoon sugar
- 1/4 cup chopped' onion
- 2 tablespoons tomato sauce
- 1 tablespoon soy sauce
- 2 tablespoons butter
- 1/2 cup water
- 1/4 teaspoon salt
- 1/2 teaspoon black pepper

Directions:
1. Cut the beef tenderloin into thick slices then rub with soy sauce, salt, black pepper, sugar, onion and tomato sauce. Place butter in the inner pot of an Instant Pot then select *Sauté* setting
2. Stir in the seasoned beef then sauté until wilted. Press the *Cancel* button
3. Pour water over the beef then cover and seal the Instant Pot properly. Closet the steam valve.
4. Select *Manual* setting and cook the beef on high. Set the time to 22 minutes
5. Once it is done; naturally release the Instant Pot and open the lid. Arrange the beef to a serving dish then serve with sautéed carrots and fried potatoes

Nutrition Facts:
Calories: 299; Net Carbs: 2.9g; Total Fat: 19.6g; Protein: 26g; Carbs: 3.6g

French Style Beef Chuck Roast

(Prep + Cooking Time: 55 minutes | Serves: 3)

Ingredients:
- 2-pound. beef chuck roast
- 2 carrots; peeled and cut into 1-inch pieces
- 2 garlic cloves; minced
- 2 cups beef broth
- 2 tablespoons unsalted butter
- 1 yellow onion; cut in 4 pieces
- 1 tablespoon fresh lemon juice
- Salt and Pepper to taste

Directions:
1. Season beef with salt and pepper, add lemon juice and toss to coat.
2. Add butter to the Instant Pot and press *Sauté* button (*Normal* preset), wait till you see Hot on the display.
3. Add onion and cook for 2 to 3 minutes. Add garlic and cook for 1 more minute.
4. Press *Cancel* and add broth and beef. Close the lid and turn the vent to *Sealed*. Press *Pressure Cook* (Manual) button, use *+* or *-* button to set the timer for 40 minutes. Use *Pressure level* button to set Pressure to *HIGH*.
5. Once the timer is up; press *Cancel* button and turn the steam release handle to *Venting* position for quick release, until the float valve drops down.
6. Open the lid; Add carrots to the Instant pot and press *Sauté* button, adjust to *Less*.
7. Cook for 10 minutes with the lid open. Add more salt if needed and serve.

Nutrition Facts:
Calories: 674 g; Total Fat: 50.6 g; Total Carbohydrate: 5 g; Protein: 36.4

Steamed Ground Beef Vegetables

(Prep + Cooking Time: 20 minutes | Serves: 2)

Ingredients:
- 1/2 lb. ground beef
- 1/4 teaspoon nutmeg
- 1/4 cup carrot sticks
- 1/4 teaspoon salt
- 1/2 cup broccoli florets
- 1/4 cup chopped' onion
- 2 teaspoons minced' garlic
- 1 teaspoon olive oil
- 1/4 teaspoon pepper

Directions:
1. Pour olive oil into the inner pot of an Instant Pot then select *Sauté* setting. Stir in chopped' onion, minced' garlic and ground beef then sauté until wilted and aromatic. Press the *Cancel* button
2. Transfer the half-cooked beef to a disposable aluminum pan then mix with broccoli florets and chopped' carrots.
3. Season with salt, pepper and nutmeg then stir until combined
4. Pour water into the Instant Pot then place a trivet in it. Put the disposable aluminum pan with beef and vegetables on the trivet then cover and seal the Instant Pot properly. Close the steam valve
5. Select *Steam* setting on the Instant Pot and cook the beef on high for 10 minutes
6. Once it is done; naturally release the Instant Pot and remove the aluminum pan out of the Instant Pot.
7. Transfer the beef and vegetables to a serving dish and serve right away

Nutrition Facts:
Calories: 374; Net Carbs: 3.8g; Total Fat: 30.5g; Protein: 19.2g; Carbs: 5.1g;

Delightful Red Wine Flank Steak

(Prep + Cooking Time: 25 minutes | Serves: 2)

Ingredients:
- 1/2 lb. flank steak
- 1/4 teaspoon oregano
- 1/4 teaspoon cumin
- 1/4 cup tomato sauce
- 1/4 cup dry red wine
- 1 teaspoon vinegar
- 1/4 teaspoon pepper
- 1/2 cup water
- 1/4 cup chopped' onion
- 1 bay leaf
- 1/4 teaspoon salt
- 1½ tablespoons canola oil
- 1½ teaspoons minced' garlic

Directions:
1. Combine salt with onion, minced' garlic, oregano, cumin, tomato sauce, vinegar and pepper. Mix well. Cut the flank steak into pieces then rub with the spice mixture. Let it sit for 5 minutes
2. Now, pour canola oil into the inner pot of an Instant Pot then select *Sauté* setting
3. Stir in the seasoned flank steak and sauté until wilted and no longer pink. Press the *Cancel* button.
4. Pour water and red wine over the flank steak then add a bay leaf on top
5. Cover and seal the Instant Pot properly then close the steam valve
6. Select *Manual* setting and cook the flank steak on high for 15 minutes

7. Once it is done; naturally release the Instant Pot and open the lid. Transfer the cooked flank steak to a serving dish and serve

Nutrition Facts:
Calories: 245; Net Carbs: 3.8g; Total Fat: 12.2g; Protein: 0.8g; Carbs: 4.9g;

Beef Meatballs

(Prep + Cooking Time: 30 minutes | Serves: 3)

Ingredients:
- 1-pound ground beef
- 14-ounce tomato sauce
- 1/2 tablespoon olive oil
- 1/2 teaspoon dried oregano
- 1/2 egg
- 1/2 tablespoon flaxseed meal
- 1 tablespoon grated Parmesan cheese
- Salt and Black pepper to taste

Directions:
1. In a bowl; combine the Parmesan cheese with the ground beef, oregano, egg, salt, pepper and flaxseed.
2. Use this mixture to make small meatballs of 1-inch diameter.
3. Add the oil to the instant pot and select the *Sauté* function, Put the meatballs into the oil and sauté until they turn brown.
4. Stir in the tomato sauce and water then secure the lid.
5. Cook on *Manual* setting for 6 minutes at *HIGH* pressure. Natural release the steam for 5 minutes then remove the lid. Serve warm.

Nutrition Facts:
Calories: 358, Fat: 15g, Carbs: 3.1g, Protein: 50.6g

Beef Meatloaf

(Prep + Cooking Time: 50 minutes | Serves: 3)

Ingredients:
- 1-pound. ground beef
- 2 tablespoons tomato sauce
- 1/2 teaspoon Italian seasoning
- 2 tablespoons ketchup
- 3 tablespoons onion; chopped
- 2 garlic cloves; minced
- 1/3 cup breadcrumbs
- 1 egg
- 1/2 teaspoon paprika
- 1 tablespoon olive oil
- 1 cup water
- Salt and Pepper to taste

Directions:
1. Mix all ingredients (except for oil, water and ketchup) in a mixing bowl. Mould the mixture into a form of a loaf.
2. Add oil to Instant Pot and press "Sauté" button (*Normal* preset), wait till you see Hot on the display. Add meatloaf and cook for 2 to 3 minutes on each side.
3. Take two pieces of foil, put them on top of each other. Put the meatloaf on top and fold the foil a bit to make a pan for a meatloaf.
4. Add water to the Instant pot; add the meatloaf in foil. Close the lid and turn the vent to *Sealed*. Press *Meat/Stew* button and adjust to *Normal* preset.
5. Once the timer is up; press *Cancel* button and turn the steam release handle to *Venting* position for quick release, until the float valve drops down. Open the lid and serve.

Nutrition Facts: Calories: 364 g; Total Fat: 14 g; Total Carbohydrate: 13.7 g; Protein: 53.3

Coffee Pulled Beef

(Prep + Cooking Time: *4 hours* | **Serves:** *2)*

Ingredients:
- 3/4 lb. beef tenderloin
- 3/4 tablespoon Worcestershire sauce
- 1/2 cup brewed coffee
- 1/2 teaspoon pepper
- 2 teaspoons minced' garlic
- 1 teaspoon olive oil
- 1/4 teaspoon salt

Directions:
1. Pour olive oil into the inner pot of an Instant Pot then select *Sauté* setting. Stir in minced' garlic then sauté until lightly golden brown and aromatic. Press the *Cancel* button
2. Place beef tenderloin in the inner pot of an Instant Pot then pour brewed coffee over the beef
3. Season with Worcestershire sauce, pepper and salt then cover and seal the Instant Pot properly
4. Select *Slow cook* setting on the Instant Pot and cook the beef on low. Set the time to 4 hours
5. Once it is done; naturally release the Instant Pot and open the lid
6. Take the cooked beef out of the Instant Pot and place on a flat surface. Let it cool for a few minutes. Shred the cooked beef then transfer to a serving dish

Nutrition Facts:
Calories: 302; Net Carbs: 2.2g; Total Fat: 14.4g; Protein: 37.8g; Carbs: 2.4g;

Cheesy Beef Roll

(Prep + Cooking Time: *24 minutes* | **Serves:** *2)*

Ingredients:
- 3/4 lbs. ground beef
- 2 tablespoons diced' onion
- 2 tablespoons fresh milk
- 2 tablespoons flour
- 3/4 teaspoon Worcestershire sauce
- 1 egg white
- 2 tablespoons ketchup
- 1/4 cup grated Mozzarella cheese
- 1/4 teaspoon salt
- 1/4 teaspoon pepper

Directions:
1. Combine ground beef with egg white, diced' onion, fresh milk, flour, Worcestershire sauce, salt, pepper and ketchup in a bowl then mix well
2. Spread the beef mixture on a sheet of aluminum foil then add grated Mozzarella cheese on top
3. Carefully roll the beef and wrap with aluminum foil. Bind the beef roll tightly then set aside
4. Pour water into the Instant Pot then place a trivet in it. Put the wrapped beef roll on the trivet then cover and seal the Instant Pot properly. Close the steam valve
5. Select *Steam* setting on the Instant Pot and cook the beef on high for 18 minutes.
6. Once it is done; naturally release the Instant Pot and open the lid
7. Remove the beef roll from the Instant Pot and let it cool. After a few minutes, unwrap the beef roll then cut into thick slices
8. Arrange the sliced beef rolls on a serving dish then serve right away

Nutrition Facts:
Calories: 387; Net Carbs: 6.1g; Total Fat: 29.9g; Protein: 22.1g; Carbs: 6.6g;

Beef Bulgogi Tender

(Prep + Cooking Time: 26 minutes | Serves: 2)

Ingredients:
- 1/2 lb. beef sirloin
- 1 teaspoon garlic powder
- 2 tablespoons chopped' leek
- 3/4 tablespoon sesame oil
- 1/2 tablespoon brown sugar
- 1 tablespoon soy sauce
- 1/2 cup chopped' onion
- 1/4 teaspoon salt
- 1/4 cup water
- 1/4 teaspoon pepper

Directions:
1. Cut the beef sirloin into thin slices then place in the inner pot of an Instant Pot. Drizzle soy sauce and sesame oil over the beef then sprinkle brown sugar, salt, pepper and garlic powder on top
2. Pour water into the Instant Pot then cover and seal it properly. Close the steam valve
3. Select *Manual* setting and cook the Instant Pot on high. Set the time to 14 minutes
4. Once it is done; quick release the Instant Pot and open the lid
5. Now, stir in chopped' onion and leek to the Instant Pot then cook the beef on *Sauté* setting for 5 minutes.
6. Transfer the cooked beef to a serving dish then serve immediately. If you like, you can also sprinkle sesame seeds on top for garnish

Nutrition Facts:
Calories: 289; Net Carbs: 6.5g; Total Fat: 12.2g; Protein: 35.6g; Carbs: 7.5g;

Beef Bourguignon

(Prep + Cooking Time: 50 minutes | Serves: 2)

Ingredients:
- 1/2-pound beef stew meat
- 2 bacon slices
- 1 garlic clove; minced
- 1 large potato; cubed
- 1 medium onion; chopped
- 1 tablespoon parsley
- 1/2 tablespoon honey
- 1 tablespoon thyme
- 1/2 cup beef stock
- 1/2 cup red wine
- 2 medium carrots; chopped
- 1/2 tablespoon olive oil

Directions:
1. Switch on the pot after placing it on a clean and dry platform. Press *Sauté* cooking function.
2. Open the lid; add the oil and beef in the pot; cook for 3-4 minutes to cook well and evenly browned. Set aside.
3. Add the bacon and onion and sauté until onion is translucent. Add beef and the rest of the ingredients.
4. Close the pot by closing the top lid. Also, ensure to seal the valve.
5. Press *Manual* cooking function and set cooking time to 30 minutes. It will start cooking after a few minutes. Let the pot mix cook under pressure until the timer reads zero.
6. Press *Cancel* cooking function and press *Natural release* setting.
7. It will take 8-10 minutes for natural pressure release. Open the pot and serve warm.

Nutrition Facts: Calories: 558; Fat: 16.5g; Carbohydrates: 46.5g; Fiber: 7g; Protein 42g

Beef Sirloin Recipe

(Prep + Cooking Time: 1 hour | Serves: 8)

Ingredients:
- 6-pound beef top sirloin steak
- 4 teaspoon garlic powder
- 8 minced garlic cloves
- 1 cup butter
- Salt and Pepper to taste

Directions:
1. Select the *Sauté* function on the instant pot.
2. Pour in the oil and add the sirloin steaks, Cook for 5 minutes, Let the meat brown on each side,
3. Stir in all the remaining Ingredients and secure the lid.
4. Switch the cooker to the *meat stew* mode and cook for 30 minutes. When it beeps; *Natural Release* the steam and remove the lid. Serve hot.

Nutrition Facts:
Calories: 865, Fat: 44.3g, Carbs: 2g, Protein: 103.9g

Cheesy Beef Casserole

(Prep + Cooking Time: 20 minutes | Serves: 4)

Ingredients:
- 1/2 (15 ounce) can diced tomatoes
- 1/2 (15 ounce) can tomato sauce
- 1-pound. lean ground beef
- 1 (3 ounce) package cream cheese; softened
- 1/2 box shell pasta
- 1 onion; chopped
- 1/2 cup cheddar cheese; grated
- 2 cups beef broth
- 1 teaspoon olive oil
- 1/2 cup cottage cheese
- 1/2 green bell pepper; seeded and chopped
- Salt and Pepper to taste

Directions:
1. Add oil to Instant Pot and press "Sauté" button (*Normal* preset), wait till you see Hot on the display. Add onion and cook for 1 to 2 minutes until soft.
2. Add beef and cook for 3-4 minutes until no longer pink. Season with salt and pepper.
3. Add tomato sauce, diced tomatoes, bell peppers, cottage cheese and cream cheese to the Instant pot. Mix well and press *Cancel* button.
4. Add pasta and beef broth, make sure there is enough liquid to cover the pasta.
5. Close the lid and turn the vent to *Sealed*. Press *Pressure Cook* (Manual) button, use *+* or *-* button to set the timer for 5 minutes. Use *Pressure level* button to set Pressure to *HIGH*.
6. Once the timer is up; press *Cancel* button and turn the steam release handle to *Venting* position for quick release, until the float valve drops down.
7. Open the lid; Add cheddar cheese to the pot and stir until melted.

Nutrition Facts:
Calories: 749 g; Total Fat: 28.3 g; Total Carbohydrate: 38 g; Protein: 63

Beef Fritters in Gravy

(Prep + Cooking Time: 30 minutes | Serves: 2)

Ingredients:
- 1/2 lb. ground beef
- 2 shallots
- 2 candlenuts
- 2 cloves garlic
- 1/2 teaspoon coriander
- 1/4 teaspoon turmeric
- 1/4 teaspoon ginger
- 1/4 teaspoon cumin
- 1 egg
- 1/4 cup water
- 4 tablespoons coconut milk
- 1/2 teaspoon vegetable oil
- 1 lemon grass
- 1 bay leaf
- 1-inch galangal
- 1/4 teaspoon pepper
- 1/4 teaspoon salt

Directions:
1. Pour water into the Instant Pot then place a trivet in it. Now, combine ground beef with egg then mix well.
2. Shape the beef mixture into medium fritter forms then arrange on the trivet
3. Cover the Instant Pot with the lid and seal it properly. Close the steam valve
4. Select *Steam* menu and cook the beef fritters on high for 10 minutes.
5. In the meantime, place shallots, candlenuts and garlic in a food processor then process until smooth.
6. Once the Instant Pot beeps, quick release the Instant Pot and open the lid
7. Take the trivet out of the Instant Pot then place the beef fritters on a plate. Wipe and clean the Instant Pot.
8. Pour vegetable oil into the inner pot of an Instant Pot then select *Sauté* menu
9. Stir in spice mixture and sauté until aromatic. Pour coconut milk into the Instant Pot then add lemon grass, bay leaf, galangal, coriander, cumin, pepper, turmeric, ginger and salt. Stir well
10. Put the beef fritters in the gravy then cook for 3 minutes. Once it is done; transfer the beef fritters to a serving dish and drizzle the gravy over the meatballs

Nutrition Facts:
Calories: 356; Net Carbs: 5.8g; Total Fat: 23.6 g; Protein: 28.2g; Carbs: 8.8g;

Coconut Spiced Beef

(Prep + Cooking Time: 25 minutes | Serves: 2)

Ingredients:
- 1/2 lb. beef tenderloin
- 2 cloves
- 1/4 teaspoon nutmeg
- 1 tablespoon fried sliced shallots
- 4 tablespoons coconut milk
- 1/2 teaspoon vegetable oil
- 1/2 teaspoon shrimp paste
- 2 shallots
- 2 cloves garlic
- 1 lemon grass
- 1 bay leaf
- 1/2 teaspoon ginger
- 1/4 cup water
- 1 kaffir lime leaf
- 1/4 teaspoon turmeric
- 1/4 teaspoon salt
- 1/4 teaspoon pepper

Directions:
1. Cut the beef tenderloin into thin slices then set aside. Place shallots, garlic, shrimp paste and turmeric in a food processor then process until smooth
2. Pour water into the inner pot of an Instant Pot then select *Sauté* setting on the Instant Pot
3. Stir in spice mixture then sauté until aromatic. Add sliced beef to the Instant Pot then sauté until wilted and no longer pink. Press the *Cancel* button
4. Pour water and coconut milk into the Instant Pot and season the beef with lemon grass, bay leaf, ginger, lime leaf, cloves, nutmeg, salt and pepper
5. Cover the Instant Pot with the lid and seal it properly. Close the steam valve.
6. Select *Manual* setting and cook the beef on high for 20 minutes
7. Once the beef is done, naturally release the Instant Pot and open the lid. Transfer the beef to a serving dish and serve.

Nutrition Facts:
Calories: 275; Net Carbs: 6.5g; Total Fat: 15.4g; Protein: 26.5g; Carbs: 7.6g;

Beef Teriyaki

(Prep + Cooking Time: 25 minutes | Serves: 2)

Ingredients:
- 1/2 lb. beef sirloin
- 1 teaspoon vegetable oil
- 1/2 teaspoon ginger
- 1/2 teaspoon soy sauce
- 1/2 teaspoon pepper
- 1/4 cup chopped' onions
- 1/4 cup water
- 1 teaspoon cornstarch
- 1 teaspoon sesame seeds
- 1 teaspoon sugar

Directions:
1. Cut the beef sirloin into very thin slices then set aside. Pour vegetable oil into the inner pot of an Instant Pot then select *Sauté* menu
2. Stir in chopped' onion and sauté until wilted aromatic. Add sliced beef to the Instant Pot then sauté until wilted and no longer pink. Press the *Cancel* button
3. Pour water into the Instant Pot and season the beef with ginger, soy sauce, pepper and sugar
4. Cover the Instant Pot with the lid properly and close the steam valve.
5. Select *Manual* menu on the Instant Pot and cook the beef for 15 minutes
6. Once it is done; quick release the Instant Pot then open the lid
7. Take about 3 tablespoons of gravy and mix with cornstarch. Pour the cornstarch mixture over the beef and stir well
8. Select *Sauté* menu again and cook the beef for another 2 minutes or until the gravy is thickened. Transfer the beef together with the gravy to a serving dish then sprinkle sesame seeds on top

Nutrition Facts:
Calories: 181; Net Carbs: 6.3g; Total Fat: 6.9g; Protein: 23.6g; Carbs: 7.1g;

Tomato Beef Stew

(Prep + Cooking Time: 4 hours | Serves: 2)

Ingredients:
- 3/4 lb. stew meat
- 1/4 cup tomato puree
- 3/4 cup water
- 3 tablespoons balsamic vinegar
- 1/4 teaspoon thyme
- 1/4 teaspoon oregano
- 1/4 cup chopped' onion
- 1/4 teaspoon rosemary
- 1 teaspoon olive oil
- 2 teaspoons minced' garlic

Directions:
1. Pour olive oil into the inner pot of an Instant Pot then select *Sauté* setting. Add chopped' onion and minced' garlic to the Instant Pot then sauté until just aromatic
2. Now, stir in stew meat and sauté until wilted and no longer pink. Press the *Cancel* button
3. Add tomato puree, water, balsamic vinegar, thyme, oregano and rosemary to the Instant Pot then cover and seal the Instant Pot properly. Close the steam valve
4. Select *Slow cook* setting on the Instant Pot and cook the beef on low. Set the time to 4 hours.
5. Once it is done; naturally release the Instant Pot and open the lid. Transfer the cooked beef to a serving dish then serve

Nutrition Facts:
Calories: 228; Net Carbs: 4.4g; Total Fat: 10g; Protein: 27.9g; Carbs: 5.6g;

Beef Polenta

(Prep + Cooking Time: 15 minutes | Serves: 2)

Ingredients:
- Cooked beef meal of your choice
- 2 cups vegetable broth
- 1/4 teaspoon cayenne pepper
- 1 teaspoon oregano
- 1 teaspoon cumin
- 1/2 teaspoon smoked paprika
- 1 tablespoon chili powder
- 1/4 cup cilantro; chopped
- 2 teaspoons garlic; minced
- 1 bunch green onion; sliced
- 1 cup cornmeal
- 2 cups boiling water

Directions:
1. Place your Instant Pot on a flat kitchen surface', plug it and turn it on.
2. To start making the recipe, press *Sauté* button. Add the oil, garlic and onions; cook for 2-3 minutes to soften the ingredients.
3. Add the broth, cornmeal, spices, boiling water and cilantro and stir well. Carefully close its lid and firmly lock it. Then after, seal the valve too.
4. To start making the recipe, press *Manual* button. Now you have to set cooking time', set the timer for 5 minutes. Allow the pot to cook the mixture until the timer goes off.
5. Turn off the pot and press *Cancel. * Allow the built up pressure to vent out naturally', it will take 8-10 minutes to completely release inside pressure.
6. Open its lid and transfer the cooked mixture into serving container/containers. Serve warm with your favorite beef meal!

Nutrition Facts:
Calories 136; Fat: 1.2g; Carbohydrates: 25.3g; Fiber: 1.6g; Protein 3g

Sweet Beef Ribs in Sweet Gravy

*(**Prep + Cooking Time:** 25 minutes | **Serves:** 2)*

Ingredients:
- 1/2 lb. beef ribs
- 1 lemon grass
- 2 teaspoons sliced shallots
- 1/4 teaspoon pepper
- 2 teaspoons minced' garlic
- 1/2 teaspoon brown sugar
- 1 tablespoon soy sauce
- 1/4 teaspoon ginger
- 1/4 teaspoon cinnamon
- 1/4 cup coconut milk
- 1/4 cup water
- 1 bay leaf
- 1/4 teaspoon salt

Directions:
1. Chop the beef ribs then place in the Instant Pot. Drizzle coconut milk, soy sauce and water over the beef then season with minced' garlic, sliced shallots, pepper, ginger, cinnamon, brown sugar and salt on top
2. Add lemon grass and bay leaf to the Instant Pot then cover and seal it properly. Close the steam valve
3. Select *Pressure cook* setting on the Instant Pot and cook the beef on high for 25 minutes
4. Once it is done; naturally release the Instant Pot and open the lid. Transfer the cooked beef and the gravy to a serving dish then serve warm

Nutrition Facts:
Calories: 325; Net Carbs: 4.8g; Total Fat: 25.9g; Protein: 17.7g; Carbs: 5.9g;

Pork Recipes

Lettuce Pork Wraps Recipe

(Prep + Cooking Time: 65 minutes | Serves: 6)

Ingredients:
- 3-pound bone-in pork shoulder
- 1/2 teaspoon dried oregano
- 1 ¼ chopped onion.
- 1 ¼ pinches cayenne
- 1 ¼ tablespoon olive oil
- 1 ¼ oranges
- 6 lettuce leaves
- 3/4 teaspoon garlic powder
- 3/4 teaspoon ground cumin
- 1/2 teaspoon black pepper
- 3/4 teaspoon sea salt

Directions:
1. Put all the Ingredients in with the pork and mix well. Refrigerate overnight.
2. Heat the oil in the instant pot using the *Sauté* function.
3. Put the marinated pork into the oil and sear for 10 minutes,
4. Pour in 2 cups of water and secure the lid, Select the *Manual* function and cook for 45 minutes at medium pressure,
5. Release the pressure for 10 minutes using Natural release. Serve the cooked pork on lettuce leaves,

Nutrition Facts:
Calories: 514, Fat: 35.5g, Carbs: 7.6g, Protein: 39.2g

Pork Congee

(Prep + Cooking Time: 50 minutes | Serves: 2)

Ingredients:
- 1-pound pork bones
- 1-pound pork shank
- 1/4 teaspoon sesame oil
- 6 ½ cups cold running tap water
- 3-century eggs; make small pieces
- 2 thin slices ginger
- 1 cup jasmine rice
- Pork seasoning:
- A dash of ground white pepper
- Salt to taste

Directions:
1. Place your Instant Pot on a flat kitchen surface', plug it and turn it on.
2. Open the lid and one by one add the rice, pork, bones, ginger and water in the pot.
3. Carefully close its lid and firmly lock it. Then after, seal the valve too.
4. To start making the recipe, press *Manual* button. Now you have to set cooking time', set the timer for 35 minutes.
5. Allow the pot to cook the mixture until the timer goes off.
6. Turn off the pot and press *Cancel.* Allow the built up pressure to vent out naturally', it will take 8-10 minutes to completely release inside pressure.
7. Open its lid and remove the bones and pork shank; shred the pork and season it with ground white pepper, 1/2-teaspoon salt and 1/4 teaspoon sesame oil.
8. Add the eggs and stir well until you get the desired consistency. Top with green onions and serve warm!

Nutrition Facts:
Calories: 414; Fat: 18g; Carbohydrates: 15.2g; Fiber: 0.5g; Protein 47.3g

Pulled Pork Garlic

(Prep + Cooking Time: 5 hours | Serves: 2)

Ingredients:
- 3/4 lb. pork tenderloin
- 1/2 cup coconut water
- 1/2 teaspoon pepper
- 1/2 teaspoon garlic powder
- 3 teaspoons minced' garlic
- 1/4 teaspoon salt

Directions:
1. Place the pork tenderloin in the inner pot of an Instant Pot then season with minced' garlic, garlic powder, pepper and salt
2. Pour coconut water over the pork tenderloin then cover and seal the Instant Pot properly. Close the steam valve
3. Select *Slow cook* setting on the Instant Pot and cook the pork tenderloin on low. Set the time to 5 hours.
4. Once it is done; naturally release the Instant Pot and open the lid
5. Take the cooked pork out of the Instant Pot and place on a flat surface. Let it cool for about 15 minutes. Using a fork shred the cooked pork then transfer to a serving dish

Nutrition Facts:
Calories: 265; Net Carbs: 3.5g; Total Fat: 6.1g; Protein: 45.4g; Carbs: 4.5g;

Pulled Pork BBQ

(Prep + Cooking Time: 30 minutes | Serves: 2)

Ingredients:
- 1/2 lb. pork butt
- 1 tablespoon apple cider vinegar
- 3/4 teaspoon garlic powder
- 1 tablespoon honey
- 1/4 cup water
- 1/2 tablespoon Worcestershire sauce
- 1/2 teaspoon mustard
- 1 tablespoon ketchup
- 1/4 teaspoon salt

Directions:
1. Combine ketchup with honey, Worcestershire sauce, apple cider vinegar, garlic powder, mustard and salt. Stir until incorporated
2. Rub the pork butt with the spice mixture then place in the inner pot of an Instant Pot.
3. Pour water into the Instant Pot then cover the Instant Pot properly. Close the steam valve
4. Select *Manual* setting on the Instant Pot then cook the pork on high for 25 minutes
5. Once it is done; naturally release the Instant Pot and open the lid.
6. Take the pork out of the Instant Pot and place on a flat surface. Let it cool for a few minutes
7. Using a fork shred the pork and place on a serving dish. Drizzle the liquid over the pulled pork then serve

Nutrition Facts:
Calories: 152; Net Carbs: 6.1g; Total Fat: 15.1g; Protein: 13.8g; Carbs: 6.9g;

Honey Glazed Pork Roast Recipe

(Prep + Cooking Time: 40 minutes | Serves: 2)

Ingredients:
- 1-pound pork roast
- 2 tablespoons parmesan cheese; grated
- 1 tablespoon soy sauce
- 2 tablespoons raw honey
- 1/2 cup water
- 1/2 tablespoon garlic; minced
- 1/2 tablespoon dry basil
- 1/2 tablespoon cornstarch
- 1/2 tablespoon olive oil
- Salt as per taste preference

Directions:
1. Switch on the pot after placing it on a clean and dry platform.
2. Open the pot lid and place the above-mentioned ingredients in the cooking pot area. Give the ingredients a little stir. Close the pot by closing the top lid. Also, ensure to seal the valve.
3. Press *Meat* cooking function and set cooking time to 35 minutes. It will start cooking after a few minutes. Let the pot mix cook under pressure until the timer reads zero.
4. Press *Cancel* cooking function and press *Natural release* setting.
5. It will take 8-10 minutes for natural pressure release. Open the pot and serve warm.

Nutrition Facts:
Calories: 652; Fat: 29.5g; Carbohydrates: 20g; Fiber: 0.5g; Protein 68g

Pork in Coconut Gravy

(Prep + Cooking Time: 4 hours | Serves: 2)

Ingredients:
- 1/2 lb. pork shoulder
- 1/4 teaspoon coriander
- 1/4 teaspoon candlenut
- 1 lemon grass
- 2 tablespoons chopped' shallot
- 2 teaspoons minced' garlic
- 1 teaspoon olive oil
- 1/4 cup coconut milk
- 3/4 cup water

Directions:
1. Cut the pork shoulder into medium cubes then set aside. Pour olive oil into the inner pot of an Instant Pot then select *Sauté* setting
2. Add chopped' shallot and minced' garlic to the Instant Pot then sauté until just aromatic
3. Now, stir in pork shoulder cubes and sauté until wilted and no longer pink. Press the *Cancel* button
4. Add coconut milk, water, coriander, candlenut and lemon grass to the Instant Pot then cover and seal the Instant Pot properly. Close the steam valve
5. Select *Slow cook* setting on the Instant Pot and cook the pork on low. Set the time to 4 hours.
6. Once it is done; naturally release the Instant Pot and open the lid. Transfer the cooked pork to a serving dish then serve

Nutrition Facts:
Calories: 377; Net Carbs: 3.9g; Total Fat: 30.8g; Protein: 20g; Carbs: 4.5g;

Pork Stew with Canola

(Prep + Cooking Time: 25 minutes | Serves: 2)

Ingredients:
- 1/2 lb. pork tenderloin
- 1/4 teaspoon oregano
- 1 bay leaf
- 1/4 teaspoon salt
- 1/4 cup water
- 1/4 teaspoon black pepper
- 1½ tablespoons canola oil
- 1½ teaspoons minced' garlic

Directions:
1. Combine salt with minced' garlic, oregano and black pepper
2. Mix well, Cut the pork tenderloin into pieces then rub with the spice mixture. Let it sit for 5 minutes.
3. Now, pour canola oil into the inner pot of an Instant Pot then select *Sauté* setting
4. Stir in the seasoned pork tenderloin and sauté until wilted and no longer pink. Press the *Cancel* button.
5. Pour water over the pork then add bay leaf on top. Cover and seal the Instant Pot properly then close the steam valve
6. Select *Manual* setting and cook the pork on high for 15 minutes
7. Once it is done; naturally release the Instant Pot and open the lid. Transfer the cooked pork to a serving dish and serve

Nutrition Facts:
Calories: 186; Net Carbs: 0.7g; Total Fat: 9.6g; Protein: 24.2g; Carbs: 1g;

Pork Bites Oregano

(Prep + Cooking Time: 25 minutes | Serves: 2)

Ingredients:
- 1/2 lb. boneless pork shoulder
- 1/2 teaspoon cayenne powder
- 1/4 cup chopped' onion
- 1 bay leaf
- 1½ teaspoons chili powder
- 3/4 teaspoon cumin
- 3/4 teaspoon coriander
- 3/4 tablespoon olive oil
- 1 teaspoon paprika
- 3/4 teaspoon oregano
- 1/2 teaspoon salt
- 1/4 teaspoon cinnamon
- 2 teaspoons minced' garlic
- 3 tablespoons lemon juice
- 1/4 teaspoon pepper

Directions:
1. Combine salt with pepper, cumin, paprika, chili powder, oregano and cayenne powder then mix well.
2. Cut the boneless pork shoulder into bite sizes then rub with the spice mixture. Set aside. Pour olive oil into the inner pot of an Instant Pot then select *Sauté* menu
3. Stir in pork and sauté until wilted and no longer pink. Take the pork out of the Instant Pot then place on a plate. Leave the oil in the Instant Pot
4. Add chopped' onion and minced' garlic to the Instant Pot then sauté until lightly golden brown and aromatic.
5. Return the pork to the Instant Pot then pour orange juice over the pork.

6. Season with cinnamon and bay leaf then cover the Instant Pot with the lid. Seal it properly and close the steam valve
7. Select *Manual* setting on the Instant Pot and cook the pork on high for 20 minutes.
8. Once it is done; naturally release the Instant Pot and open the lid. Transfer the cooked pork to a serving dish then serve

Nutrition Facts:
Calories: 368; Net Carbs: 3.7g; Total Fat: 29.3g;; Protein: 20.2g; Carbs: 6g

Rice and Ham Treat

(Prep + Cooking Time: 8 minutes | Serves: 2)

Ingredients:
- 2 tablespoons scallions; sliced
- 1/2 cup matchstick carrots
- 1 ½ cup water
- 1 ½ cup brown rice
- 1 tablespoon soy sauce
- 1/2 cup ham; diced
- 1 tablespoon butter

Directions:
1. Switch on the pot after placing it on a clean and dry platform.
2. Open the pot lid and put the above-mentioned ingredients in the cooking pot area. Give the ingredients a little stir.
3. Close the pot by closing the top lid. Also, ensure to seal the valve. Press *Manual* cooking function and set cooking time to 6 minutes.
4. It will start cooking after a few minutes. Let the pot mix cook under pressure until the timer reads zero.
5. Press *Cancel* cooking function and press *Quick release* setting.
6. Open the instant pot; fluff the mix and serve warm.

Nutrition Facts:
Calories: 116; Fat: 6g; Carbohydrates: 12g; Fiber: 2.5g; Protein 4g

Pork Chili Tomato

(Prep + Cooking Time: 25 minutes | Serves: 2)

Ingredients:
- 1/2 lb. ground pork
- 1/2 teaspoon paprika
- 1/2 teaspoon cumin
- 1/4 cup chopped' onion
- 1/4 teaspoon coriander
- 1/2 teaspoon oregano
- 2 tablespoons chili powder
- 1/4 cup diced' tomatoes
- 1/2 cup vegetable broth
- 1 tablespoon olive oil
- 2 teaspoons minced' garlic
- 1 tablespoon tomato paste
- 1/2 teaspoon salt

Directions:
1. Pour olive oil into the inner pot of an Instant Pot then select *Sauté* setting. Stir in chopped' onion and minced' garlic then sauté until aromatic and lightly golden brown
2. Add ground pork to the Instant Pot and sauté until the pork is no longer pink. Press the *Cancel* button.
3. Season the ground pork with salt, chili powder, cumin, paprika, coriander and oregano then pour vegetable broth over the ground pork

4. Cover the Instant Pot with the lid and seal it properly. Close the steam valve
5. Select *Manual* setting and cook the ground pork for 15 minutes
6. Once it is done; quick release the Instant Pot and open the lid.
7. Add diced' tomatoes to the Instant Pot then stir well. Select * Sauté* setting again and cook the pork uncovered for another 2 minutes or until the tomatoes are wilted
8. Transfer the cooked pork to a serving dish then serve. Enjoy the pork with taco or use it as a sandwich filling.

Nutrition Facts:
Calories: 281; Net Carbs: 5.8g; Total Fat: 12.9g; Protein: 32.9g; Carbs: 9.8g;

Pork Belly Paprika

*(**Prep + Cooking Time:** 25 minutes | **Serves:** 2)*

Ingredients:
- 1/4 lb. pork belly
- 1/4 cup water
- 1/4 cup white wine
- 2 teaspoons minced' garlic
- 1 tablespoon coconut oil
- 1/4 teaspoon thyme
- 1/4 teaspoon salt
- 1 teaspoon paprika

Directions:
1. Cut the pork belly into medium pieces then rub with salt, paprika, thyme and minced' garlic. Set aside. Pour water and white wine into the inner pot of an Instant Pot then place the seasoned pork belly in it
2. Cover the Instant Pot with the lid and seal it properly. Close the steam valve
3. Select *Manual* setting on the Instant Pot and cook the pork belly on high. Set the time to 15 minutes
4. Once it is done; naturally release the Instant Pot and open the lid. Transfer the cooked pork belly to a serving dish then serve

Nutrition Facts:
Calories: 352; Net Carbs: 1.9g; Total Fat: 22.2g; Protein: 26.5g; Carbs: 2.4g;

Pineapple Pork

*(**Prep + Cooking Time:** 35 minutes | **Serves:** 2)*

Ingredients:
- 1/2-pounds. pork tenderloin; sliced
- 1/2 cup tomato puree
- 1/2 teaspoon nutmeg
- 1/2 teaspoon cinnamon
- 1 cup unsweetened pineapple juice
- 1/2 cup pineapple chunks
- 2 cloves
- 1/4 cup chopped onion
- 1/2 teaspoon rosemary

Directions:
1. Switch on the pot after placing it on a clean and dry platform.
2. Open the pot lid and place the above-mentioned ingredients in the cooking pot area. Give the ingredients a little stir. Do not add the chunks.
3. Close the pot by closing the top lid. Also, ensure to seal the valve. Press *Manual* cooking function and set cooking time to 25 minutes.
4. It will start cooking after a few minutes. Let the pot mix cook under pressure until the timer reads zero.

5. Press *Cancel* cooking function and press *Quick release* setting. Open the instant pot; add the chunks and serve warm.

Nutrition Facts:
Calories: 292; Fat: 5g; Carbohydrates: 30g; Fiber: 3.5g; Protein 31.5g

Sweet Pork Tender

(Prep + Cooking Time: 30 minutes | Serves: 2)

Ingredients:
- 1/2 lb. pork tenderloin
- 2 teaspoons minced' garlic
- 2 teaspoons sliced shallots
- 1 lemon grass
- 1/2 cup coconut water
- 1/4 teaspoon cinnamon
- 1/2 teaspoon sugar
- 1 bay leaf
- 1/4 teaspoon ginger
- 1/4 teaspoon salt
- 1/4 teaspoon pepper

Directions:
1. Cut the pork into medium cubes then place in the Instant Pot. Pour coconut water over the pork then season with minced' garlic, sliced shallots, pepper, ginger, cinnamon, sugar and salt
2. Add lemon grass and bay leaf to the Instant Pot then cover and seal it properly. Close the steam valve.
3. Select *Pressure cook* setting on the Instant Pot and cook the pork on high for 25 minutes
4. Once it is done; naturally release the Instant Pot and open the lid. Transfer the cooked pork without the gravy to a serving dish and serve

Nutrition Facts:
Calories: 188; Net Carbs: 4.7g; Total Fat: 4.2g; Protein: 30.5g; Carbs: 5.8g;

Classic Sweet Pork Ribs

(Prep + Cooking Time: 30 minutes | Serves: 3)

Ingredients:
- 1 ½ pounds pork spareribs
- 1 cup beef broth
- 1 teaspoon garlic powder
- 1/2 cup ketchup
- 2 tablespoons brown sugar
- 1/2 onion; chopped
- 1 teaspoon paprika
- 1/4 cup chili sauce
- Salt and Pepper to taste

Directions:
1. Mix paprika, garlic powder, salt and pepper in a bowl. Season pork ribs with this mixture; make sure to coat the meat evenly on all sides.
2. Mix onion, ketchup, chili sauce and brown sugar in a bowl. Add broth to the Instant pot; add pork ribs and pour the sauce on top. Close the lid and turn the vent to *Sealed*.
3. Press *Pressure Cook* (Manual) button, use *+* or *-* button to set the timer for 20 minutes. Use *Pressure level* button to set Pressure to *HIGH*. If you prefer more tender (falling-off-the-bone) ribs, set the timer for 30 minutes.
4. Once the timer is up; press *Cancel* button and allow the pressure to be released naturally; until the float valve drops down. Open the lid.

Nutrition Facts:
Calories: 606 g; Total Fat: 45.8 g; Total Carbohydrate: 19.4 g; Protein: 32.9

Juicy Pork Chops

(Prep + Cooking Time: *20 minutes | **Serves:** 2)*

Ingredients:
- 1/4 lb. pork chops
- 2 tablespoons flour
- 2 tablespoons butter
- 1/4 cup chicken broth
- 1 tablespoon chopped' onion
- 1/4 teaspoon salt
- 1/4 teaspoon black pepper

Directions:
1. Roll the pork chops in the flour and make sure that it is completely coated with flour. Set aside. Place butter in the inner pot of an Instant Pot and select *Sauté* setting
2. Put the coated pork chops into the Instant Pot then cook for about 4 minutes or until both sides of the pork chops are lightly golden brown.
3. Remove the pork chops from the Instant Pot and place on a plate
4. Stir in the chopped' onion in the remaining melted butter then sauté until aromatic and lightly golden brown. Press the *Cancel* button.
5. Pour chicken broth into the Instant Pot then season with salt and pepper. Stir well
6. Return the pork to the Instant Pot then cover and seal the Instant Pot properly
7. Select *Manual* setting on the Instant Pot and cook the pork on high. Set the time to 15 minutes.
8. Once it is done; naturally release the Instant Pot and open the lid. Transfer the cooked pork chops to a serving dish then serve

Nutrition Facts:
Calories: 231; Net Carbs: 6.8g; Total Fat: 17.2g; Protein: 12.1g; Carbs: 7.2g;

Saucy Pork Meatballs

(Prep + Cooking Time: *35 minutes | **Serves:** 2)*

Ingredients:
- 3/4-pounds. ground pork
- 1/4 cup chopped onion
- 1/4 cup coconut milk
- 3/4 teaspoon brown sugar
- 1 tablespoon breadcrumb
- 1 organic egg

Directions:
1. Combine the meat with egg and breadcrumbs. Shape the mixture into balls. Switch on the pot after placing it on a clean and dry platform.
2. Open the pot lid and place the balls and milk in the cooking pot area. Add the brown sugar and chopped onion.
3. Give the ingredients a little stir. Close the pot by closing the top lid. Also, ensure to seal the valve.
4. Press *Manual* cooking function and set cooking time to 25 minutes. It will start cooking after a few minutes. Let the pot mix cook under pressure until the timer reads zero.
5. Press *Cancel* cooking function and press *Natural release* setting. It will take 8-10 minutes for natural pressure release. Open the pot and serve warm.

Nutrition Facts:
Calories: 272; Fat: 21g; Carbohydrates: 6.5g; Fiber: 1.5g; Protein 13.5g

Green Chili Pork Stew Recipe

(Prep + Cooking Time: 35 minutes | Serves: 3)

Ingredients:
- 1/2-pound. pork ribs; bone-in
- 1 tablespoon honey
- 3 cups beef broth
- 2 tablespoon oil
- 1 can green chilis; diced
- 1 tablespoon apple cider vinegar
- 1 onion; chopped
- 1 carrot; chopped
- 2 garlic cloves; chopped
- Salt and Pepper to taste

Directions:
1. Season pork ribs with salt and pepper. Add oil to Instant Pot and press "Sauté" button (*Normal* preset), wait till you see Hot on the display.
2. Add onions and garlic, cook for 2 to 3 minutes stirring constantly. Add pork ribs and cook for 3-4 more minutes until slightly brown. Press *Cancel* button.
3. Add broth, carrot, green chilis, apple cider vinegar, honey, salt and pepper.
4. Close the lid and turn the vent to *Sealed*. Press *Meat/Stew* button and adjust to *Less* preset.
5. Once the timer is up; press *Cancel* button and turn the steam release handle to *Venting* position for quick release, until the float valve drops down. Open the lid.

Nutrition Facts:
Calories: 390 g; Total Fat: 23.9 g; Total Carbohydrate: 16.1 g; Protein: 25.6

Pork Fritter

(Prep + Cooking Time: 20 minutes | Serves: 2)

Ingredients:
- 1/2 lb. ground pork
- 2 eggs
- 2 teaspoons minced' garlic
- 1/2 teaspoon coriander
- 1 tablespoon coconut milk
- 2 teaspoons sliced shallots
- 1/4 teaspoon cumin
- 1/4 teaspoon pepper
- 1 tablespoon breadcrumbs
- 1/4 teaspoon ginger
- 1/4 teaspoon turmeric
- 1/4 teaspoon salt

Directions:
1. Crack the eggs then place in a bowl. Season the eggs with sliced shallot, minced' garlic, coriander, cumin, pepper, turmeric, ginger and salt then stir well
2. Pour the egg mixture over the ground pork then add breadcrumbs and coconut milk into the bowl. Mix until combined.
3. Shape the pork mixture into medium fritter forms then set aside
4. Pour water into the Instant Pot and place a trivet in it. Arrange the pork fitters on the trivet then cover and seal the Instant Pot
5. Select *Manual* setting on the Instant Pot and cook the pork fritters on high for 15 minutes.
6. Once it is done; naturally release the Instant Pot and open the lid
7. Remove the pork fritters from the Instant Pot and arrange on a serving dish. Serve and enjoy with tomato or barbecue sauce, as you desired

Nutrition Facts: Calories: 339; Net Carbs: 5.9g; Total Fat: 22.5g; Protein: 26.7g; Carbs: 6.5g

Cheesy Pork Bombs

(Prep + Cooking Time: 20 minutes | Serves: 2)

Ingredients:
- 1/2 lb. ground pork
- 2 tablespoons diced' onion
- 2 tablespoons fresh milk
- 2 tablespoons chopped' red chilies
- 1/4 cup Mozzarella cheese cubes
- 1 tablespoon flour
- 3/4 teaspoon Worcestershire sauce
- 1 egg white
- 1/4 teaspoon salt
- 1/4 teaspoon pepper

Directions:
1. Combine ground pork with egg white, diced' onion, fresh milk, flour, Worcestershire sauce, salt and pepper.
2. Mix well using your hand, shape the pork mixture into medium balls. Fill each ball with red chili and Mozzarella cubes. Set aside
3. Pour water into the Instant Pot and place a trivet in it. Arrange the pork balls on the trivet then cover and seal the Instant Pot properly. Close the steam valve
4. Select *Steam* setting on the Instant Pot and cook the pork balls on high for 15 minutes.
5. Once it is done; naturally release the Instant Pot and open the lid
6. Remove the pork balls from the Instant Pot and place on a serving dish. Let them cool.
7. Serve and enjoy with any kind of sauce, as you desired

Nutrition Facts:
Calories: 146; Net Carbs: 6.2g; Total Fat: 7.9g; Protein: 11.2g; Carbs: 7.3g;

Cheesy Pork Macaroni

(Prep + Cooking Time: 25 minutes | Serves: 2)

Ingredients:
- 1/4 lb. ground pork
- 1/4 cup grated cheddar
- 1/4 cup cooked macaroni
- 1 tablespoon olive oil
- 2 tablespoons diced' mushroom
- 2 eggs
- 2 teaspoons garlic powder
- 1/2 teaspoon pepper

Directions:
1. Combine the entire ingredients except cheese in a bowl then mix well. Transfer the mixture in a disposable aluminum pan then spread evenly
2. Sprinkle grated cheddar cheese on top then set aside. Pour water into the Instant Pot and place a trivet in it.
3. Place the disposable aluminum pan on the trivet then cover and seal the Instant Pot properly
4. Select *Manual* setting on the Instant Pot and cook the pork on high for 20 minutes
5. Once it is done; naturally release the Instant Pot then open the lid. Take the disposable aluminum pan out of the Instant Pot and let it sit for a few minutes

Nutrition Facts:
Calories: 368; Net Carbs: 3.4g; Total Fat: 30.7g; Protein: 19.2g; Carbs: 3.8g

Spicy and Sour Pork Ribs

(Prep + Cooking Time: 30 minutes | Serves: 2)

Ingredients:
- 3/4 lb. pork ribs
- 2 cloves garlic
- 1 lemon grass
- 1/2 teaspoon tamarind
- 3 tablespoons coconut milk
- 1 teaspoon cayenne
- 2 shallots
- 1/4 cup water
- 1 tablespoon red chili flakes
- 1/2 teaspoon turmeric
- 1/4 teaspoon ginger
- 1/4 teaspoon salt

Directions:
1. Place red chili flakes, cayenne, shallots, garlic, turmeric, ginger, tamarind water and salt in a food processor. Process until smooth
2. Chop the pork ribs then place in the inner pot of an Instant Pot. Add the spice mixture to the Instant Pot then pour coconut milk and water over the pork ribs. Stir well
3. Cover the Instant Pot with the lid then seal it properly. Close the steam valve
4. Select *Pressure cook* setting on the Instant Pot then cook the pork ribs on high. Set the time to 25 minutes.
5. Once it is done; naturally release the Instant Pot then open the lid. Transfer the cooked pork ribs and the gravy to a serving dish then serve warm

Nutrition Facts:
Calories: 398; Net Carbs: 6.9g; Total Fat: 25.2g; Protein: 36.1g; Carbs: 8.2g

Pork Baby Back Ribs

(Prep + Cooking Time: 45 minutes | Serves: 2)

Ingredients:
- 2-pound. rack of baby back ribs
- 2 tablespoons BBQ rub
- 1 tablespoon liquid smoke
- 1 cup BBQ sauce
- 1/2 onion
- 2 cups water
- Salt and Pepper to taste

Directions:
1. Season baby back ribs with barbecue rub, salt and pepper, sprinkle both sides with liquid smoke.
2. Pour water into Instant Pot and insert a trivet. Put seasoned ribs bones and onion on the trivet.
3. Close the lid and turn the vent to *Sealed*. Press *Pressure Cook* (Manual) button, use *+* or *-* button to set the timer for 25 minutes. Use *Pressure level* button to set Pressure to *HIGH*.
4. Once the timer is up; press *Cancel* button and allow the pressure to be released naturally; until the float valve drops down.
5. Open the lid; Top cooked ribs with BBQ sauce and put on a baking sheet.
6. Preheat the oven to 375 F and cook the ribs for 5-10 minutes. Serve with more BBQ sauce.

Nutrition Facts:
Calories: 559 g; Total Fat: 37.1 g; Total Carbohydrate: 23.9 g; Protein: 30.1

Taco Pork Bowl Recipe

(Prep + Cooking Time: 1 hour 10 minutes | Serves: 8)

Ingredients:
- 2-pound pork sirloin roast; thickly sliced
- 20-ounce green chili tomatillo salsa
- 2 teaspoon cumin powder
- 2 teaspoon garlic powder
- 2 teaspoons black pepper
- 2 tablespoons olive oil
- 2 teaspoon salt

Directions:
1. Put the garlic powder, salt, pepper and ground cumin in a bowl and mix together
2. Put the pork in the bowl and dredge it in the spice mixture. Pour the oil into the instant pot and select the *Sauté* function.
3. Place the pork in the oil then add the tomatillo salsa.
4. Secure the lid and cook for 45 minutes at *HIGH* pressure using the *Manual* function.
5. Release the steam naturally for 15 minutes then remove the lid. Serve warm.

Nutrition Facts:
Calories: 295, Fat: 14.3g, Carbs: 6.1g, Protein: 32.6g

Loin Pork with Herbed Butter and Veggies

(Prep + Cooking Time: 1 hour 10 minutes | Serves: 3)

Ingredients:
- 1 (3/4-pound) pork tenderloin
- 1 tablespoon fresh herbs (sage; thyme and chives), chopped
- 2 tablespoons lemon juice
- 1 celery stalk; sliced
- 1 red onion; diced
- 2 tablespoons olive oil
- 2 garlic cloves; minced
- 2 carrots; sliced or cubed
- 1 cup chicken stock
- 1/4 cup softened unsalted butter
- 2 teaspoons dried rosemary
- Salt and Pepper to taste

Directions:
1. Mix oil, lemon juice, minced garlic, rosemary, salt and pepper in a bowl. Pour stock into the Instant pot and add pork loin.
2. Pour lemon juice mixture over the pork. Close the lid and turn the vent to *Sealed*.
3. Press *Pressure Cook* (Manual) button, use *+* or *-* button to set the timer for 30 minutes. Use *Pressure level* button to set Pressure to *HIGH*.
4. Once the timer is up; press *Cancel* button and turn the steam release handle to *Venting* position for quick release, until the float valve drops down.
5. Open the lid; Add onion, celery and carrots and close the lid again. Press *Pressure Cook* (Manual) button, use *+* or *-* button to set the timer for 6 minutes. Use *Pressure level* button to set Pressure to *HIGH*.
6. Once the timer is up; press *Cancel* button and turn the steam release handle to *Venting* position for quick release, until the float valve drops down.
7. Open the lid; Now make the herbed butter by simply mixing softened butter with herbs. Slice pork and serve with butter and veggies on top.

Nutrition Facts:
Calories: 450 g; Total Fat: 39 g; Total Carbohydrate: 7.5 g; Protein: 20.3

Pork Stew in Sweet Ginger Soy

(Prep + Cooking Time: 25 minutes | Serves: 2)

Ingredients:
- 1/2 lb. pork sirloin
- 3 tablespoons chopped' leek
- 1/4 cup water
- 2 tablespoons soy sauce
- 1/2 teaspoon ginger
- 1/2 teaspoon pepper
- 1 teaspoon cornstarch
- 1 teaspoon sesame seeds
- 1 teaspoon vegetable oil
- 1/4 cup chopped' onions
- 1 teaspoon sugar
- 1 tablespoon oyster sauce
- 1/4 teaspoon salt

Directions:
1. Cut the pork into very thin slices then set aside. Pour vegetable oil into the inner pot of an Instant Pot then select *Sauté* menu
2. Stir in chopped' onion and sauté until wilted aromatic. Add sliced pork to the Instant Pot then sauté until wilted and no longer pink. Press the *Cancel* button
3. Pour water into the Instant Pot and season the pork with soy sauce, ginger, pepper, sugar, oyster sauce and salt.
4. Cover the Instant Pot with the lid properly and close the steam valve
5. Select *Manual* menu on the Instant Pot and cook the pork for 15 minutes
6. Once it is done; quick release the Instant Pot then open the lid
7. Take about 3 tablespoons of gravy and mix with cornstarch
8. Pour the cornstarch mixture over the pork and stir well. add chopped' leek to the Instant Pot
9. Select *Sauté* menu again and cook the pork for another 2 minutes or until the gravy is thickened. Transfer the pork together with the gravy to a serving dish then sprinkle sesame seeds on top

Nutrition Facts:
Calories: 253; Net Carbs: 7g; Total Fat: 13.1g; Protein: 24.7g; Carbs: 7.9g;

Mustard Pork Chops

(Prep + Cooking Time: 30 minutes | Serves: 2)

Ingredients:
- 2 pork chops
- 1/2 teaspoon paprika
- 1/2 teaspoon thyme
- 1 teaspoon apple cider vinegar
- 1 tablespoon mustard
- 1 tablespoon olive oil
- 1/2 cup chicken stock
- 1/4 cup heavy cream
- 2 tablespoons lemon juice
- Salt and Pepper to taste

Directions:
1. Season pork chops with salt, pepper, paprika and thyme.
2. Add oil to Instant Pot and press "Sauté" button (*Normal* preset), wait till you see Hot on the display.
3. Add pork chops and cook for 2 to 3 minutes on both sides until slightly brown. Mix stock, vinegar, mustard, heavy cream and lemon juice in a bowl, add to the Instant pot.
4. Close the lid and turn the vent to *Sealed*. Press *Pressure Cook* (Manual) button, use *+* or *-* button to set the timer for 15 minutes. Use *Pressure level* button to set Pressure to *HIGH*.

5. Once the timer is up; press *Cancel* button and turn the steam release handle to *Venting* position for quick release, until the float valve drops down.
6. Open the lid; Serve chops with the sauce from the Instant pot.

Nutrition Facts:
Calories: 331 g; Total Fat: 27.2 g; Total Carbohydrate: 2 g; Protein: 19.1

Lime Ginger Pork

(Prep + Cooking Time: 40 minutes | Serves: 2)

Ingredients:
- 3/4-pound. pork loin
- 2 garlic cloves; minced
- 1 teaspoon fresh ginger; grounded
- 2 tablespoons honey
- 1 tablespoon Worcestershire Sauce
- 1/2 lime; juiced
- 1 tablespoon cornstarch or agar agar
- 1 cup water
- 1 tablespoon olive oil
- Salt and Pepper to taste

Directions:
1. Add oil to Instant Pot and press "Sauté" button (*Normal* preset), wait till you see Hot on the display.
2. Season pork with salt and pepper, then put it into Instant pot. Cook for 2-5 minutes both sides. Press *Cancel* button.
3. Mix honey, Worcestershire sauce, lime juice, garlic cloves and ginger in a bowl. Pour the mixture over pork, add water.
4. Close the lid and turn the vent to *Sealed*. Press *Meat/Stew* button and adjust to *Less* preset.
5. Once the timer is up; press *Cancel* button and turn the steam release handle to *Venting* position for quick release, until the float valve drops down.
6. Open the lid; Transfer the pork to a plate and press "Sauté" button, adjust to *Less*.
7. Add cornstarch to the cooker. Stir until the sauce thickens. Pour over the pork and serve.

Nutrition Facts:
Calories: 442 g; Total Fat: 23.4 g; Total Carbohydrate: 15.1 g; Protein: 41.5

Pork Roast Rosemary

(Prep + Cooking Time: 25 minutes | Serves: 2)

Ingredients:
- 1/2 lb. boneless pork roast
- 1½ tablespoons butter
- 1½ teaspoons brown sugar
- 1/4 cup chopped' onion
- 1/2 teaspoon mustard
- 1 tablespoon rosemary
- 2 teaspoons minced' garlic
- 1/2 cup chopped' carrots
- 2 tablespoons chopped' celeries
- 1/4 cup apple juice
- 2 teaspoons Worcestershire sauce
- 1/2 teaspoon salt
- 1/4 teaspoon pepper

Directions:
1. Cut the pork loin into small pieces then set aside. Place butter in the inner pot of an Instant Pot then select *Sauté* menu
2. Stir in pork loin pieces and sauté until wilted. Press the *Cancel* button

3. Sprinkle chopped' carrots and onion then season with salt, pepper, minced' garlic, brown sugar, mustard, Worcestershire sauce and rosemary
4. Pour apple juice over the pork then cover the Instant Pot properly. Close the steam valve.
5. Select *Pressure cook* menu and cook the pork on high. Set the time to 25 minutes
6. Once it is done; naturally release the Instant Pot and open the lid. Transfer the cooked pork to a serving dish then serve

Nutrition Facts: Calories: 137; Net Carbs: 5.6g; Total Fat: 5.2g; Protein: 17.8g; Carbs: 6.7g;

Garlic Pork Rinds

(Prep + Cooking Time: 20 minutes | Serves: 2)

Ingredients:
- 1/2 lb. pork rinds
- 1/4 teaspoon ginger
- 3 teaspoons minced' garlic
- 1/2 cup water
- 3 tablespoons soy sauce
- 1/4 teaspoon salt
- 1/2 teaspoon pepper

Directions:
1. Cut the pork rinds into medium cubes then rub with minced' garlic, soy sauce, salt, pepper and ginger. Let it sit for about 10 minutes. Pour water into the inner pot of an Instant Pot then place the seasoned pork rinds in it
2. Cover the Instant Pot with the lid and seal it properly. Close the steam valve
3. Select *Manual* setting on the Instant Pot and cook the pork rinds on high. Set the time to 15 minutes.
4. Once it is done; naturally release the Instant Pot and open the lid. Transfer the cooked pork rinds to a serving dish then serve

Nutrition Facts: Calories: 621; Net Carbs: 3.2g; Total Fat: 37.6g; Protein: 69.4g; Carbs: 3.7g

Spicy Pork Ribs

(Prep + Cooking Time: 55 minutes | Serves: 3)

Ingredients:
- 2-pound pork ribs
- 1/2 teaspoon garlic powder
- 1/4 teaspoon coriander powder
- 1/4 cup tomato ketchup
- 1/4 teaspoon black pepper
- 1/2 teaspoon onion powder
- 1/4 teaspoon liquid smoke
- 3/4 tablespoon red wine vinegar
- 1/2 teaspoon ground mustard
- 3/4 teaspoon erythritol
- 1/2 teaspoon allspice
- 1/2 teaspoon salt

Directions:
1. Add all the dry spices to the pork and marinate for 1 hour.
2. In a different bowl; mix the mustard, vinegar, ketchup and liquid smoke to prepare a sauce,
3. Place the marinated ribs in the instant pot and pour the sauce over it.
4. Secure the lid and select the *Manual* function. Cook for 35 minutes at *HIGH* pressure,
5. Natural release the steam for 5 minutes then remove the lid.
6. Transfer the ribs to a platter, Cook the remaining sauce in the pot on the *Sauté* setting for 5 minutes, to serve; drizzle the sauce over the ribs,

Nutrition Facts: Calories: 852, Fat: 53.8g, Carbs: 7.3g, Protein: 80.7g

Pork Ribs Barbecue

(Prep + Cooking Time: 25 minutes | Serves: 2)

Ingredients:
- 3/4 lb. pork ribs
- 1/4 cup red wine vinegar
- 1/2 teaspoon onion powder
- 1/2 teaspoon garlic powder
- 1/4 teaspoon paprika
- 1/4 teaspoon mustard
- 1/4 teaspoon cinnamon
- 1/2 teaspoon chili powder
- 1/2 cup water
- 2 tablespoons tomato sauce
- 2 tablespoons ketchup
- 2 tablespoons brown sugar
- 1/2 teaspoon salt
- 1/2 teaspoon pepper

Directions:
1. Pour water into the inner pot of an Instant Pot then place a trivet in it
2. Now, rub the pork ribs with salt, pepper and garlic powder then place on the trivet. Cover and seal the Instant Pot properly then close the steam valve
3. Select *Pressure cook* setting on the Instant Pot and cook the pork on high. Set the time to 10 minutes
4. In the meantime, combine tomato sauce with ketchup, brown sugar, red wine vinegar, paprika, mustard, cinnamon, chili powder and onion powder. Stir well
5. Once the pork is done, quick release the Instant Pot and open the lid.
6. Take the pork out of the Instant Pot and glaze with the sauce mixture
7. Wrap the glazed pork with aluminum foil then return it back to the Instant Pot. Place on the trivet.
8. Select *Manual* setting and cook the wrapped pork on high for another 10 minutes
9. Once it is done; naturally release the Instant Pot and open the lid
10. Remove the wrapped pork from the Instant Pot and let it cool for a few minutes. Unwrap the pork then place on a serving dish
11. Cut into thick slices then serve. Enjoy right away. The pork barbecue is best to be served with mashed potatoes

Nutrition Facts:
Calories: 354; Net Carbs: 6.7g; Total Fat: 19.9g; Protein: 35.4g; Carbs: 7.8g;

Pulled Pork

(Prep + Cooking Time: 50 minutes | Serves: 2)

Ingredients:
- 1-pound pork belly; make cubes
- 1 ½ teaspoons black pepper
- 1 tablespoon cornstarch
- 1/2 cup beef broth
- 1/2 cup chopped onion
- 3 tablespoons water
- 1 teaspoon thyme
- 1/4 teaspoon salt

Directions:
1. Switch on the pot after placing it on a clean and dry platform.
2. Open the pot lid and place the above-mentioned ingredients in the cooking pot area. Give the ingredients a little stir. Do not add the water and cornstarch.
3. Close the pot by closing the top lid. Also, ensure to seal the valve. Press *Manual* cooking function and set cooking time to 35 minutes.

4. It will start cooking after a few minutes. Let the pot mix cook under pressure until the timer reads zero. Press *Cancel* cooking function and press *Quick release* setting.
5. Open the pot. Combine cornstarch with water then stir into the Instant Pot. Add the liquid over the pork then serve warm!

Nutrition Facts:
Calories: 188; Fat: 15g; Carbohydrates: 8g; Fiber: 1.5g; Protein 4.5g

Pork Chops with Cinnamon

(Prep + Cooking Time: 25 minutes | Serves: 2)

Ingredients:
- 1/2 lb. pork chops
- 1/4 teaspoon cinnamon
- 1/2 apple
- 1 teaspoon brown sugar
- 1 tablespoon butter
- 1/4 teaspoon nutmeg
- 1/2 cup water
- 1/4 teaspoon salt
- 1/4 teaspoon pepper

Directions:
1. Rub the pork chops with salt and pepper then let it sit. Meanwhile, cut the apple into slices then place in a bowl
2. Sprinkle brown sugar, cinnamon and nutmeg over the sliced apple then toss to combine
3. Now, pour water into the inner pot of an Instant Pot then sprinkle the sliced apple in it
4. After that; place the seasoned pork chops on top then cover and seal the Instant Pot properly. Close the steam valve.
5. Select *Manual* setting on the Instant Pot and cook the pork chops on high for 20 minutes
6. Once it is done; naturally release the Instant Pot and open the lid. Transfer the cooked pork chops to a serving dish then garnish with the apples

Nutrition Facts:
Calories: 267; Net Carbs: 7g; Total Fat: 16.6g; Protein: 21.1g; Carbs: 8.5g;

Mushroom Tomato Pork Meatloaf

(Prep + Cooking Time: 25 minutes | Serves: 2)

Ingredients:
- 3/4 lbs. ground pork
- 1/2 teaspoon ginger
- 1/4 teaspoon nutmeg
- 1/2 cup chopped' mushrooms
- 3/4 teaspoon Worcestershire sauce
- 1/4 teaspoon salt
- 1/4 cup diced' tomatoes
- 1 egg white
- 2 tablespoons diced' onion
- 1/2 tablespoon flour
- 1/4 teaspoon pepper

Directions:
1. Combine ground beef with egg white, diced' onion, flour, Worcestershire sauce, salt, pepper, mushrooms and carrots in a bowl then mix well
2. Transfer the pork mixture to loaf pan then spread evenly. Pour water into the Instant Pot then place a trivet in it
3. Put the beef loaf on the trivet then cover and seal the Instant Pot properly. Close the steam valve
4. Select *Steam* setting on the Instant Pot and cook the pork on high for 20 minutes

5. Once it is done; naturally release the Instant Pot and open the lid.
6. Remove the pork loaf from the Instant Pot and let it cool for a few minutes
7. Now, take the pork loaf out of the loaf pan then place on a flat surface. Cut the pork loaf into thick slices then arrange on a serving dish

Nutrition Facts:
Calories: 378; Net Carbs: 4.5g; Total Fat: 24.3g; Protein: 33g; Carbs: 5g;

Pork Sausages and Mushrooms Recipe

(Prep + Cooking Time: 55 minutes | Serves: 2)

Ingredients:
- 6-ounce pork sausages
- 1/2 cup marinara sauce
- 2 large Portobello mushrooms
- 1/2 cup shredded mozzarella cheese
- 1/4 cup chopped parsley
- 1/2 cup whole milk ricotta cheese

Directions:
1. Stuff each mushroom with pork sausage,
2. Place the ricotta cheese over the sausages and carve a dent in the center.
3. Drizzle the marinara sauce over the ricotta cheese,
4. Cover with mozzarella cheese on top and place the mushrooms in the instant pot.
5. Secure the lid; select the *Manual* function and cook for 35 minutes at *HIGH* pressure. Natural release the steam then remove the lid. Serve immediately.

Nutrition Facts:
Calories: 624, Fat: 41.7g, Carbs: 27.2g, Protein: 34.9g

Tropical Pork Stew

(Prep + Cooking Time: 20 minutes | Serves: 2)

Ingredients:
- 1/2 lb. pork sirloin
- 1/4 teaspoon oregano
- 1 tablespoon soy sauce
- 1/2 cup water
- 1/2 cup chopped' pineapple
- 1/4 tablespoon honey
- 1/2 teaspoon ginger
- 2 tablespoons chopped' onion
- 1 teaspoon red chili
- 1/4 teaspoon salt
- 1/4 teaspoon pepper

Directions:
1. Cut the pork sirloin into slices then place in the inner pot of an Instant Pot
2. Pour water over the pork then season it with soy sauce, ginger, chopped' onion, red chili, salt, pepper and oregano
3. Sprinkle chopped' pineapple on top then cover and seal the Instant Pot properly. Close the steam valve.
4. Select *Manual* setting on the Instant Pot and cook the pork on high. Set the time to 15 minutes.
5. Once it is done; naturally release the Instant Pot and open the lid. Transfer the cooked pork to a serving dish then drizzle honey on top

Nutrition Facts:
Calories: 250; Net Carbs: 5.9g; Total Fat: 10.1g; Protein: 23.4g; Carbs: 6.7g

Pork and Beef Gumbo Recipe

(Prep + Cooking Time: 25 minutes | Serves: 3)

Ingredients:
- 1/4-pound ground pork
- 1/4-pound grass-fed ground beef
- 1/4 tablespoon olive oil
- 1/4 tablespoon chili powder
- 1/4 tablespoon ground cumin
- 1 chopped tomatillo.
- 1/8 chopped yellow onion.
- 1/2 chopped jalapeño pepper.
- 1/2 minced garlic clove
- 2 tablespoon shredded cheddar cheese
- 6-ounce sugar-free tomato sauce
- 1 tablespoon water
- Salt and black pepper

Directions:
1. Put the oil and all the Ingredients into the instant pot.
2. Stir well and secure the lid, Set the cooker to *Slow cook* at high heat for 4 hours,
3. Natural release the steam and remove the lid. Serve hot.

Nutrition Facts:
Calories: 181, Fat: 8.5g, Carbs: 4.8g, Protein: 20.4g

BBQ Pork Ribs Recipe

(Prep + Cooking Time: 1 hour 45 minutes | Serves: 4)

Ingredients:
- 2-pound baby back pork ribs
- 1/2 teaspoon ground cumin
- 1/2 teaspoon brown sugar
- 1/2 teaspoon garlic powder
- 2 tablespoon apple cider vinegar
- 2 cup apple juice
- 1/4 cup BBQ sauce
- 1/4 cup tomato ketchup
- 1 tablespoon Worcestershire sauce
- 1 tablespoon liquid smoke
- 1/2 teaspoon black pepper
- 1 teaspoon salt

Directions:
1. Combine the salt, pepper, brown sugar, cumin and garlic powder in a bowl to prepare the seasoning.
2. Add pork and mix well.
3. Now put the seasoned pork, apple cider vinegar, liquid smoke and apple juice into the instant pot.
4. Cook for 20 minutes at *HIGH* pressure using the *meat stew* function.
5. Natural release the steam for 15 minutes then remove the lid, Stir in the Worcestershire sauce BBQ sauce and the tomato ketchup. Allow to cool before serving.

Nutrition Facts:
Calories: 746, Fat: 54.5g, Carbs: 25.2g, Protein: 36.6g

Soups and Stews

Chicken and Radish Soup

(Prep + Cooking Time: 26 minutes | Serves: 2)

Ingredients:
- 1/4 lb. boneless chicken breast
- 1 medium carrot
- 1½ cups water
- 1/4 lb. radish
- 2 teaspoons minced' garlic
- 2 tablespoons chopped' onions
- 2 tablespoons chopped' celery stalk
- 1/4 teaspoon oregano
- 1/4 teaspoon chopped' parsley
- 1/4 teaspoon dried thyme
- 1/4 teaspoon dried rosemary
- 1 bay leaf
- 1/4 teaspoon salt
- 1/4 teaspoon pepper

Directions:
1. Cut the radish and carrots into thick slices then place in the inner pot of an Instant Pot. Cut the boneless chicken breast into small chunks then sprinkle over the radish.
2. Season with oregano, chopped' parsley, thyme, rosemary, minced' garlic and chopped' onion
3. Pour water into the Instant Pot then cover it with the lid. Seal the Instant Pot properly and close the steam valve
4. Select *Soup* setting on the Instant Pot and cook the chicken soup for 22 minutes.
5. Once the soup is done, quick release the Instant Pot then open the lid
6. Add chopped' celery stalk to the soup then stir until wilted. Transfer the soup to a serving bowl then serve warm.

Nutrition Facts: Calories: 142; Net Carbs: 5.3g; Total Fat: 4.4g; Protein: 17.5g; Carbs: 7.7g;

Celery Soup

(Prep + Cooking Time: 6 minutes | Serves: 4)

Ingredients:
- 1½ cups diced' celeries
- 2 tablespoons fresh milk
- 1 teaspoon minced' garlic
- 1 bay leaf
- 1½ cups vegetable broth
- 1 tablespoon chopped' parsley
- 1½ tablespoons butter
- 1/4 cup chopped' onion
- 1/4 teaspoon salt
- 1/4 teaspoon pepper

Directions:
1. Place butter in the inner pot of an Instant Pot then select *Sauté* setting. Stir in minced' garlic, chopped' onion and celeries then sauté until wilted. Press the *Cancel* button
2. Pour vegetable broth over the celeries then add bay leaf, salt, fresh milk and pepper. Stir well
3. Cover the Instant Pot with the lid and seal it properly.
4. Select *Manual* setting and cook the celeries for 4 minutes. Once it is done; naturally release the Instant Pot and open the lid
5. Using an immersion blender blend the soup until smooth. Transfer the soup to a serving bowl then top with chopped' parsley

Nutrition Facts: Calories: 110; Net Carbs: 4.2g; Total Fat: 7.3g; Protein: 5.1g; Carbs: 6g;

Coconut Squash Soup

(Prep + Cooking Time: 40 minutes | Serves: 2)

Ingredients:
- 1 ½–pound cubed butternut squash
- 1 minced garlic clove
- 1/4 cup coconut milk
- 1 ½ cup water
- 1/2 tablespoon curry powder
- 1/2 minced onion
- 1 teaspoon olive oil

Directions:
1. Add olive oil in the instant pot and set the pot on sauté mode.
2. Add onion and sauté until tender. Add curry powder and garlic and sauté for a minute.
3. Add butternut squash, water; and salt and stir well, Seal pot with lid and select soup setting and set timer for 25 minutes.
4. Release pressure using quick release method than open the lid.
5. Using blender puree the soup until smooth and creamy.
6. Add coconut milk and stir well.

Nutrition Facts:
Calories: 260, Fat: 10.1g, Carbs: 45.4g, Protein: 4.7g

Chicken Zucchini Noodles Soup

(Prep + Cooking Time: 15 minutes | Serves: 2)

Ingredients:
- 1/2 lb. bone-in chicken breast
- 1/4 teaspoon garlic powder
- 1 teaspoon soy sauce
- 1/4 teaspoon oregano
- 2 medium zucchinis
- 2 tablespoons chopped' onion
- 1 tablespoon butter
- 1 cup water
- 1/4 cup chopped' carrots
- 2 tablespoons diced' celeries
- 1/4 teaspoon salt

Directions:
1. Cut the chicken into medium chunks then set aside. Place butter in the inner pot of an Instant Pot then select *Sauté* setting
2. Stir in chopped' carrots, diced' celeries and chopped' onion to the Instant Pot then sauté until wilted and aromatic. Press the *Cancel* button
3. Add chopped' chicken to the Instant Pot then pour water over the chicken.
4. Season with salt, garlic powder, soy sauce and oregano the mix well.
5. Cover the Instant Pot with the lid then seal it properly. Close the steam valve
6. Select *Soup* setting on the Instant Pot and cook the chicken soup on high for 8 minutes.
7. In the meantime, peel the zucchinis and discard the seeds
8. Using a julienne peeler cut the zucchinis into noodle form then set aside
9. Once the soup is done, quick release the Instant Pot then open the lid
10. Stir in zucchini noodles then stir until wilted. Transfer the chicken noodle soup to a soup bowl then serve immediately

Nutrition Facts:
Calories: 226; Net Carbs: 6.6g; Total Fat: 7.7g; Protein: 30g; Carbs: 9.6g

Black Bean Soup

(Prep + Cooking Time: 47 minutes | Serves: 2)

Ingredients:
- 1 cup black beans; soaked overnight and drained
- 2 cups water
- 1 tablespoon olive oil
- 1 teaspoon cumin seeds
- 1 medium onion; chopped
- 1 teaspoon lemon juice
- 1 tablespoon garlic paste
- 1 tablespoon ginger paste
- 1 teaspoon red chili powder
- 1/2 teaspoon ground turmeric
- 1/2 teaspoon garam masala
- 2 teaspoons ground coriander
- Salt as per taste preference

Directions:
1. Switch on the pot after placing it on a clean and dry platform. Press *Sauté* cooking function.
2. Open the lid; add the oil and cumin seeds in the pot; cook for 30 seconds. Add the onion, garlic, spices and ginger; cook for 3-4 minutes to cook well and soften.
3. Mix in the chickpeas and water. Close the pot by closing the top lid. Also, ensure to seal the valve.
4. Press *Bean/Chili* cooking function and set cooking time to 30 minutes. It will start cooking after a few minutes. Let the pot mix cook under pressure until the timer reads zero.
5. Press *Cancel* cooking function and press *Natural release* setting.
6. It will take 8-10 minutes for natural pressure release. Open the instant pot; mix the lemon juice and serve warm.

Nutrition Facts: Calories: 437; Fat: 9g; Carbohydrates: 68.5g; Fiber: 16.5g; Protein 22g

Thai Style Chicken Soup

(Prep + Cooking Time: 20 minutes | Serves: 4)

Ingredients:
- 1 cup chicken breast 1-inch slices
- 1 onion; chopped
- 1 tablespoon oil
- 1 jalapeno; chopped
- 1 tablespoon curry paste
- 1 can full fat coconut milk
- 1 zucchini; spiralized
- 1 tablespoon fish sauce
- 1/2 lime; juiced
- 4 cups chicken broth
- Salt; to taste

Directions:
1. Add oil to Instant Pot and press "Sauté" button (*Normal* preset), wait till you see Hot on the display. Add onion, cook for 2 to 3 minutes until soft.
2. Add jalapeno and garlic, cook for 1 to 2 more minutes. Add chicken, curry paste and coconut milk, sauté for another 2 to 3 minutes.
3. Press *Cancel* button, add fish sauce, broth and salt. Close the lid and turn the vent to *Sealed*. Press *Pressure Cook* (Manual) button, use *+* or *-* button to set the timer for 5 minutes. Use *Pressure level* button to set Pressure to *HIGH*.
4. Once the timer is up; press *Cancel* button and turn the steam release handle to *Venting* position for quick release, until the float valve drops down.
5. Open the lid; Add zoodles to the Instant pot and mix well, keep mixing for 1 to 2 minutes. Serve soup with lime juice.

Nutrition Facts: Calories: 319 g; Total Fat: 22.8 g; Total Carbohydrate: 10.8 g; Protein: 19.5

Lentils Chicken Soup

(Prep + Cooking Time: 24 minutes | Serves: 2)

Ingredients:
- 1/4 lb. boneless chicken breast
- 2 tablespoons uncooked lentils
- 2 tablespoons diced' onions
- 1/4 cup half and half
- 1½ cups chicken broth
- 1/4 teaspoon salt
- 1/4 teaspoon pepper

Directions:
1. Cut the boneless chicken breast into small cubes then place in the inner pot of an Instant Pot
2. Add uncooked lentils, salt, pepper and diced' onions to the Instant Pot then pour chicken broth over the chicken. Mix well.
3. Cover the Instant Pot with the lid and seal it properly. Close the steam valve
4. Select *Manual* setting on the Instant Pot and cook the chicken on high for 10 minutes
5. Once it is done; naturally release the Instant Pot then open the lid. Add half and half to the Instant Pot then mix well
6. Press *Sauté* button on the Instant Pot then cook the chicken soup for about 2 minutes. Bring to a simmer. Transfer the chicken soup to a serving bowl then serve

Nutrition Facts:
Calories: 151; Net Carbs: 6.1g; Total Fat: 3.4g; Protein: 19.9g; Carbs: 10g

Salmon Stew

(Prep + Cooking Time: 15 minutes | Serves: 3)

Ingredients:
- 1-pound cubed salmon fillet
- 1 chopped onion
- 1 cup fish broth
- 1 tablespoon butter
- Salt and Pepper to taste

Directions:
1. Add all ingredients into the instant pot and stir well to mix.
2. Seal pot with lid and select *HIGH* pressure for 6 minutes.
3. Allow to release pressure naturally then Open the lid; Stir well and serve.

Nutrition Facts:
Calories: 261, Fat: 13.7g, Carbs: 3.7g, Protein: 31.4g

Carrot Tarragon Soup Recipe

(Prep + Cooking Time: 16 minutes | Serves: 4)

Ingredients:
- 2 ½ cups raw carrots; chopped
- 2 sprigs fresh tarragon
- 2 tablespoons butter
- 5-ounce Greek yoghurt
- 1 onion; chopped
- 4 cups vegetable stock or water
- Salt and Pepper to taste

Directions:
1. Add butter to Instant Pot and press "Sauté" button (*Normal* preset), wait till you see Hot on the display.
2. Add onion and cook for 2 to 3 minutes until soft. Add carrots, stock, tarragon, salt and pepper to the pot. Press *Cancel* button.
3. Press *Pressure Cook* (Manual) button, use *+* or *-* button to set the timer for 3 minutes. Use *Pressure level* button to set Pressure to *HIGH*.
4. Once the timer is up; press *Cancel* button and turn the steam release handle to *Venting* position for quick release, until the float valve drops down.
5. Open the lid.
6. Remove a small part of liquid from the pot (the amount depends on the preferable soup thickness). Puree soup with an immersion blender until smooth.
7. Adjust salt and pepper if needed and serve with yogurt on top.

Nutrition Facts:
Calories: 129 g; Total Fat: 8.4 g; Total Carbohydrate: 11.2 g; Protein: 3.1

Pork Ribs Soup with Green Collard

(Prep + Cooking Time: 26 minutes | Serves: 2)

Ingredients:
- 3/4 lb. pork ribs
- 1 teaspoon sliced shallots
- 1/2 teaspoon ginger
- 1/4 teaspoon nutmeg
- 1 cup water
- 1/4 cup chopped' collard
- 1/4 teaspoon salt
- 1/4 teaspoon pepper

Directions:
1. Place pork ribs in the inner pot of an Instant Pot then season with sliced shallots, ginger, nutmeg, salt and pepper
2. Pour water into the Instant Pot then cover and seal it properly. Select *Pressure cook* setting and cook the pork ribs on high for 20 minutes
3. Once it is done; quick release the Instant Pot and open the lid
4. Add chopped' green collard to the Instant Pot then select *Sauté* setting
5. Cook the soup for a minute or until the green collard is just wilted. Transfer the soup to a bowl then serve immediately

Nutrition Facts:
Calories: 471; Net Carbs: 0.8g; Total Fat: 30.3g; Protein: 45.3g; Carbs: 1.2g;

Onion Soup

(Prep + Cooking Time: 10 minutes | Serves: 4)

Ingredients:
- 1 cup sliced onions
- 1/2 tablespoon thyme
- 1/4 teaspoon pepper
- 1½ cups vegetable broth
- 2 tablespoons butter
- 1/4 cup white wine
- 1/2 tablespoon Worcestershire sauce
- 1 bay leaf
- 1/2 teaspoon salt

Directions:
1. Place butter in the inner pot of an Instant Pot then select *Sauté* setting
2. Stir in sliced onion then sauté until wilted and aromatic. Press the *Cancel* button
3. Now, pour vegetables broth over the onions and season with salt, white wine. Thyme, pepper and bay leaf.
4. Cover the Instant Pot and seal it properly. Select *manual* setting and cook the soup for 6 minutes. Once it is done; quick release the Instant Pot and open the lid
5. Using an immersion blender blend the soup until smooth and creamy then transfer to a soup bowl. Serve and enjoy with sliced baguette

Nutrition Facts:
Calories: 160; Net Carbs: 6.8g; Total Fat: 11.7g; Protein: 0.9g; Carbs: 8.4g;

Chicken Noodle Soup

(Prep + Cooking Time: 18 minutes | Serves: 3)

Ingredients:
- 2 boneless chicken thighs; cubed
- 2 cups uncooked egg noodles
- 1 celery stalk; sliced
- 3 cups chicken stock
- 1 onion; diced
- 2 carrots; sliced
- 1 bay leaf
- 1/2 teaspoon salt
- 1/2 teaspoon black pepper

Directions:
1. Combine all ingredients in Instant Pot. Close lid and set cooking time for 8 minutes.
2. Discard bay leaf and Serve hot.

Nutrition Facts:
Calories: 311; Fat: 17.31 g; Carbohydrates: 17.68 g; Fiber: 1.3 g; Protein: 20.21 g

Sweet Potato Stew

(Prep + Cooking Time: 20 minutes | Serves: 3)

Ingredients:
- 7-ounce coconut milk
- 7-ounce diced tomatoes
- 1/2 diced bell pepper
- 1/2 diced zucchini
- 1 minced garlic clove
- 1 diced sweet potato
- 1 lime juice
- 1/2 tablespoon minced ginger
- 1 diced onion
- 1 tablespoon red curry paste
- 1/2 teaspoon turmeric
- 1 teaspoon curry powder
- 1 tablespoon olive oil
- 1/2 teaspoon sea salt

Directions:
1. Add oil into the instant pot and set on sauté mode.
2. When instant pot display reads hot then add onion and sauté until translucent.
3. Add garlic and ginger and sauté for a minute, Add remaining ingredients and mix well. Seal pot with lid and select *HIGH* pressure for 5 minutes.
4. Release pressure using quick release method than open the lid. Stir well and serve.

Nutrition Facts:
Calories: 251, Fat: 20.6g, Carbs: 16.7g, Protein: 3.5g

Chicken and Vegetable Soup

***(Prep + Cooking Time:** 35 minutes | **Serves:** 4)*

Ingredients:
- 1/2-pound. chicken meat; cooked, shredded
- 1/2 celery; diced
- 1 onion; chopped
- 1 carrot; diced
- 7-ounce mushrooms; sliced
- 5 cups chicken stock
- 2 garlic cloves; chopped
- 1 teaspoon thyme
- 1 teaspoon rosemary
- 2 bay leaves
- 2 tablespoons olive oil
- Salt and Pepper to taste

Directions:
1. Add oil to Instant Pot and press "Sauté" button (*Normal* preset), wait till you see Hot on the display.
2. Add carrots and onion, cook for 2 to 3 more minutes. Add garlic, celery and mushrooms and cook for 3 more minutes.
3. Press *Cancel* button and add chicken to the Instant pot; also stock, thyme, rosemary, bay leaves, salt and pepper.
4. Close the lid and turn the vent to *Sealed*. Press *Soup/Broth* button and adjust to *Less* preset.
5. Once the timer is up; press *Cancel* button and turn the steam release handle to *Venting* position for quick release, until the float valve drops down. Open the lid.

Nutrition Facts: Calories: 216 g; Total Fat: 11 g; Total Carbohydrate: 5.4 g; Protein: 24

Beef Soup

***(Prep + Cooking Time:** 25 minutes | **Serves:** 2)*

Ingredients:
- 1/2 lb. beef sirloin
- 2 kluwak nuts
- 1/4 teaspoon ginger
- 1/2-inch galangal
- 1/2 teaspoon coriander
- 1/4 teaspoon cumin
- 1 lemon grass
- 3 kaffir lime leaves
- 2 cloves garlic
- 2 shallots
- 1/2 cup water
- 1/4 teaspoon turmeric
- 1/2 teaspoon salt

Directions:
1. Soak the kluwak nuts in water and wait until the water turns into black
2. Place garlic, shallots, turmeric, ginger, coriander and cumin in a food processor then process until smooth. Now, cut the beef into slices then place in the inner pot of an Instant Pot
3. Pour kluwak water over the beef then season with spice mixture, galangal, lemon grass, lime leaves and salt. Stir well.
4. Cover the Instant Pot with the lid then seal it properly. Close the steam valve.
5. Select *Manual* setting on the Instant Pot and cook the beef on high. Set the time to 20 minutes
6. Once the beef is done, naturally release the Instant Pot and open the lid
7. Transfer the beef and the gravy to a serving bowl and serve immediately. Enjoy the black beef soup with a bowl of brown rice

Nutrition Facts: Calories: 154; Net Carbs: 6.4g; Total Fat: 4.2g Protein: 23.6g; Carbs: 6.6g

Oxtail Soup

*(**Prep + Cooking Time:** 28 minutes | **Serves:** 2)*

Ingredients:
- 3/4 lb. oxtails
- 1 clove
- 2 tablespoons chopped' carrots
- 1 tablespoon chopped' celeries
- 1 cup water
- 1/4 teaspoon nutmeg
- 1/4 teaspoon salt
- 1/4 teaspoon pepper

Directions:
1. Place oxtails in the inner pot of an Instant Pot then season with nutmeg, salt, pepper and clove
2. Pour water into the Instant Pot then cover and seal it properly. Select *Pressure cook* setting and cook the oxtails on high. Set the time to 20 minutes
3. Once it is done; quick release the Instant Pot and open the lid.
4. Add chopped' carrots and celeries to the Instant Pot then select *Sauté* setting
5. Cook the soup for another 3 minutes or until the carrots are tender enough. Transfer the soup to a bowl then serve immediately

Nutrition Facts:
Calories: 426; Net Carbs: 0.8g; Total Fat: 22.7g; Protein: 52.7g; Carbs: 1.2g

Chicken Mushroom Soup

*(**Prep + Cooking Time:** 18 minutes | **Serves:** 2)*

Ingredients:
- 1/2 lb. boneless chicken breast
- 1/4 cup heavy cream
- 1/4 cup diced' mushrooms
- 1/2 cup water
- 2 tablespoons diced' carrots
- 1 teaspoon minced' garlic
- 1/4 teaspoon salt
- 1/4 teaspoon black pepper

Directions:
1. Cut boneless chicken breast into small dices then place in the inner pot of an Instant Pot. Add minced' garlic, salt and black pepper then pour water over the chicken
2. Cover the Instant Pot with the lid and seal it properly. Close the steam valve.
3. Select *Pressure* menu on the Instant Pot then cook the soup on high for 10 minutes
4. Once it is done; quick release the Instant Pot then open the lid. Stir in heavy cream then add diced' mushrooms and carrots to the soup.
5. Close the Instant Pot properly and cook on high pressure for 3 minutes
6. Once it is done; quick release the Instant Pot then open the lid. Transfer the creamy soup to a serving bowl then serve warm

Nutrition Facts:
Calories: 217; Net Carbs: 1.2g; Total Fat: 11.6g; Protein: 25.5g; Carbs: 1.6;

Creamy Cauliflower Soup

(Prep + Cooking Time: 10 minutes | Serves: 4)

Ingredients:
- 1½ cups cauliflower florets
- 1 cup vegetable broth
- 2 teaspoons minced' garlic
- 1/4 cup cream cheese
- 1/4 cup chopped' onion
- 1/4 teaspoon salt
- 1/2 teaspoon pepper

Directions:
1. Place cauliflower florets in the inner pot of an Instant Pot then add minced' garlic, chopped' onion, salt and pepper
2. Pour vegetable broth over the cauliflower florets then cover and seal the Instant Pot properly
3. Select *Manual* setting on the Instant Pot and cook the cauliflower florets on high for 6 minutes.
4. Once it is done; quick release the Instant Pot and open the lid. Stir in cream cheese and mix until combined
5. Using an immersion blender blend the soup until smooth. Transfer the soup to a serving bowl and serve

Nutrition Facts:
Calories: 150; Net Carbs: 5.4g; Total Fat: 10.9g; Protein: 6.5g; Carbs: 7.8g;

Mexican Style Beef Soup

(Prep + Cooking Time: 20 minutes | Serves: 4)

Ingredients:
- 7-ounce ground beef
- 4 cups beef broth
- 1 teaspoon olive oil
- 3 ounces cream cheese
- 2 garlic cloves; minced
- 1 teaspoon chili powder
- 1 teaspoon ground cumin
- 1/2 cup heavy cream
- Salt and Pepper to taste

Directions:
1. Add oil to Instant Pot and press "Sauté" button (*Normal* preset), wait till you see Hot on the display.
2. Add beef and cook for about 5-7 minutes. Drain extra grease from the pot.
3. Press *Cancel* and add cream cheese, garlic, chili powder, ground cumin, heavy cream, salt, pepper and broth. Close the lid and turn the vent to *Sealed*.
4. Press *Pressure Cook* (Manual) button, use *+* or *-* button to set the timer for 5 minutes. Use *Pressure level* button to set Pressure to *HIGH*.
5. Once the timer is up; press *Cancel* button and allow the pressure to be released naturally; until the float valve drops down. Open the lid and serve.

Nutrition Facts:
Calories: 606 g; Total Fat: 45.8 g; Total Carbohydrate: 19.4 g; Protein: 32.9

Spicy Beef Soup

(Prep + Cooking Time: 28 minutes | Serves: 2)

Ingredients:
- 1 lb. beef tenderloin
- 1/4 cup green tomatoes
- 1 cup water
- 2 teaspoons tamarind
- 1 teaspoon soy sauce
- 2 teaspoons sliced garlic
- 2 teaspoons sliced shallots
- 2 teaspoons red chili flakes
- 1/2 teaspoon salt

Directions:
1. Cut the beef tenderloin into medium pieces then place in the inner pot of an Instant Pot
2. Sprinkle sliced garlic, sliced shallots, red chili flakes, salt and green tomatoes to the Instant Pot
3. Add tamarind and soy sauce to the Instant Pot then pour water over the beef. Cover the Instant Pot with the lid and seal it properly. Close the steam valve
4. Select *Manual* setting and cook the beef on high for 22 minutes
5. Once it is done; naturally release the Instant Pot and open the lid. Transfer the soup to a serving dish then serve warm

Nutrition Facts:
Calories: 216; Net Carbs: 6.9g; Total Fat: 8.3g; Protein: 26.5g; Carbs: 8.1g;

Carrot Soup

(Prep + Cooking Time: 15 minutes | Serves: 3)

Ingredients:
- 1-pound quartered carrots
- 3 cup chicken stock
- 1 teaspoon paprika
- 1 teaspoon ground cumin
- 2 teaspoon minced garlic
- 2 tablespoon Dijon mustard
- 1/4 cup butter
- Salt and Pepper to taste

Directions:
1. Add 1 cup water into the instant pot and place trivet into the pot.
2. Arrange carrots on top of carrots, Seal pot with lid and select *HIGH* pressure for 1 minute.
3. Release pressure using quick release method than open the lid.
4. Transfer carrots on a dish. Clean instant pot and dry with paper towel, Add butter into the instant pot and set the pot on sauté mode.
5. Once butter is melted then add remaining ingredients and stir in cooked carrots.
6. Seal pot with lid and select *HIGH* pressure for 4 minutes, Allow to release pressure naturally then open the lid.
7. Puree the soup using a blender until smooth and creamy. Serve hot and enjoy.

Nutrition Facts:
Calories: 222, Fat: 16.6g, Carbs: 17.5g, Protein: 2.9g

Tomato Soup

***(Prep + Cooking Time:** 15 minutes | **Serves:** 3)*

Ingredients:
- 15-ounce diced tomatoes
- 15-ounce tomato puree
- 4 tablespoon cashew
- 1 ½ cup vegetable stock
- 1/2 tablespoon dried basil
- 1 ½ tablespoon quick oats
- 2 minced garlic cloves
- Salt and Pepper to taste

Directions:
1. Add all ingredients except pepper and salt into the instant pot and stir well.
2. Seal pot with lid and select *HIGH* pressure for 4 minutes, Allow to release pressure naturally then open the lid.
3. Puree the soup using a blender until smooth. Season with pepper and salt.

Nutrition Facts:
Calories: 166, Fat: 6.5g, Carbs: 26.8g, Protein: 5.9g

Chicken Corn Soup

***(Prep + Cooking Time:** 23 minutes | **Serves:** 2)*

Ingredients:
- 1/2 lb. boneless chicken breast
- 2 tablespoons chopped' leek
- 1 tablespoon sliced shallots
- 1/4 teaspoon nutmeg
- 2 cups water
- 1 egg
- 1/4 cup corn kernels
- 1/4 cup diced' carrots
- 1/4 teaspoon pepper
- 1/2 teaspoon salt

Directions:
1. Place corn kernels in the inner pot of an Instant Pot. Cut the boneless chicken breast into small dices then add to the Instant Pot
2. Pour water into the Instant Pot then season with shallots, salt, nutmeg and pepper
3. Cover the Instant Pot and seal it properly. Close the steam valve.
4. Select *Pressure* menu on the Instant Pot then cook the soup on high for 15 minutes
5. Once it is done; naturally release the Instant Pot then open the lid.
6. Stir in carrots and chopped' leek to the soup then press the *Sauté* button. Bring to boil
7. In the meantime, crack the egg then place in a bowl. Stir until beaten.
8. Once the soup is boiled, drizzle beaten egg over the soup then stir vigorously
9. Wait until the egg is set then press the *Cancel* button. Transfer the soup to a soup bowl then serve immediately.

Nutrition Facts:
Calories: 173; Net Carbs: 6g; Total Fat: 4.1g; Protein: 28.8g; Carbs: 7.1g;

Carrot Soup

(Prep + Cooking Time: 37 minutes | Serves: 2)

Ingredients:
- 1/2-pound carrots; peeled and chopped
- 1/2 tablespoon Sriracha
- 7-ounce canned unsweetened coconut milk
- 1 cup chicken broth
- 1 tablespoon fresh cilantro; chopped
- 1 tablespoon unsalted butter
- ⅛ teaspoon brown sugar
- 1/2 teaspoon fresh ginger; minced
- 1 garlic clove; minced
- 1 small onion; chopped
- Pepper and salt as per taste preference

Directions:
1. Switch on the pot after placing it on a clean and dry platform. Press *Sauté* cooking function.
2. Open the lid; add the butter and onions in the pot; cook for 2-3 minutes to cook well and soften.
3. Add the ginger and garlic and cook for 1 minute. Add the carrots, salt and black pepper and cook for another 2 minutes.
4. Mix in the coconut milk, broth and Sriracha. Close the pot by closing the top lid. Also, ensure to seal the valve.
5. Press *Manual* cooking function and set cooking time to 6 minutes. It will start cooking after a few minutes. Let the pot mix cook under pressure until the timer reads zero.
6. Press *Cancel* cooking function and press *Natural release* setting. It will take 8-10 minutes for natural pressure release.
7. Open the pot and mix in the sugar. With an immersion blender, puree the soup. Serve immediately; top with some cilantro.

Nutrition Facts: Calories 364; Fat: 30.5g; Carbohydrates: 21.5g; Fiber: 5g; Protein 6g

Salmon Soup with Basil

(Prep + Cooking Time: 7 minutes | Serves: 2)

Ingredients:
- 1/2 lb. salmon fillet
- 1 cup fresh basil
- 2 teaspoons sliced shallots
- 1 teaspoon sliced garlic
- 1/4 teaspoon ginger
- 1/4 teaspoon tamarind
- 1 tablespoon lemon juice
- 1 cup water
- 1/4 cup chopped' green tomatoes
- 1 bay leaf
- 1/2 teaspoon salt

Directions:
1. Cut the salmon fillet into medium cubes then place in the inner pot of an Instant Pot
2. Pour water over the salmon then add green tomatoes, fresh basil, sliced shallot, garlic, ginger, bay leaf, salt, tamarind and lemon juice
3. Cover the Instant Pot with the lid and seal it properly. Select *Soup* setting on the Instant Pot and cook the salmon on high for 4 minutes
4. Once it is done; naturally release the Instant Pot and open the lid. Transfer the soup to a serving bowl then serve warm

Nutrition Facts: Calories: 166; Net Carbs: 3g; Total Fat: 7.2g; Protein: 22.9; Carbs: 3g;

Cheesy Broccoli Soup

(Prep + Cooking Time: 7 minutes | Serves: 4)

Ingredients:
- 1/2 lb. broccoli florets
- 1/4 teaspoon nutmeg
- 1/2 teaspoon garlic powder
- 1 cup vegetable broth
- 1 tablespoon butter
- 1/4 cup grated cheddar cheese
- 1/4 cup chopped' onion
- 1/4 teaspoon pepper
- 1/4 teaspoon paprika
- 1/4 teaspoon salt

Directions:
1. Place butter in the inner pot of an Instant Pot then select *Sauté* setting. Once the butter is melted, stir in chopped' onion then sauté until wilted and aromatic. Press the *Cancel* button
2. Pour vegetable broth into the Instant Pot then season the broccoli with pepper, paprika, salt, nutmeg and garlic powder. Stir well
3. Cover the Instant Pot with the lid and seal it properly. Select *Manual* setting and cook the broccoli for 5 minutes
4. Once it is done; naturally release the Instant Pot and open the lid. Using an immersion blender blend the soup until smooth then transfer to a serving bowl

Nutrition Facts: Calories: 177; Net Carbs: 6.9g; Total Fat: 11.7g;; Protein: 9.6g; Carbs: 10.5g;

Beef in Turmeric Yellow Soup

(Prep + Cooking Time: 20 minutes | Serves: 2)

Ingredients:
- 1/2 lb. beef sirloin
- 2 shallots
- 2 cloves garlic
- 2 candlenuts
- 1/2 teaspoon turmeric
- 1 cup water
- 2 tablespoons beansprouts
- 1 lemon grass
- 1 kaffir lime leaf
- 1 teaspoon vegetable oil
- 1/4 teaspoon pepper
- 1/4 teaspoon salt

Directions:
1. Cut the beef sirloin into thin slices then set aside. Place shallots, garlic, candlenuts and turmeric in a food processor then process until smooth.
2. Pour vegetable oil into the inner pot of an Instant Pot and select *Sauté* setting
3. Stir in the spice mixture then sauté until aromatic. Now, add sliced beef to the Instant Pot together with lemon grass and lime leaf. Sauté until just wilted then press the *Cancel* button
4. Pour water over the beef and season with salt and pepper.
5. Cover the Instant Pot with the lid and seal it properly. Close the steam valve
6. Select *Manual* setting and cook the beef on high for 15 minutes.
7. Once it is done; quickly release the Instant Pot and open the lid
8. Add beansprouts to the soup and stir until wilted. Transfer the soup to a bowl then serve immediately

Nutrition Facts: Calories: 259; Net Carbs: 6.1g; Total Fat: 14.9g; Protein: 25.8g; Carbs: 7.9g;

Beef Stew

(Prep + Cooking Time: 55 minutes | Serves: 2)

Ingredients:

- 1/2-pound beef stew meat; cut into cubes
- 1 tablespoon hot sauce
- 2 medium potatoes; chopped
- 1 small onion; chopped
- 1 celery stalk; chopped
- 1 tablespoon olive oil
- 1/2 teaspoon garlic powder
- 2 carrots; peeled and chopped
- 1 cups kale leaves; trimmed and chopped
- 1 ½ cups beef broth
- Pepper and salt as per taste preference

Directions:

1. Switch on the pot after placing it on a clean and dry platform. Press *Sauté* cooking function.
2. Open the lid; add the oil and beef in the pot; cook for 4-5 minutes to cook well and turn browned evenly.
3. Mix in the remaining ingredients. Close the pot by closing the top lid. Also, ensure to seal the valve.
4. Press *Meat/Stew* cooking function and set cooking time to 40 minutes.
5. It will start cooking after a few minutes. Let the pot mix cook under pressure until the timer reads zero.
6. Press *Cancel* cooking function and press *Quick release* setting. Open the pot and serve warm.

Nutrition Facts: Calories: 504; Fat: 15.5g; Carbohydrates: 46.5g; Fiber: 8g; Protein 42.5g

Elbow Pasta Soup

(Prep + Cooking Time: 16 minutes | Serves: 2)

Ingredients:

- 14 ounces tomatoes; diced
- 1/2 cup elbow pasta
- 2 cups chicken broth
- 1 cup cooked white beans
- 1 carrot; diced
- 1 teaspoon dried basil
- 1 tablespoon olive oil
- 1 teaspoon dried oregano
- 2 garlic cloves; minced
- 1 bay leaf
- 1 onion; diced
- 1/4 cup fresh spinach
- Pepper and salt as per taste preference

Directions:

1. Switch on the pot after placing it on a clean and dry platform. Press *Sauté* cooking function.
2. Open the lid; add the oil, carrot, onion, garlic and celery in the pot; cook until turn tender and soft.
3. Add the oregano, basil, pepper and salt. Mix the tomatoes, spinach, bone broth, pasta and bay leaf.
4. Close the pot by closing the top lid. Also, ensure to seal the valve. Press *Manual* cooking function and set cooking time to 6 minutes.
5. It will start cooking after a few minutes. Let the pot mix cook under pressure until the timer reads zero.
6. Press *Cancel* cooking function and press *Natural release* setting.

7. It will take 8-10 minutes for natural pressure release. Open the instant pot; add the beans and serve warm.

Nutrition Facts: Calories: 394; Fat: 3g; Carbohydrates: 58g; Fiber: 9.5g; Protein 20.5g

Pork Soup

(Prep + Cooking Time: 15 minutes | Serves: 2)

Ingredients:
- 1 ½ cups cabbage; chopped
- 1/2 teaspoon ground ginger
- 1 small onion; chopped
- 1/2-pound ground pork
- 2 cups low-sodium chicken broth
- 1 tablespoon soy sauce
- 1 cup carrot; peeled and shredded
- 1 tablespoon olive oil
- Fresh pepper as per taste preference

Directions:
1. Switch on the pot after placing it on a clean and dry platform. Press *Sauté* cooking function.
2. Open the lid; add the oil and meat in the pot; cook for 4-5 minutes to cook well and turn browned evenly.
3. Mix in the remaining ingredients. Close the pot by closing the top lid. Also, ensure to seal the valve.
4. Press *Manual* cooking function and set cooking time to 25 minutes.
5. It will start cooking after a few minutes. Let the pot mix cook under pressure until the timer reads zero.
6. Press *Cancel* cooking function and press *Quick release* setting. Open the pot and serve warm.

Nutrition Facts:
Calories: 294; Fat: 11g; Carbohydrates: 14.5g; Fiber: 3.5g; Protein 34g

Chicken Soup

(Prep + Cooking Time: 20 minutes | Serves: 2)

Ingredients:
- 1-pound chopped chicken
- 1 teaspoon cinnamon
- 1 teaspoon coriander
- 1 tablespoon olive oil
- 1 tablespoon fish sauce
- 1 teaspoon ginger
- 1 tablespoon sugar
- 1/4 cup chopped onion
- 3 cups low sodium chicken broth
- 2 teaspoons minced garlic
- 1/2 cup chopped cilantro
- 3/4 teaspoon salt

Directions:
1. Switch on the pot after placing it on a clean and dry platform. Press *Sauté* cooking function.
2. Open the lid; add the butter, garlic and onions in the pot; cook for 2-3 minutes to cook well and soften.
3. Mix in the chopped chicken, ginger, cilantro, sugar, cinnamon, coriander, fish sauce and salt.
4. Pour chicken broth and stir gently. Close the pot by closing the top lid. Also, ensure to seal the valve.
5. Press *Manual* cooking function and set cooking time to 15 minutes. It will start cooking after a few minutes. Let the pot mix cook under pressure until the timer reads zero.
6. Press *Cancel* cooking function and press *Natural release* setting.

7. It will take 8-10 minutes for natural pressure release. Open the pot and serve warm.

Nutrition Facts: Calories: 288; Fat: 14.5g; Carbohydrates: 23g; Fiber: 2.5g; Protein 16.5g

Delightful Goulash

*(**Prep + Cooking Time:** 20 minutes | **Serves:** 3)*

Ingredients:
- 1/2-pound cubed beef
- 3-ounce egg noodles
- 1/2 chopped onion
- 1 tablespoon olive oil
- 3 cup chicken broth
- 7-ounce diced tomatoes
- 1 ½ tablespoon paprika
- 1 teaspoon minced garlic
- 1/8 teaspoon pepper
- 1/2 teaspoon salt

Directions:
1. Add oil into the instant pot and set the instant pot on sauté mode.
2. When instant pot display reads hot then add garlic, onion; and meat and sauté until meat is browned.
3. Add paprika, broth, pasta, tomatoes, pepper; and salt. Stir well, Seal pot with lid and select *HIGH* pressure for 5 minutes.
4. Release pressure using quick release method than open the lid. Stir well and serve.

Nutrition Facts: Calories: 291, Fat: 11.8g, Carbs: 15.4g, Protein: 30.5g

Beef Stew

*(**Prep + Cooking Time:** 40 minutes | **Serves:** 6)*

Ingredients:
- 1-pound cubed beef
- 3 sliced carrots
- 1 tablespoon red pepper flakes
- 2 sliced garlic cloves
- 1/2 cup dry red wine
- 2 tablespoon butter
- 5-ounce mixed wild mushrooms
- 1 diced yellow onion
- 1 cup diced potatoes
- 4 cup beef broth
- 1 tablespoon red wine vinegar
- 4 cup water
- 1 can diced tomatoes
- 1 cup green beans

Directions:
1. Turn the Sauté function in the Mini Instant Pot and add the butter. Let it melt; and add the onions and sauté them until they are soft for about 3 minutes.
2. Gradually; add the beef cubes and season them with pepper and salt.
3. The beef should be brown on all sides. It will take about 5-7 minutes for the beef to be brown.
4. Add garlic and cook until you have a nice flavor. This will take about a minute.
5. Pour the red wine over the beef and use a wooden spatula to scrap the sides.
6. Now you need to turn off the Mini Instant Pot and add rest of the ingredients.
7. Secure the lid tightly and set the temperature to High Pressure. Put the Mini Pot in Manual mode for 15 minutes.
8. Once the cooking time ends, you can release the steam. Remove the bay leaf.
9. Serve this amazing beef stew and enjoy it with your family.

Nutrition Facts: Calories: 222, Fat: 10g, Carbs: 11.7g, Protein: 19.2g

Cabbage Tomato Soup

(Prep + Cooking Time: 25 minutes | Serves: 4)

Ingredients:
- 1 chopped cabbage head
- 28-ounce chopped tomatoes
- 3 tablespoon Apple cider vinegar
- 4 minced garlic cloves
- 3 cup chicken broth
- 3 chopped celery stalks
- 3 chopped carrots
- 1 tablespoon lemon juice
- 1 chopped onion

Directions:
1. Add all ingredients into the instant pot and stir well, Seal pot with lid and select *HIGH* pressure for 15 minutes.
2. Release pressure using quick release method than open the lid. Stir and serve.

Nutrition Facts:
Calories: 155, Fat: 1.3g, Carbs: 29.8g, Protein: 8.7g

Chicken Lentil Soup

(Prep + Cooking Time: 45 minutes | Serves: 4)

Ingredients:
- 1/2-pound dried lentils
- 6-ounce skinless chicken thighs
- 1/2 chopped onion
- 3 ½ cup water
- 1/4 teaspoon paprika
- 1/2 teaspoon garlic powder
- 1 diced tomato
- 2 tablespoon chopped cilantro
- 1/8 teaspoon oregano
- 1/2 teaspoon cumin
- 1 chopped scallion
- 1/4 teaspoon salt

Directions:
1. Add all ingredients into the instant pot and stir well.
2. Seal pot with lid and select soup mode and set the timer for 30 minutes.
3. Allow to release pressure naturally then Open the lid; Shred the chicken using a fork and stir well.

Nutrition Facts:
Calories: 293, Fat: 3.9g, Carbs: 36.5g, Protein: 27.5g

Fish and Seafood

Mahi Mahi Fillets

(Prep + Cooking Time: 25 minutes | Serves: 4)

Ingredients:
- 6 mahi-mahi fillets
- 28-ounce diced tomatoes
- 1 sliced onion
- 3 tablespoon butter
- 2 tablespoon lemon juice
- 1 teaspoon dried oregano
- Salt and Pepper to taste

Directions:
1. Add butter into the instant pot and set the pot on sauté mode.
2. When instant pot display reads hot then add onion and sauté for 2 minutes.
3. Add remaining ingredients except for mahi-mahi fillets and sauté for 3 minutes.
4. Now add fish fillets and seal pot with lid. Set instant pot on *HIGH* pressure for 8 minutes, Release pressure using quick release method than open the lid. Serve hot and enjoy.

Nutrition Facts:
Calories: 268, Fat: 8.8g, Carbs: 13.1g, Protein: 33.8g

Sour and Sweet Fish

(Prep + Cooking Time: 20 minutes | Serves: 3)

Ingredients:
- 1-pound fish chunks
- 1/2 tablespoon sugar
- 1 tablespoon olive oil
- 1 tablespoon vinegar
- 1 tablespoon soy sauce
- Salt and Pepper to taste

Directions:
1. Add oil into the instant pot and set the instant pot on sauté mode.
2. When instant pot display reads hot then add fish chunks and sauté for 3 minutes.
3. Add the rest of the ingredients as you stir to mix, Seal pot with lid and select *HIGH* pressure for 6 minutes.
4. Allow to release pressure naturally then open the lid. Stir well and serve.

Nutrition Facts:
Calories: 402, Fat: 23.3g, Carbs: 28.1g, Protein: 22.5g

Dijon Lemon Whitefish

(Prep + Cooking Time: 15 minutes | Serves: 2)

Ingredients:
- 2 big whitefish fillets
- 2 tablespoons Dijon mustard
- 1/2 teaspoon black pepper
- 1 teaspoon horseradish; grated
- 1 tablespoon fresh lemon juice
- 1 teaspoon fresh ginger; grated
- 1 lemon; sliced
- 1 cup water
- 1/2 tablespoon olive oil
- 1/2 teaspoon salt

Directions:
1. Mix Dijon mustard, horseradish and lemon juice in a bowl.
2. Season white fish fillets with salt and pepper and add to the Dijon marinade. Let it marinate for 20 minutes.
3. Add water to the Instant pot and place a steamer rack inside. Put the fish fillets on the rack and pour the marinade on top.
4. Close the lid and turn the vent to *Sealed*. Press *Pressure Cook* (Manual) button, use *+* or *-* button to set the timer for 4 minutes. Use *Pressure level* button to set Pressure to *HIGH*.
5. Once the timer is up; press *Cancel* button and allow the pressure to be released naturally; until the float valve drops down.
6. Open the lid; Serve with lemon slices on top.

Nutrition Facts:
Calories: 176 g; Total Fat: 14.4 g; Total Carbohydrate: 7 g; Protein: 1.2

Ricotta and Tomatoes Shrimps Recipe

(Prep + Cooking Time: 17 minutes | Serves: 3)

Ingredients:
- 1/2-pound. shrimps; peeled and deveined
- 2 garlic cloves; minced
- 4 tablespoons ricotta cheese
- 1 onion; diced
- 14.5-ounce can diced tomatoes
- 2 tablespoons grass-fed butter
- 1 tablespoon salt-free Italian seasoning
- 1/2 teaspoon cayenne pepper
- Salt; to taste

Directions:
1. Add butter to Instant Pot and press "Sauté" button (*Normal* preset), wait till you see Hot on the display.
2. Add garlic, cook for 30 seconds-1 minute until fragrant. Add onion, tomatoes, Italian seasoning, cayenne and salt. Add shrimps and mix well.
3. Close the lid and turn the vent to *Sealed*. Press *Pressure Cook* (Manual) button, use *+* or *-* button to set the timer for 5 minutes. Use *Pressure level* button to set Pressure to *HIGH*.
4. Once the timer is up; press *Cancel* button and turn the steam release handle to *Venting* position for quick release, until the float valve drops down.
5. Open the lid; Serve shrimps with ricotta cheese on top over noodles.

Nutrition Facts:
Calories: 260 g; Total Fat: 19.7 g; Total Carbohydrate: 11.9 g; Protein: 20.4

Tasty Spicy Mussels Mania

(Prep + Cooking Time: 10 minutes | Serves: 3)

Ingredients:
- 2-pounds' mussels; scrubbed
- 14 ounces' tomatoes; chopped
- 2 tablespoons olive oil
- 2 garlic cloves; minced
- 1/2 cup chicken stock
- 1/2 teaspoon red pepper flakes
- 2 teaspoons dried oregano
- 1 yellow onion; chopped

Directions:
1. Place your Instant Pot on a flat kitchen surface', plug it and turn it on.
2. To start making the recipe, press *Sauté* button. Add the pepper flakes, garlic and onions; cook for 2-3 minutes to soften the ingredients.
3. Add the tomatoes, oregano, stock and mussels; combine well. Carefully close its lid and firmly lock it. Then after, seal the valve too.
4. To start making the recipe, press *Manual* button. Now you have to set cooking time', set the timer for 2 minutes. Allow the pot to cook the mixture until the timer goes off.
5. Turn off the pot and press *Cancel.* Allow the built up pressure to vent out naturally', it will take 8-10 minutes to completely release inside pressure.
6. Open its lid and transfer the cooked mixture into serving container/containers. Serve warm!

Nutrition Facts:
Calories: 291; Fat: 10g; Carbohydrates: 11.2g; Fiber: 2g; Protein 38.7g

Simple Swordfish Fra Diavolo

(Prep + Cooking Time: 15 minutes | Serves: 2)

Ingredients:
- 1-pound swordfish steaks
- 1/2 teaspoon red pepper flakes
- 4 garlic cloves; minced
- 1/2 teaspoon black pepper
- 1 can whole peeled tomatoes; crushed
- 2 tablespoons olive oil
- 1/2 teaspoon salt

Directions:
1. Set the Instant Pot to *Sauté* mode. Add garlic and red pepper flakes and cook until fragrant. Add tomatoes, salt and pepper.
2. Place swordfish in the sauce. Flip once to coat. Close lid and set cooking time to 3 minutes.
3. After cooking time, use the quick release to remove steam. Serve with pasta.

Nutrition Facts:
Calories: 427; Fat: 28.88 g; Carbohydrates: 5.81 g; Fiber: 2.1 g; Protein: 45.81 g

Coconut Scallops Curry Recipe

(Prep + Cooking Time: 25 minutes | Serves: 4)

Ingredients:
- 1–pound scallops
- 1 cup coconut milk
- 1 ½ cup chicken broth
- 1 teaspoon curry powder
- 1 teaspoon vinegar
- 1 teaspoon soy sauce
- 1/2 teaspoon nutmeg powder
- 1/2 cup Thai red curry paste
- 1 tablespoon olive oil
- 1/2 teaspoon salt

Directions:
1. Set instant pot on sauté mode and add olive oil into the pot.
2. When instant pot display reads hot then add scallops and sauté for 3 minutes.
3. Add remaining ingredients and stir well, Seal pot with lid and select *HIGH* pressure for 6 minutes.
4. Release pressure using quick release method than open the lid.

Nutrition Facts:
Calories: 405, Fat: 28.2g, Carbs: 12.7g, Protein: 22.4g

Raspberry Sauce Salmon Recipe

(Prep + Cooking Time: 15 minutes | Serves: 2)

Ingredients:
- 1 leek; chopped
- 1 cup clam juice
- 1 tablespoon parsley; chopped
- 1 tablespoon lemon juice
- black pepper; to taste
- 1 cup red raspberries; minced
- 1 tablespoon cider vinegar
- 1 tablespoon olive oil
- 1/3 cup dill; chopped
- 1 teaspoon sherry
- 2 salmon steaks
- 2 garlic cloves; minced
- a pinch of sea salt

Directions:
1. Mix raspberries and vinegar in a bowl and stir well. Add salmon, stir, cover and keep in the fridge for 2 hours.
2. Add oil to Instant Pot and press "Sauté" button (*Normal* preset), wait till you see Hot on the display.
3. Add garlic, parsley and leek, stir and cook for 2 minutes with the lid open. Add lemon juice, clam juice, salt, pepper, cherry and dill, stir and cook for 2 minutes.
4. Add salmon steaks with the raspberry sauce, stir. Close the lid and turn the vent to *Sealed*.
5. Press *Pressure Cook* (Manual) button, use *+* or *-* button to set the timer for 4 minutes. Use *Pressure level* button to set Pressure to *HIGH*.
6. Once the timer is up; press *Cancel* button and turn the steam release handle to *Venting* position for quick release, until the float valve drops down.
7. Open the lid; Serve with steamed vegetables and rice on the side.

Nutrition Facts:
Calories: 160 g; Total Fat: 25 g; Total Carbohydrate: 5 g; Protein: 12

Steamed Tilapia

(Prep + Cooking Time: 13 minutes | Serves: 2)

Ingredients:
- 3 sprigs fresh dill
- 4 tilapia fillets
- 1/2 teaspoon black pepper
- Juice of 1 lemon
- 1/2 tablespoon olive oil
- 1/2 teaspoon salt
- 4 garlic cloves

Directions:
1. Place the fillets on top of a sheet of aluminum foil. Season on both sides with lemon, olive oil, salt and pepper.
2. Place garlic and dill on top of the fish. Add another sheet of aluminum foil on top and fold in the edges to seal.
3. Pour 2 cups of water into the Instant Pot and add the foil package. Close the lid and set the cooking time for 3 minutes at *HIGH* pressure. Use quick release to remove the steam.

Nutrition Facts:
Calories: 269; Fat: 7.46 g; Carbohydrates: 4.14 g; Fiber: 0.4 g; Protein: 47.14 g

Broccoli Salmon Meal

(Prep + Cooking Time: 16 minutes | Serves: 2)

Ingredients:
- 2 salmon fillets; skin on
- 1 cup baby carrots
- 1 cinnamon stick
- 1 cup water
- 2 cups broccoli florets
- 1 bay leaf
- Some lime wedges for serving
- 1 tablespoon canola oil
- 3 cloves
- pepper and salt as needed

Directions:
1. Place your Instant Pot on a flat kitchen surface', plug it and turn it on. Open the lid and one by one add the cinnamon, water, cloves and bay leaf in the pot.
2. Add the steamer basket, add the salmon inside, season with salt and pepper and brush it with the oil.
3. Add the carrots and broccoli to the basket. Carefully close its lid and firmly lock it. Then after, seal the valve too.
4. To start making the recipe, press *Manual* button. Now you have to set cooking time', set the timer for 6 minutes. Allow the pot to cook the mixture until the timer goes off.
5. Turn off the pot and press *Cancel.* Allow the built up pressure to vent out naturally', it will take 8-10 minutes to completely release inside pressure.
6. Open its lid and transfer the cooked mixture into serving container/containers. Serve warm with steamed carrots and broccoli and fresh lime wedges.

Nutrition Facts:
Calories: 421; Fat: 18g; Carbohydrates: 42.3g; Fiber: 16.2g; Protein 32.4g

Sweet Caramel Salmon

(Prep + Cooking Time: 20 minutes | Serves: 2)

Ingredients:
- 3/4-pound. salmon fillets
- 1/4 teaspoon lemon zest
- 1/4 teaspoon pepper
- 1/2 teaspoon ginger
- 1 tablespoon fish sauce
- 2 tablespoons soy sauce
- 2 tablespoons brown sugar
- 1 teaspoon vegetable oil
- 1 tablespoon lemon juice

Directions:
1. Season the salmon with pepper and salt. Set aside. In a bowl mix the vegetable oil with brown sugar, fish sauce, soy sauce, ginger, lemon zest and lemon juice.
2. Switch on the pot after placing it on a clean and dry platform. Press *Sauté* cooking function.
3. Open the lid; add the oil mix in the pot; cook for 2 minutes to caramelize. Add the salmon. Close the pot by closing the top lid. Also, ensure to seal the valve.
4. Press *Manual* cooking function and set cooking time to 5 minutes. It will start cooking after a few minutes. Let the pot mix cook under pressure until the timer reads zero.
5. Press *Cancel* cooking function and press *Natural release* setting.
6. It will take 8-10 minutes for natural pressure release. Open the pot and serve warm with the liquid.

Nutrition Facts:
Calories: 294; Fat: 12.5g; Carbohydrates: 11g; Fiber: 0.5g; Protein 34g

Fish Boil

(Prep + Cooking Time: 19 minutes | Serves: 3)

Ingredients:
- 2-pounds' whitefish
- 1-pound small red potatoes; halved
- 2 carrots; sliced
- 1/2 teaspoon pepper
- 2 stalks celery; sliced
- 1 lemon; halved
- 1 large onion; diced
- 4 cups water
- 1 teaspoon salt

Directions:
1. Place water, potatoes, carrots, onion, lemon, salt and pepper into the Instant Pot.
2. Close the lid and set the cooking time for 7 minutes. Use quick release to remove the steam.
3. Add the whitefish to the pot. Close the lid and set the cooking time for 2 minutes. Use quick release to remove the steam. Serve with buttered rolls.

Nutrition Facts:
Calories: 405; Fat: 13.54 g; Carbohydrates: 23.29 g; Fiber: 2.9 g; Protein: 46.08 g

Asian Salmon

(Prep + Cooking Time: 15 minutes | Serves: 2)

Ingredients:
- 2 salmon fillets; boneless
- 2 tablespoons lemon juice
- 1 teaspoon sesame seeds
- 8 ounces broccoli
- 8 ounces cauliflower florets
- 2 tablespoons coconut aminos
- 1 cup water
- a pinch of sea salt and black pepper

Directions:
1. Mix coconut aminos and lemon juice in a bowl, whisk well.
2. Season salmon fillets with salt and pepper. Put the fish, broccoli and cauliflower florets onto a plate and pour the lemon mixture on top; Let it marinate for 10-15 minutes.
3. Pour water into your Instant pot; add the steamer basket. Add salmon and veggies to the basket and close the lid.
4. Close the lid and turn the vent to *Sealed*. Press *Pressure Cook* (Manual) button, use *+* or *-* button to set the timer for 5 minutes. Use *Pressure level* button to set Pressure to *HIGH*.
5. Once the timer is up; press *Cancel* button and turn the steam release handle to *Venting* position for quick release, until the float valve drops down.
6. Open the lid; Serve with salad on the side.

Nutrition Facts:
Calories: 315 g; Total Fat: 22.3 g; Total Carbohydrate: 14.2 g; Protein: 30.4

Honey Shrimps

(Prep + Cooking Time: 16 minutes | Serves: 2)

Ingredients:
- 1/2-pound. large shrimps; peeled
- 2 teaspoons parsley; dried
- 1 teaspoon olive oil
- 1 tablespoon honey
- 1 garlic clove; minced
- 2 tablespoons lemon juice; freshly squeezed
- 2 teaspoons soy sauce
- 1/2 cup water
- 2 teaspoons Creole seasoning

Directions:
1. Add oil to Instant Pot and press "Sauté" button (*Normal* preset), wait till you see Hot on the display.
2. Add shrimps and garlic to the Instant pot and sauté for 2 to 3 minutes. Press *Cancel* button.
3. Mix honey, Creole seasoning, dried parsley, lemon juice and soy sauce in a bowl.
4. Add water to the Instant pot and pour honey mixture on top of shrimps. Close the lid and turn the vent to *Sealed*.
5. Press *Pressure Cook* (Manual) button, use *+* or *-* button to set the timer for 3 minutes. Use *Pressure level* button to set Pressure to *HIGH*.
6. Once the timer is up; press *Cancel* button and turn the steam release handle to *Venting* position for quick release, until the float valve drops down.
7. Open the lid; Serve topped with extra chopped parsley.

Nutrition Facts:
Calories: 152 g; Total Fat: 2.5 g; Total Carbohydrate: 12 g; Protein: 21.9

Shrimp Scampi

(Prep + Cooking Time: 15 minutes | Serves: 2)

Ingredients:
- 3/4–pound jumbo shrimp
- 2 chopped garlic cloves
- 1 teaspoon lemon juice
- 2 tablespoon chopped parsley
- 3 tablespoon butter
- 2 tablespoons dry white wine
- 1/8 teaspoon black pepper
- 1 teaspoon kosher salt

Directions:
1. Add shrimp, garlic, wine, pepper; and salt into the instant pot and stir well.
2. Seal pot with lid and select *HIGH* pressure for 1 minute.
3. Release pressure using quick release method than open the lid.
4. Transfer shrimp to a bowl; leaving juices behind.
5. Set pot on sauté mode and simmer liquid until reduced half.
6. Add butter and stir until melted. Return shrimp to pot and stir well, Add lemon juice and parsley and toss to combine.

Nutrition Facts:
Calories: 293, Fat: 17.4g, Carbs: 1.8g, Protein: 30.9g

Mussels Tomatino

(Prep + Cooking Time: 13 minutes | Serves: 2)

Ingredients:
- 2-pounds fresh mussels; cleaned and rinsed
- 1/2 tablespoon dried parsley
- 1/2 tablespoon pepper
- 1 cup diced tomatoes
- 1/2 cup white wine
- Salt as per taste preference

Directions:
1. Switch on the pot after placing it on a clean and dry platform.
2. Pour the tomatoes into the Instant Pot with the juices and add the wine. Add the pepper, salt and parsley.
3. Place the mussels in a steamer basket and lower it to the liquid.
4. Close the pot by closing the top lid. Also, ensure to seal the valve. Press *Manual* cooking function and set cooking time to 3 minutes.
5. It will start cooking after a few minutes. Let the pot mix cook under pressure until the timer reads zero.
6. Press *Cancel* cooking function and press *Quick release* setting. Open the pot and serve warm with garlic bread.

Nutrition Facts:
Calories: 446; Fat: 10.5g; Carbohydrates: 22.5g; Fiber: 2g; Protein 55g

Steamed Clams

(Prep + Cooking Time: 15 minutes | Serves: 3)

Ingredients:
- 1–pound mushy shell clams
- 1/4 cup lemon juice
- 2 tablespoon Melted butter
- 1 teaspoon garlic powder
- 1/4 cup white wine

Directions:
1. In a bowl; mix together white wine, lemon juice, garlic powder; and butter and set aside.
2. Place trivet into the instant pot then add white wine mixture to the pot.
3. Arrange clams on the trivet. Seal pot with lid and select *HIGH* pressure for 3 minutes, allow to release pressure naturally then open the lid.

Nutrition Facts:
Calories: 159, Fat: 7.9g, Carbs: 4.4g, Protein: 13.7g

Bacon and Clam Chowder

(Prep + Cooking Time: 11 minutes | Serves: 2)

Ingredients:
- 1 cup chopped' clams
- 1 tablespoon diced' celeries
- 2 tablespoons butter
- 1/4 cup chopped' onion
- 1/4 teaspoon salt
- 1/2 teaspoon thyme
- 1 teaspoon minced' garlic
- 1/2 cup clam juice
- 2 tablespoons diced' bacon
- 1/4 cup half and half
- 1/4 teaspoon pepper

Directions:
1. Place butter in the inner pot of an Instant Pot then select *Sauté* button
2. Stir in bacon, minced' garlic and onion then sauté until aromatic and lightly golden brown. Press the *Cancel*
3. button
4. Now, add chopped' clams, diced' celeries and thyme to the Instant Pot then season with salt and pepper.
5. Cover the Instant Pot and seal it properly. Select *Manual* setting on the Instant Pot and cook the clams for 3 minutes
6. Once it is done; quick release the Instant Pot and open the lid. Add half and half to the Instant Pot and stir well
7. Select *Sauté* setting and cook the clams for another 2 minutes. Once it is done; transfer the clams to a serving dish then serve

Nutrition Facts:
Calories: 231; Net Carbs: 6.1g; Total Fat: 13.3g; Protein: 21.7; Carbs: 6.5g

Sesame Anchovies

(Prep + Cooking Time: 9 minutes | Serves: 2)

Ingredients:
- 1 cup anchovies; dried
- 2 garlic cloves; minced
- 1 tablespoon water
- 1 tablespoon sesame seed oil
- 1/2 tablespoon vegetable oil
- Black sesame seeds to serve
- Roasted sesame seeds to serve
- 1 tablespoon sugar

Directions:
1. In a bowl of medium size, thoroughly mix the water, garlic and sugar; combine and set aside.
2. Place your Instant Pot on a flat kitchen surface', plug it and turn it on. To start making the recipe, press *Sauté* button. Add the anchovies; cook for 1 minute.
3. Add vegetable oil, stir and cook for 1 minute more. Add the sugar mix. Carefully close its lid and firmly lock it. Then after, seal the valve too.
4. To start making the recipe, press *Manual* button. Now you have to set cooking time', set the timer for 2 minutes. Allow the pot to cook the mixture until the timer goes off.
5. Turn off the pot and press *Cancel.* Allow the built up pressure to vent out naturally', it will take 8-10 minutes to completely release inside pressure.
6. Open its lid and transfer the cooked mixture into serving container/containers. Add the sesame oil, black sesame seeds and roasted seeds', stir and serve warm!

Nutrition Facts:
Calories 232; Fat: 17g; Carbohydrates: 7.4g; Fiber: 1.2g; Protein 10.6g

Cheesy Crab Quiche

(Prep + Cooking Time: 8 minutes | Serves: 2)

Ingredients:
- 1/4 cup crabmeat
- 1/2 teaspoon paprika
- 2 eggs
- 1/2 cup half and half
- 1/4 teaspoon salt
- 1/2 cup grated cheddar cheese
- 1/2 cup chopped' onion
- 1/2 teaspoon pepper

Directions:
1. Crack the eggs then place in a bowl. Add half and half to the egg then season with salt, pepper and paprika.
2. Stir in crabmeat and onion to the egg mixture then mix until combined
3. Pour the egg and crab mixture into a small disposable aluminum pan then sprinkle grated cheddar cheese on top
4. Pour water into the Instant Pot and put a trivet in it. Place the aluminum pan with crab mixture on the trivet then cover and seal the Instant Pot properly
5. Select *Manual* setting on the Instant Pot and cook the quiche on high for 25 minutes
6. Once it is done; naturally release the Instant Pot and open the lid. Remove the aluminum pan from the Instant Pot and let it sit for a few minutes until warm

Nutrition Facts:
Calories: 276; Net Carbs: 5.8g; Total Fat: 20.9g; Protein: 15.7; Carbs: 6.8g;

Mussel Garlic

(Prep + Cooking Time: 11 minutes | Serves: 2)

Ingredients:
- 2 cups fresh mussels
- 1 tablespoon chopped' parsley
- 1 tablespoon butter
- 1/4 cup vegetable broth
- 1/4 cup white wine
- 1 tablespoon lemon juice
- 1 teaspoon shallot
- 1 teaspoon minced' garlic

Directions:
1. Discard the shell of the shell of the mussels then place in the inner pot of an Instant Pot
2. Add butter, shallot and minced' garlic then pour vegetable broth and white wine over the mussels.
3. Cover the Instant Pot and seal it properly. Select *Manual* setting on the Instant Pot and cook the mussels on high. Set the time to 4 minutes
4. Once it is done; quick release the Instant Pot and open the lid
5. Drizzle lemon juice over the mussels and stir well. Transfer mussels and the gravy to a serving dish then sprinkle chopped' parsley on top

Nutrition Facts:
Calories: 201; Net Carbs: 6.9g; Total Fat: 9.4g; Protein: 18.8; Carbs: 7g;

Lobster Meat with Mayo

(Prep + Cooking Time: 15 minutes | Serves: 2)

Ingredients:
- 1 lb. lobster tails
- 2 cups ice water
- 2 tablespoon lemon juice
- 1 teaspoon sliced scallions
- 1/4 cup mayonnaise
- 1/2 cup chicken broth
- 1/2 teaspoon salt

Directions:
1. Pour chicken broth into the inner pot of an Instant Pot then add sliced scallions. Season with salt then stir until dissolved

2. Place a trivet in the Instant Pot and put then lobster tails on it
3. Cover the Instant Pot and seal it properly. Select *Pressure cook* setting and cook the lobster tail for 5 minutes.
4. Once it is done; quick release the Instant Pot and open the lid
5. Take the lobster tail out of the Instant Pot and quickly put into the ice water. Let it sit for a minute.
6. Using a kitchen shear cut the vertebrae of the lobster tails to remove the meat
7. Cut the lobster meat into small chunks and place in a bowl
8. Pour mayonnaise and lemon juice over the lobster meat then mix well. Serve with potato chips

Nutrition Facts:
Calories: 314; Net Carbs: 3g; Total Fat: 12.3g; Protein: 44.7; Carbs: 3.1g;

Sweet Brown Calamari

(Prep + Cooking Time: 4 hours | Serves: 2)

Ingredients:
- 1/2 lb. fresh squids
- 3 teaspoons oyster sauce
- 1 bay leaf
- 1½ teaspoons brown sugar
- 3 teaspoons soy sauce
- 1/4 cup water
- 1/4 teaspoon ginger
- 1 teaspoon minced' garlic

Directions:
1. Wash and clean the squids then discard the head. Place the squids in the inner pot of an Instant Pot then add ginger, minced' garlic, brown sugar and bay leaf to the Instant Pot
2. Pour water, soy sauce and oyster sauce over the squids then cover and seal the Instant Pot properly.
3. Select *Slow cook* setting on the Instant Pot and cook the squids on low. Set the time to 4 hours
4. Once it is done; naturally release the Instant Pot and open the lid. Transfer the cooked squids to a serving dish then serve

Nutrition Facts:
Calories: 140; Net Carbs: 7g; Total Fat: 1.8g; Protein: 20; Carbs: 7.1g;

Savory Crab Legs

(Prep + Cooking Time: 14 minutes | Serves: 2)

Ingredients:
- 3/4 lb. fresh crab legs
- 1/4 teaspoon salt

Directions:
1. Pour water into an Instant Pot and place a trivet in it. Arrange the crab legs on the trivet then sprinkle salt on top
2. Cover the Instant Pot and seal it properly. Select *Manual* setting on the Instant Pot and cook the crab legs for 4 minutes
3. Once it is done; naturally release the Instant Pot and open the lid. Transfer the cooked crab to a serving dish then serve immediately

Nutrition Facts: Calories: 195; Net Carbs: 1g; Total Fat: 11.5g; Protein: 20.5; Carbs: 1g;

Garlic Lemon Shrimp

(Prep + Cooking Time: 15 minutes | Serves: 3)

Ingredients:
- 1-pound large shrimp
- 3 tablespoon Butter
- 4 minced garlic cloves
- 1 teaspoon paprika
- 2 sliced lemons

Directions:
1. Set instant pot on sauté mode and add butter into the pot.
2. When instant pot display reads hot then add garlic and sauté for 1 minute.
3. Add shrimp, paprika; and lemon slices; and stirs well, Seal pot with lid and select *HIGH* pressure for 4 minutes.
4. Allow to release pressure naturally then open the lid.

Nutrition Facts:
Calories: 231, Fat: 11.6g, Carbs: 4.4g, Protein: 28.8g

Rosemary Salmon Recipe

(Prep + Cooking Time: 20 minutes | Ser...

Ingredients:
- 4 salmon filets
- 2 lemons
- 1/2 cup chopped shallots
- 4 Roma tomatoes
- 2 cup...
- 4 spr...
- Pepp...

Directions:
1. Slice the tomatoes and the lemons. Make two foil pouches by a... each.
2. Arrange the salmon down on the foil and mix with pepper and... ingredients equally.
3. Fold up the foil, so it creates a secure package. Switch on the pot after placing it on a clean and dry platform.
4. Pour the water into the pot. Arrange the trivet inside it*, arrange the pockets over the trivet. Close the pot by closing the top lid. Also, ensure to seal the valve.
5. Press *Manual* cooking function and set cooking time to 10 minutes. It will start cooking after a few minutes. Let the pot mix cook under pressure until the timer reads zero.
6. Press *Cancel* cooking function and press *Quick release* setting. Open the pot and serve warm.

Nutrition Facts:
Calories 292; Fat: 22g; Carbohydrates: 13g; Fiber: 2g; Protein 54.5g

White Wine Haddock

(Prep + Cooking Time: 16 minutes | Serves: 2)

Ingredients:
- 4 fillets of haddock
- 4 green onions
- 1 cup white wine
- 2 lemons
- 2 tablespoons olive oil
- 1-inch fresh ginger; chopped
- Pepper and salt as per taste preference

Directions:
1. Rub the olive oil into the fish fillets and sprinkle them with pepper and salt. Juice your lemons and zest one lemon.
2. Switch on the pot after placing it on a clean and dry platform. Open the pot lid and place everything except fish in the cooking pot area. Give the ingredients a little stir.
3. Place the fish in a steamer basket and lower it to the liquid. Close the pot by closing the top lid. Also, ensure to seal the valve.
4. Press *Manual* cooking function and set cooking time to 8 minutes. It will start cooking after a few minutes. Let the pot mix cook under pressure until the timer reads zero.
5. Press *Cancel* cooking function and press *Quick release* setting. Open the pot and serve warm with the veggie salad or rice.

Nutrition Facts:
Calories: 274; Fat: 8.5g; Carbohydrates: 5.5g; Fiber: 1.5g; Protein 32g

Mushroom Stuffed Squids

(Prep + Cooking Time: 14 minutes | Serves: 2)

Ingredients:
- 1/2 lb. chopped' mushrooms
- 1/2 lb. fresh shrimps
- 2 eggs
- 1 teaspoon garlic powder
- 1/2 tablespoon butter
- 1/4 teaspoon salt
- 1/4 teaspoon pepper

Directions:
1. Wash and rinse the squids then discard the ink. Set aside. Place chopped' mushroom in a food processor then add eggs to it
2. Season with garlic powder, salt and pepper then process until smooth
3. Fill each squid with the mushroom mixture then prick each squid with a toothpick
4. Pour water into an Instant Pot then place a trivet in it. Arrange the stuffed squids on the trivet then baste with butter
5. Cover the Instant Pot with the lid and seal it properly. Close the steam valve
6. Select *Pressure cook* setting on the Instant Pot and cook the stuffed squids for 15 minutes.
7. Once it is done; naturally release the Instant Pot and open the lid. Take the cooked stuffed squids out of the Instant Pot and place on a serving dish

Nutrition Facts:
Calories: 253; Net Carbs: 5.7g; Total Fat: 9.5g; Protein: 35.2; Carbs: 7g;

Coconut Shrimp Curry

(Prep + Cooking Time: 10 minutes | Serves: 2)

Ingredients:
- 1-pound frozen shrimp
- 2 tablespoon coconut milk
- 3/4 cup onion masala
- 1/2 teaspoon garam masala
- 2 tablespoon chopped cilantro
- 1/8 teaspoon cayenne
- 1/2 cup water
- 1/2 teaspoon salt

Directions:
1. Add all ingredients into the instant pot except coconut milk and cilantro.
2. Stir well and seal pot with lid and select *HIGH* pressure for 1 minute.
3. Release pressure using quick release method than Open the lid; Stir in coconut milk and garnish with cilantro.

Nutrition Facts:
Calories: 276, Fat: 7.7g, Carbs: 3g, Protein: 46.7g

Salmon Dinner

(Prep + Cooking Time: 15 minutes | Serves: 3)

Ingredients:
- 1-pound salmon fillet
- 1 teaspoon red chili powder
- 1 minced garlic clove
- 1 teaspoon ground cumin
- Salt and Pepper to taste

Directions:
1. Pour 1 ½ cups water into the instant pot and place trivet into the pot.
2. In a small bowl, mix together all ingredients except salmon.
3. Rub salmon pieces with spice mixture and place on top of the trivet.
4. Seal pot with lid and select steam mode and set the timer for 2 minutes, Release pressure using quick release method than open the lid. Serve hot and enjoy.

Nutrition Facts:
Calories: 207, Fat: 9.7g, Carbs: 1.1g, Protein: 29.6g

Braised Cod

(Prep + Cooking Time: 10 minutes | Serves: 2)

Ingredients:
- 1-pound cod; cut into 4 filets
- 1 bag (10 ounces) frozen peas
- 1 teaspoon oregano
- 1 sprig fresh rosemary
- 2 garlic cloves; smashed
- 1 cup fresh parsley
- Pepper and salt as per taste preference
- 1 cup white wine
- 1 teaspoon paprika

Directions:
1. In a bowl, mix the wine, herbs, salt and spices together.
2. Add the liquid into the Instant Pot and add the peas.
3. Arrange the fish into a steamer basket and lower it to the liquid.
4. Close the pot by closing the top lid. Also, ensure to seal the valve.

5. Press *Manual* cooking function and set cooking time to 5 minutes. It will start cooking after a few minutes. Let the pot mix cook under pressure until the timer reads zero.
6. Press *Cancel* cooking function and press *Quick release* setting. Open the pot and serve warm.

Nutrition Facts:
Calories: 234; Fat: 1.5g; Carbohydrates: 13.5g; Fiber: 44g; Protein 30g

Salmon Rice

(Prep + Cooking Time: 10 minutes | Serves: 2)

Ingredients:
- 2 wild salmon fillets
- 1/2 teaspoon saffron
- 1/2 cup jasmine rice
- 1 tablespoon butter
- 1/2 cup veggie stock mix; dried
- 1 cup chicken stock
- Salt and black pepper as needed

Directions:
1. Place your Instant Pot on a flat kitchen surface', plug it and turn it on.
2. Open the lid and one by one add the stock, soup mix, rice, saffron and butter in the pot.
3. Add the steamer basket in your pot, place salmon inside, season with salt and pepper. Carefully close its lid and firmly lock it. Then after, seal the valve too.
4. To start making the recipe, press *Manual* button. Now you have to set cooking time', set the timer for 5 minutes. Allow the pot to cook the mixture until the timer goes off.
5. Turn off the pot and press *Cancel. * Allow the built up pressure to vent out naturally', it will take 8-10 minutes to completely release inside pressure.
6. Open its lid and transfer the cooked mixture into serving container/containers. Serve the salmon with rice on the side.

Nutrition Facts:
Calories: 286; Fat: 12.4g; Carbohydrates: 18g; Fiber: 0.7g; Protein 24.6g

Chili Snapper

(Prep + Cooking Time: 37 minutes | Serves: 2)

Ingredients:
- 2 teaspoons sugar
- 1 garlic clove; minced
- 1/2 teaspoon ginger; grated
- 1 tablespoon soy sauce
- 1 green onion; chopped
- 2 teaspoons sesame seeds; toasted
- 1 teaspoon sesame oil
- 1 red snapper; cleaned
- 3 tablespoons chili paste
- 2 cups water
- A pinch of sea salt

Directions:
1. Make some slits into the snapper and season with some salt and leave aside for 25-30 minutes.
2. Place your Instant Pot on a flat kitchen surface', plug it and turn it on. Pour the water into the pot. Arrange the steamer basket in the pot and add the fish over the trivet.
3. Rub the snapper with the chili paste. Carefully close its lid and firmly lock it. Then after, seal the valve too.
4. To start making the recipe, press *Manual* button. Now you have to set cooking time', set the timer for 12 minutes. Allow the pot to cook the mixture until the timer goes off.

5. Turn off the pot and press *Cancel.* Allow the built up pressure to vent out naturally', it will take 8-10 minutes to completely release inside pressure.
6. Open its lid and transfer the cooked mixture into serving container/containers.
7. In a bowl of medium size, thoroughly mix the sugar with soy sauce, garlic, ginger, sesame seeds, sesame oil and green onion. Serve the fish with the prepared sauce!

Nutrition Facts:
Calories: 186; Fat: 12g; Carbohydrates: 23.5g; Fiber: 1g; Protein 6.2g

Calamari with Anchovies

(Prep + Cooking Time: 20 minutes | Serves: 2)

Ingredients:
- 1/2 lb. fresh squids
- 1/2 teaspoon olive oil
- 1/4 cup diced' tomatoes
- 1/4 cup white wine
- 1/2 teaspoon minced' garlic
- 3 tablespoons chopped' parsley
- 2 anchovies
- 1/2 teaspoon red chili flakes
- 1 tablespoon lemon juice
- 1/4 teaspoon salt
- 1/4 teaspoon pepper

Directions:
1. Remove the squid's head and discard the ink. Wash the squids and cut into rings then set aside.
2. Pour olive oil into the inner pot of an Instant Pot then select *Sauté* setting. Stir in minced' garlic then sauté until aromatic and lightly golden brown
3. Now, add the squids to the Instant Pot then pour white wine over the squids. Sauté a bit then press the *Cancel* button
4. Add the remaining ingredients to the Instant Pot then cover and seal it properly
5. Select *Pressure cook* setting on the Instant Pot and cook the squids for 15 minutes. Once it is done; transfer the squids to a serving dish and serve

Nutrition Facts:
Calories: 199; Net Carbs: 6.8g; Total Fat: 4.8g; Protein: 24.9g; Carbs: 7.5g;

Thai Style Scallops with Oranges

(Prep + Cooking Time: 16 minutes | Serves: 2)

Ingredients:
- 1/2-pound. sea scallops; cleaned
- 1/4 teaspoon mustard
- 1/2 jalapeno pepper; seedless and minced
- 3 tablespoons extra virgin olive oil
- 1/3 cup water or broth
- 2 oranges; sliced
- 1 tablespoon rice vinegar
- a pinch cayenne pepper
- Salt and Pepper to taste

Directions:
1. Pulse jalapeno with 2 tablespoons olive oil, mustard, black pepper, salt and vinegar in a blender.
2. Season scallops with cayenne pepper. Add 1 tablespoon oil to Instant Pot and press "Sauté" button (*Normal* preset), wait till you see Hot on the display.
3. Add scallops and cook them with the lid open for 3 minutes on each side.
4. Press *Cancel* button. Add water or broth, jalapeno sauce, orange slices and close the lid, turn the vent to *Sealed*.

5. Press *Pressure Cook* (Manual) button, use *+* or *-* button to set the timer for 6 minutes. Use *Pressure level* button to set Pressure to *HIGH*.
6. Once the timer is up; press *Cancel* button and turn the steam release handle to "Venting" position for quick release, until the float valve drops down. Open the lid and serve.

Nutrition Facts:
Calories: 293 g; Total Fat: 27.1 g; Total Carbohydrate: 13.8 g; Protein: 20

Flavors Cod Recipe

(Prep + Cooking Time: 25 minutes | Serves: 2)

Ingredients:
- 2 cod steaks
- 1/4 cup sherry
- 1/2 tablespoon soy sauce
- 2 tablespoon lemon pepper seasoning
- 1 tablespoon balsamic vinegar

Directions:
1. Mix together in a bowl; sherry, lemon pepper seasoning, soy sauce; and balsamic vinegar.
2. Add cod steaks and marinate for 20 minutes.
3. Transfer marinated cod steaks in the instant pot. Seal pot with lid and select *HIGH* pressure for 6 minutes, allow to release pressure naturally then open the lid.

Nutrition Facts:
Calories: 60, Fat: 0.3g, Carbs: 4.5g, Protein: 10.5 g

Tuna in Red Sauce

(Prep + Cooking Time: 15 minutes | Serves: 2)

Ingredients:
- 1/2 lb. fresh tuna
- 1 kaffir lime leaf
- 3 cloves garlic
- 4 shallots
- 1/2 teaspoon turmeric
- 1 bay leaf
- 1/4 cup cayenne pepper

Directions:
1. Place garlic, shallots, cayenne pepper and turmeric in a food processor then process until smooth.
2. Rub the tuna with the spice mixture then place on a sheet of aluminum foil. Put bay leaf and kaffir lime leaf on top then wrap the tuna with aluminum foil
3. Pour water into an Instant Pot and put a trivet in it. Place the wrapped tuna on the trivet then cover and seal the Instant Pot properly.
4. Select *Steam* setting on the Instant Pot and cook the tuna for 10 minutes
5. Once it is done; naturally release the Instant Pot and open the lid. Remove the wrapped tuna from the Instant Pot and let it cool for a few minutes
6. Unwrap the tuna then transfer to a serving dish. Serve and enjoy with a plate of brown rice.

Nutrition Facts:
Calories: 156; Net Carbs: 6.4g; Total Fat: 2.3g; Protein: 26.7; Carbs: 8.3g;

Masala Shrimps Curry

(Prep + Cooking Time: 8 minutes | Serves: 2)

Ingredients:
- 1/2 lb. fresh shrimps
- 2 tablespoons heavy cream
- 1/4 teaspoon garam masala
- 1/4 teaspoon curry
- 1/4 teaspoon cayenne
- 1/2 cup chopped' onion
- 1/4 cup water
- 1/4 teaspoon salt

Directions:
1. Peel the shrimps and discard the head. Place the shrimps in the inner pot of an Instant Pot then sprinkle chopped' onion, garam masala, curry, salt and cayenne into the Instant Pot
2. Pour water over the shrimps then cover and seal the Instant Pot properly
3. Select *Manual* setting and cook the shrimps on high for 2 minutes.
4. Once it is done; quick release the Instant Pot and open the lid. Select *Sauté* setting on the Instant Pot and stir in heavy cream. Cook the shrimps for a minute more
5. Transfer the shrimps to a serving dish and serve immediately

Nutrition Facts:
Calories: 200; Net Carbs: 4.3g; Total Fat: 7.6g; Protein: 26.5; Carbs: 5.1g;

Jalapeno Shrimp

(Prep + Cooking Time: 15 minutes | Serves: 2)

Ingredients:
- 1-pound frozen shrimp; peeled and deveined
- 1 lemon; juiced
- 1 teaspoon cayenne pepper
- 2 cloves garlic; minced
- 1 sweet onion; minced
- 1 jalapeno pepper; minced
- 1 teaspoon black pepper
- 1 teaspoon white pepper
- 1 can diced tomatoes (15 ounces)

Directions:
1. Allow the frozen shrimp to rest at room temperature for 15 minutes. Switch on the pot after placing it on a clean and dry platform.
2. Open the pot lid and place the above-mentioned ingredients in the cooking pot area.
3. Give the ingredients a little stir. Close the pot by closing the top lid. Also, ensure to seal the valve.
4. Press *Manual* cooking function and set cooking time to 5 minutes. It will start cooking after a few minutes. Let the pot mix cook under pressure until the timer reads zero.
5. Press *Cancel* cooking function and press *Quick release* setting. Open the pot and serve warm.

Nutrition Facts:
Calories: 172; Fat: 2.5g; Carbohydrates: 10g; Fiber: 2.5g; Protein 26g

Delightful Paella

(Prep + Cooking Time: 18 minutes | Serves: 2)

Ingredients:
- 1/2-pound. big shrimps; deveined
- 1 cup risotto rice
- 1/4 cup white wine
- 1/4 cup parsley; chopped
- 2 tablespoons butter
- 1 small onion; chopped
- 1 cup chicken broth
- a pinch of saffron
- 1 lemon; quartered
- 2 garlic cloves; minced
- a pinch of red pepper; crushed
- black pepper; to taste
- a pinch of sea salt

Directions:
1. Add butter to Instant Pot and press "Sauté" button (*Normal* preset), wait till you see Hot on the display.
2. Add onion to the pot and cook until soft. Add garlic and cook for one more minute.
3. Add red pepper, saffron, salt and black pepper. Add rice and stir for about 1 minute. Add broth and wine, press *Cancel* button.
4. Put the shrimps on top. Close the lid and turn the vent to *Sealed*. Press *Pressure Cook* (Manual) button, use *+* or *-* button to set the timer for 5 minutes. Use *Pressure level* button to set Pressure to *HIGH*.
5. Once the timer is up; press *Cancel* button and turn the steam release handle to *Venting* position for quick release, until the float valve drops down.
6. Open the lid; Serve with parsley and lemon wedges on top.

Nutrition Facts:
Calories: 603 g; Total Fat: 13 g; Total Carbohydrate: 44.7 g; Protein: 31.3

Fried Sea Bass

(Prep + Cooking Time: 9 minutes | Serves: 2)

Ingredients:
- 1/2 lb. sea bass fillet
- 1/4 lb. fresh shrimps
- 1/4 cup diced' onion
- 1 tablespoon tomato paste
- 3/4 tablespoon avocado oil
- 3/4 tablespoon Cajun seasoning
- 1/2 cup water
- 1/4 teaspoon salt
- 2 tablespoons diced' celeries
- 1/2 cup diced' tomatoes
- 1/4 teaspoon pepper

Directions:
1. Sprinkle salt and pepper over the sea bass then set aside. Pour avocado oil into the inner pot of an Instant Pot and select *Sauté* setting
2. Place the seasoned sea bass in the Instant Pot and sauté for about 4 minutes or until both sides look cooked.
3. Remove the cooked sea bass from the Instant Pot and place on a serving dish
4. Now, add diced' onion to the Instant Pot and sauté until aromatic and lightly golden brown. Press the *Cancel* button
5. Add shrimps to the Instant Pot then top with Cajun seasoning, diced' celeries, diced' tomatoes and tomato paste.
6. Pour water over the ingredients then cover and seal the Instant Pot properly

7. Select *Manual* setting and cook the shrimps topping for 2 minutes
8. Once it is done; quick release the Instant Pot and open the lid. Put the shrimps and tomato over the sea bass then serve

Nutrition Facts:
Calories: 210; Net Carbs: 3.7g; Total Fat: 4.2g; Protein: 36.9g; Carbs: 5.3g;

Classic Crab Cakes with Roasted Pepper Sauce

(Prep + Cooking Time: 20 minutes | Serves: 2)

Ingredients:
- 1/2 cup jarred roasted red pepper and garlic sauce
- 2 tablespoons butter

For crab cakes:
- 1/2-pound. crab meat; free of shells
- 1 egg
- 1/4 cup breadcrumbs
- 1/2 teaspoon salt
- 1/4 cup mayonnaise
- 1 tablespoon lemon juice
- 1/4 cup water
- 1/4 teaspoon white pepper
- 2 tablespoons fresh parsley; chopped
- 3 tablespoons flour
- 1/4 teaspoon paprika

Directions:
1. Mix all crab cakes ingredients in a bowl and shape the mixture into flat cakes.
2. Add butter to Instant Pot and press "Sauté" button (*Normal* preset), wait till you see Hot on the display.
3. Cook crab cakes for about 3 minutes on each side or until lightly browned.
4. Mix red pepper and garlic sauce, mayonnaise and water in a bowl, pour into the pressure cooker. Press *Cancel* button.
5. Close the lid and turn the vent to *Sealed*. Press *Pressure Cook* (Manual) button, use *+* or *-* button to set the timer for 5 minutes. Use *Pressure level* button to set Pressure to *HIGH*.
6. Once the timer is up; press *Cancel* button and turn the steam release handle to *Venting* position for quick release, until the float valve drops down. Open the lid and serve.

Nutrition Facts:
Calories: 472 g; Total Fat: 27.4 g; Total Carbohydrate: 31.9 g; Protein: 21.1

Parmesan Tilapia Recipe

(Prep + Cooking Time: 20 minutes | Serves: 2)

Ingredients:
- 2 tilapia fillets
- 2 tablespoon mayonnaise
- 1/2 cup grated parmesan cheese
- 2 tablespoon lemon juice
- Salt and Pepper to taste

Directions:
1. In a bowl; mix lemon juice, pepper, mayonnaise; and salt and marinate tilapia in this mixture.
2. Place marinated tilapia fillets into the instant pot, Seal pot with lid and select *HIGH* pressure for 7 minutes.
   Allow to release pressure naturally then open the lid.
3. Top with grated parmesan cheese and set the pot on sauté mode for 3 minutes.

Nutrition Facts:
Calories: 345, Fat: 16.6g, Carbs: 3.9g, Protein: 48.3g

Salmon with Dill

(Prep + Cooking Time: 10 minutes | Serves: 2)

Ingredients:
- 1 tablespoon dill
- 1 tablespoon butter
- 1/4 teaspoon salt
- 3 fresh lemons
- 1/2 lb. salmon fillet
- 1/4 teaspoon pepper

Directions:
1. Season the salmon fillet with salt and pepper then set aside
2. Take a lemon and cut into halves. Squeeze the lemon then pour the juice into the inner pot of an Instant Pot.
3. Add water to the Instant Pot then put a trivet in it. Place the seasoned salmon on the trivet and baste butter over the salmon
4. Sprinkle dill over the salmon then place sliced lemon on top
5. Cover the Instant Pot and seal it properly. Select *Steam* setting and cook the salmon for 5 minutes
6. Once it is done; naturally release the Instant Pot and open the lid
7. Remove the salmon from the Instant Pot and arrange on a serving dish. Top with extra dill then serve

Nutrition Facts:
Calories: 261; Net Carbs: 6.5g; Total Fat: 17.1g; Protein: 21.4; Carbs: 9.2g;

Tasty Tangy Crabs

(Prep + Cooking Time: 8 minutes | Serves: 2)

Ingredients:
- 2 tablespoons fish sauce
- 1/4 cup butter; melted
- 1/4 teaspoon salt
- 1 ½-pounds. crabs
- 1/2 cup water
- 1 tablespoon lemon juice
- 1/4 cup minced garlic

Directions:
1. Switch on the pot after placing it on a clean and dry platform.
2. Place crabs in an Instant Pot then season with salt and garlic. Mix the fish sauce and add butter over the crabs then pour water.
3. Give the ingredients a little stir. Close the pot by closing the top lid. Also, ensure to seal the valve.
4. Press *Manual* cooking function and set cooking time to 3 minutes. It will start cooking after a few minutes. Let the pot mix cook under pressure until the timer reads zero.
5. Press *Cancel* cooking function and press *Quick release* setting. Open the instant pot; top with lemon juice and serve warm.

Nutrition Facts:
Calories: 264; Fat: 18g; Carbohydrates: 6.5g; Fiber: 0.5g; Protein 17g

Soy Honey Shrimps

***(Prep + Cooking Time:** 15 minutes | **Serves:** 2)*

Ingredients:
- 1/2 lb. fresh shrimps
- 1/2 teaspoon ginger
- 1 teaspoon vegetable oil
- 1/2 tablespoon raw honey
- 1 teaspoon minced' garlic
- 4 tablespoons soy sauce

Directions:
1. Peel the shrimps then discard the head. Place the shrimps in a zipper-lock plastic bag then pour vegetable oil, soy sauce and raw honey
2. Add minced' garlic and ginger to the plastic bag then shake until the shrimps are completely seasoned. Let it sit for about 5 minutes
3. Place the seasoned shrimps in the inner pot of an Instant Pot together with the liquid then cover and seal it properly
4. Select *Manual* setting on the Instant Pot and cook the shrimps for 4 minutes
5. Once it is done; quick release the Instant Pot and open the lid. Place the shrimps and the gravy to a serving dish then serve immediately

Nutrition Facts:
Calories: 179; Net Carbs: 5g; Total Fat: 3.8g; Protein: 27.1g; Carbs: 5.1g;

Orange Steamed Salmon

***(Prep + Cooking Time:** 8 minutes | **Serves:** 2)*

Ingredients:
- 1/2 lb. salmon fillet
- 1/2 teaspoon minced' garlic
- 3/4 orange marmalade
- 1½ teaspoons soy sauce
- 1/2 teaspoon ginger
- 1/4 teaspoon salt
- 1/4 teaspoon pepper

Directions:
1. Place soy sauce, ginger, minced' garlic, salt, pepper and orange marmalade in a zipper-lock plastic bag then stir well
2. Place the salmon fillet in the plastic bag then shake until the salmon is coated with the seasoning mixture. Marinate the salmon for 15 minutes.
3. After 15 minutes, pour water into the Instant Pot and put a trivet on it
4. Place the seasoned salmon on the rack then cover and seal the Instant Pot properly. Select *Steam* setting on the Instant Pot and steam the salmon for 3 minutes
5. Once it is done; naturally release the Instant Pot and open the lid
6. Remove the cooked salmon from the Instant Pot and arrange on a serving dish. Serve and enjoy with steamed vegetables

Nutrition Facts:
Calories: 294; Net Carbs: 5.8g; Total Fat: 16.5g; Protein: 30.4; Carbs: 6g;

Scallop Ginger with Maple Syrup

(Prep + Cooking Time: 10 minutes | Serves: 2)

Ingredients:
- 3/4 lb. jumbo scallops
- 1/2 tablespoon maple syrup
- 1/4 cup water
- 1/4 teaspoon salt
- 1/4 teaspoon ginger
- 2 tablespoons coconut milk

Directions:
1. Pour water into the inner pot of an Instant Pot then add coconut milk, ginger and salt. Stir well
2. Put the scallops into the Instant Pot then cover and seal it properly
3. Select *Manual* setting and cook the scallops for 5 minutes
4. Once it is done; naturally release the Instant Pot and open the lid. Transfer the scallops to a serving dish then drizzle maple syrup on top

Nutrition Facts:
Calories: 191; Net Carbs: 7g; Total Fat: 4.6g; Protein: 21.8; Carbs: 7.4g;

Coconut Fish Curry

(Prep + Cooking Time: 14 minutes | Serves: 2)

Ingredients:
- 1/2 lb. tuna fillet
- 2 tablespoons halved cherry tomatoes
- 1 teaspoon green chili
- 1 tablespoon lemon juice
- 2 tablespoons chopped' onion
- 1/2 teaspoon ginger
- 1/2 teaspoon coriander
- 3/4 teaspoon curry powder
- 1/4 cup coconut milk
- 1/4 cup water
- 1 teaspoon minced' garlic
- 1/4 teaspoon salt

Directions:
1. Cut the tuna fillet into cubes then place in the inner pot of an Instant Pot
2. Sprinkle green chili, cherry tomatoes, chopped' onion, minced' garlic, ginger, coriander, salt and curry powder over the tuna then pour coconut milk and water into the Instant Pot
3. Cover the Instant Pot and seal it properly. Select *Manual* setting and cook the fish for 5 minutes.
4. Once it is done; quick release the Instant Pot and open the lid
5. Drizzle lemon juice over the curry and stir well. Once it is done; transfer the fish curry to a serving dish then serve

Nutrition Facts:
Calories: 464; Net Carbs: 5.8g; Total Fat: 38.3g; Protein: 23.1; Carbs: 8g;

Marinated Shrimps

(Prep + Cooking Time: 14 minutes | Serves: 2)

Ingredients:
- 1/2 lb. fresh shrimps
- 1/4 teaspoon ginger
- 1/2 teaspoon minced' garlic
- 1 tablespoon yogurt
- 1 tablespoon butter
- 1/2 cup heavy cream
- 1/2 teaspoon cumin
- 1/2 teaspoon paprika
- 1/2 teaspoon garam masala
- 1 teaspoon lemon juice
- 1 tablespoon diced' onion
- 1/4 teaspoon red chili flakes
- 1/2 cup diced' tomatoes
- 1/4 teaspoon salt

Directions:
1. Peel the shrimps then discard the head. Put the shrimps in a zipper-lock plastic bag then add yogurt, cumin, paprika, garam masala, lemon juice, salt, ginger and minced' garlic
2. Shake until the shrimps are completely coated with the seasoning mixture. Marinate the shrimps for at least 10 minutes and set aside
3. In the meantime, place bitter in the inner pot of an Instant Pot. Select *Sauté* setting and stir in the diced' onion to the Instant Pot. Sauté until wilted and aromatic. Press the *Cancel* button
4. Add diced' tomatoes, heavy cream and red chili flakes to the Instant Pot then cover and seal it properly.
5. Select *Manual* setting and cook the sauce for 6 minutes.
6. Once it is done; quick release the Instant Pot and open the lid
7. Add the shrimps together with the marinade to the Instant Pot and stir well
8. Select *Sauté* setting on the Instant Pot and cook the shrimps for 3 minutes. Transfer the cooked shrimps and the gravy to a serving dish

Nutrition Facts:
Calories: 297; Net Carbs: 4.1g; Total Fat: 18.7g; Protein: 28.9; Carbs: 5.1g;

Snacks and Appetizers

Eggplant Tomato Spread

(Prep + Cooking Time: 18 minutes | Serves: 3)

Ingredients:
- 2 cups eggplant; chopped
- 1 cup yellow onion; chopped
- 2 minced garlic cloves
- 2 tablespoons tomato paste
- 1/4 cup vegetable stock
- 3 tablespoons olive oil
- 1 cup sweet bell pepper; chopped
- 1/4 cup sun-dried tomatoes; minced
- Black pepper and salt as needed

Directions:
1. Take your Instant Pot and place it on a clean kitchen platform. Turn it on after plugging it into a power socket.
2. Put the pot on *Sauté* mode. In the pot; add the oil and onion', cook for 2-3 minutes until the ingredients become soft.
3. Mix in the garlic, bell pepper and eggplant; stir and cook for 2 minutes more. Add the tomatoes, stock, salt, pepper and tomato paste; stir gently.
4. Close the lid and lock. Ensure that you have sealed the valve to avoid leakage.
5. Press *Manual* mode and set timer for 5 minutes. It will take a few minutes for the pot to build inside pressure and start cooking.
6. After the timer reads zero, press *Cancel* and quick release pressure. Carefully remove the lid. Serve on toasted bread as an appetizer.

Nutrition Facts:
Calories: 162; Fat: 4g; Carbohydrates: 7.5g; Fiber: 3g; Protein 8g

Bacon Muffins

(Prep + Cooking Time: 20 minutes | Serves: 3)

Ingredients:
- 4 slices precooked bacon; crumbled
- 1 green onion; diced
- 1/4 teaspoon lemon pepper seasoning
- 4 tablespoons cheddar cheese; shredded
- 4 eggs

Directions:
1. Place your Instant Pot on a flat kitchen surface', plug it and turn it on.
2. Arrange a steamer basket inside the pot and add 1 ½ cups of water. In a bowl, break 4 eggs and whisk well. Add the lemon pepper and beat everything well.
3. Divide the green onion, bacon and cheese into 4 muffin cups. Top with the egg mixture and stir to combine well.
4. Arrange the cups on the steamer basket, cover it and then lock the lid.
5. To start making the recipe, press *Manual* button. Now you have to set cooking time', set the timer for 8 minutes.
6. Turn off the pot and press *Cancel.* Quick release inside pressure. Serve warm!

Nutrition Facts:
Calories: 170; Fat: 13g; Carbohydrates: 1g; Fiber: 0g; Protein 12g

Asparagus Lemon Snack

(Prep + Cooking Time: 7 minutes | Serves: 2)

Ingredients:
- 1/4-pound Asparagus
- 2 tablespoons lemon juice
- 1 cup water
- 1 teaspoon olive oil

Directions:
1. Trim the asparagus and remove the woody parts. Add some lemon juice and olive oil over the asparagus then toss to combine.
2. Switch on the pot after placing it on a clean and dry platform.
3. Pour the water into the pot. Arrange the trivet inside it*, arrange the asparagus over the trivet. Close the pot by closing the top lid. Also, ensure to seal the valve.
4. Press *Manual* cooking function and set cooking time to 2 minutes. It will start cooking after a few minutes. Let the pot mix cook under pressure until the timer reads zero.
5. Press *Cancel* cooking function and press *Natural release* setting.
6. It will take 8-10 minutes for natural pressure release. Open the pot and serve warm.

Nutrition Facts:
Calories 38; Fat: 2.5g; Carbohydrates: 2.8g; Fiber: 1g; Protein 2g

Spicy Potato Appetizer

(Prep + Cooking Time: 30 minutes | Serves: 2)

Ingredients:
- 3 large sweet potatoes; peeled and make wedges
- 2 tablespoons vegetable oil
- 1 teaspoon paprika
- 1 tablespoon dry mango powder
- 1/2 teaspoon salt
- 1 cup water
- Cooking oil as needed.

Directions:
1. Switch on the pot after placing it on a clean and dry platform.
2. Pour 1 cup water into the pot. Arrange the trivet inside it*, arrange the wedges over the trivet.
3. Close the pot by closing the top lid. Also, ensure to seal the valve.
4. Press *Manual* cooking function and set cooking time to 15 minutes. It will start cooking after a few minutes. Let the pot mix cook under pressure until the timer reads zero.
5. Press *Cancel* cooking function and press *Quick release* setting. Open the lid and remove the water. Set aside the potato.
6. Press *Sauté* cooking function. Add the oil and potatoes in the pot; cook for 2 minutes to cook well and turn brown.
7. Combine the mango powder, salt and paprika in a bowl and mix well. Coat the wedges with this mixture and serve warm!

Nutrition Facts:
Calories: 164; Fat: 6.5g; Carbohydrates: 25.5g; Fiber: 3g; Protein 1.5g

Sweet Brussels

(Prep + Cooking Time: 9 minutes | Serves: 2)

Ingredients:
- 1/2-pound Brussels sprouts; trimmed
- 3 tablespoons orange juice
- 1 tablespoon butter
- 1 teaspoon orange zest
- 1 ½ teaspoon maple syrup
- Pinch of salt
- Pinch of pepper

Directions:
1. Switch on the pot after placing it on a clean and dry platform.
2. Open the pot lid and place the above-mentioned ingredients in the cooking pot area.
3. Give the ingredients a little stir. Close the pot by closing the top lid. Also, ensure to seal the valve.
4. Press *Manual* cooking function and set cooking time to 4 minutes. It will start cooking after a few minutes. Let the pot mix cook under pressure until the timer reads zero.
5. Press *Cancel* cooking function and press *Quick release* setting. Open the pot and serve warm.

Nutrition Facts:
Calories: 68; Fat: 4g; Carbohydrates: 6g; Fiber: 1g; Protein 2.5g

Jalapeno Dip

(Prep + Cooking Time: 40 minutes | Serves: 2)

Ingredients:
- 1 jalapeno; seeded
- 1 cup dried pinto beans; rinsed
- 1 medium onion; quartered
- 1 ½ cups water
- 2 cloves garlic; chopped
- 1/2 teaspoon chili powder
- 1/2 teaspoon cumin
- 1/4 teaspoon black pepper
- 1/4 cup salsa
- 1/2 teaspoon paprika
- 1/2 teaspoon salt

Directions:
1. Switch on the pot after placing it on a clean and dry platform.
2. Open the pot lid and place the above-mentioned ingredients in the cooking pot area.
3. Give the ingredients a little stir. Close the pot by closing the top lid. Also, ensure to seal the valve.
4. Press *Manual* cooking function and set cooking time to 28 minutes. It will start cooking after a few minutes. Let the pot mix cook under pressure until the timer reads zero.
5. Press *Cancel* cooking function and press *Quick release* setting.
6. Open the pot and blend in a blender to make a smooth paste. Enjoy with your favorite crackers or tortilla chips.

Nutrition Facts:
Calories: 288; Fat: 2g; Carbohydrates: 26.5g; Fiber: 11g; Protein 21g

Amazing Artichoke Dip with Nachos

***(Prep + Cooking Time:** 80 minutes | **Serves:** 2)*

Ingredients:
- 8 medium sized artichokes; make halves
- 1/2 cup cannellini beans; soaked for about 4 hours
- 1 cup vegetable broth
- 1/4 teaspoon ground pepper
- 1/2 cup grated ricotta cheese
- 1/2 lemon
- 2 garlic cloves; minced
- 3/4 cup plain yogurt
- 3/4 teaspoon salt
- Nachos to serve

Directions:
1. Boil artichokes in water for 30 minutes in a pan. Remove the leaves and discard the chokes.
2. Switch on the pot after placing it on a clean and dry platform.
3. Open the pot lid and place the garlic cloves, lemon, vegetable broth, artichokes and beans in the cooking pot area.
4. Give the ingredients a little stir. Close the pot by closing the top lid. Also, ensure to seal the valve.
5. Press *Manual* cooking function and set cooking time to 20 minutes. It will start cooking after a few minutes. Let the pot mix cook under pressure until the timer reads zero.
6. Press *Cancel* cooking function and press *Natural release* setting. It will take 8-10 minutes for natural pressure release.
7. Open the pot. Mix the yogurt, ground pepper, salt and cheese and mix well.
8. Add these ingredients to a blender and combine until it forms a smooth paste. Serve along with some nachos.

Nutrition Facts:
Calories: 188; Fat: 2.5g; Carbohydrates: 29.5g; Fiber: 13g; Protein 14g

Instant Asparagus

***(Prep + Cooking Time:** 13 minutes | **Serves:** 2)*

Ingredients:
- 1/2-pound asparagus spears
- 5-ounces sliced prosciutto

Directions:
1. Wrap the prosciutto slices around the asparagus. Switch on the pot after placing it on a clean and dry platform.
2. Pour 2 cups water into the pot. Arrange the trivet inside it*, arrange the asparagus over the trivet. Close the pot by closing the top lid. Also, ensure to seal the valve.
3. Press *Manual* cooking function and set cooking time to 3 minutes. It will start cooking after a few minutes. Let the pot mix cook under pressure until the timer reads zero.
4. Press *Cancel* cooking function and press *Natural release* setting.
5. It will take 8-10 minutes for natural pressure release. Open the pot and serve warm.

Nutrition Facts:
Calories: 124; Fat: 4g; Carbohydrates: 5.5g; Fiber: 2g; Protein 17g

Sweet Honey Carrots

(Prep + Cooking Time: *20 minutes* | **Serves:** *2)*

Ingredients:
- 1/2-pound carrots
- 1 tablespoon Dijon mustard
- 1/4 teaspoon paprika
- 1 teaspoon garlic; minced
- 1/2 teaspoon ground cumin
- 1 tablespoon butter
- 1 tablespoon honey
- Dash of hot sauce
- Pepper and salt as per taste preference

Directions:
1. Take the carrots and cut into quarters lengthwise and then cut each quarter in half. Switch on the pot after placing it on a clean and dry platform.
2. Pour 1 cup water into the pot. Arrange the trivet inside it*, arrange the carrots over the trivet. Close the pot by closing the top lid. Also, ensure to seal the valve.
3. Press *Manual* cooking function and set cooking time to 2 minutes. It will start cooking after a few minutes. Let the pot mix cook under pressure until the timer reads zero. Press *Cancel* cooking function and press *Quick release* setting.
4. Transfer carrots to a plate. Empty the pot, pat the pot dry. Press *Sauté* cooking function.
5. Open the lid; add the butter and other in the pot; cook for 30 seconds. Press *Cancel* and add the carrots. Toss well and serve!

Nutrition Facts:
Calories: 138; Fat: 6g; Carbohydrates: 21g; Fiber: 3.5g; Protein 1.5g

Soy Garlic Tofu

(Prep + Cooking Time: *2 hours 35 minutes* | **Serves:** *2)*

Ingredients:
- 1 container extra firm tofu; cut to make 1-inch cubes
- 1 ½ tablespoon brown sugar
- 3/4 cup ketchup
- 1/2 tablespoon apple cider vinegar
- 1 tablespoon soy sauce
- 1/4 teaspoon garlic powder
- 1/2 tablespoon red pepper flakes
- 1/4 teaspoon salt

Directions:
1. Place your Instant Pot on a flat kitchen surface', plug it and turn it on.
2. Open the lid and one by one add the mentioned ingredients in the pot. Stir to combine well. Carefully close its lid and firmly lock it. Then after, seal the valve too.
3. To start making the recipe, press *Slow Cook* button. Now you have to set cooking time', set the timer for 2 hours 30 minutes. Allow the pot to cook the mixture until the timer goes off.
4. Turn off the pot and press *Cancel*. Allow the built up pressure to vent out naturally', it will take 8-10 minutes to completely release inside pressure.
5. Open its lid and transfer the cooked mixture into serving container/containers. Serve warm!

Nutrition Facts:
Calories 433; Fat: 5.3g; Carbohydrates: 27.2g; Fiber: 4g; Protein 15g

Simple Garlic Hummus

(Prep + Cooking Time: 45minutes | Serves: 2)

Ingredients:
- 1 cup dry chickpeas
- 1/2 cup tahini
- Juice of 1 lemon
- 1/4 teaspoon cumin
- 2 cups water
- 1/2 teaspoon black pepper
- 3 garlic cloves; minced
- 1/2 teaspoon salt

Directions:
1. Place chickpeas in Instant Pot with water. Close lid and set cooking time to 35 minutes on *HIGH* pressure.
2. When steam is removed, drain beans and transfer to a food processor or blender. Add tahini, garlic, lemon, cumin, salt and pepper. Blend until smooth.
3. Season to taste with additional salt, pepper and lemon. Serve with pita bread or chips.

Nutrition Facts:
Calories: 375; Fat: 19.23 g; Carbohydrates: 39.7 g; Fiber: 9.1 g; Protein: 15.58 g

Eggplant and Green beans

(Prep + Cooking Time: 10 minutes | Serves: 2)

Ingredients:
- 1 cup chopped green beans
- 1 cup chopped eggplant
- 2 teaspoons minced garlic
- 1 tablespoon fish sauce
- 1/2 teaspoon olive oil
- 2 tablespoons soy sauce
- 1/2 cup water
- 1 tablespoon oyster sauce

Directions:
1. Switch on the pot after placing it on a clean and dry platform. Press *Sauté* cooking function.
2. Open the lid; add the oil and garlic in the pot; cook for 2 minutes to cook well and turn aromatic. Add the green beans and eggplant to the pot, Mix in the soy sauce, oyster sauce and fish sauce.
3. Add some water over the vegetables then stir well. Close the pot by closing the top lid. Also, ensure to seal the valve.
4. Press *Manual* cooking function and set cooking time to 3 minutes. It will start cooking after a few minutes. Let the pot mix cook under pressure until the timer reads zero.
5. Press *Cancel* cooking function and press *Quick release* setting. Open the pot and serve warm.

Nutrition Facts:
Calories: 46; Fat: 0.5g; Carbohydrates: 9g; Fiber: 3.5g; Protein 3g

Vegetable Dishes

Tomato Soup Black Pepper

(Prep + Cooking Time: 20 minutes | Serves: 4)

Ingredients:
- 3/4 cup roasted cherry tomatoes
- 1 tablespoon tomato paste
- 1/4 teaspoon cayenne pepper
- 1½ teaspoons olive oil
- 2 tablespoons diced' onions
- 1/2 cup heavy cream
- 1 tablespoon chopped' celeries
- 1/4 teaspoon salt
- 1 cup water
- 1 teaspoon red chili flakes
- 1/4 teaspoon pepper

Directions:
1. Pour olive oil into the inner pot then select *Sauté* setting. Stir in chopped' onion and sauté until lightly golden and aromatic. Press the *Cancel* button
2. Add chopped' roasted tomatoes, celeries, tomato paste, red chili flakes, cayenne pepper, salt and pepper then pour water over the ingredients
3. Cover the Instant Pot and seal it properly. Select *Soup* setting on the Instant Pot and cook the soup on low for 10 minutes.
4. Once it is done; quick release the Instant Pot and open the lid
5. Stir heavy cream into the Instant Pot then select *Sauté* setting. Cook the soup for 2 minutes. Using an immersion blender blend the tomato soup until smooth then transfer to a serving bowl

Nutrition Facts:
Calories: 156; Net Carbs: 6.7g; Total Fat: 13.5g; Protein: 2.1g; Carbs: 8.4g

Penne Pasta Primavera

(Prep + Cooking Time: 14 minutes | Serves: 3)

Ingredients:
- 1-pound penne pasta
- 2 zucchinis; julienned
- 1 large tomato; diced
- 1 red bell pepper; julienned
- 1 onion; sliced thin
- 2 cloves garlic; minced
- 1/2 cup grated Parmesan
- 1/2 teaspoon black pepper
- 1/4 cup fresh basil; chopped
- 2 tablespoons olive oil
- 4 cups water
- 1/2 teaspoon salt

Directions:
1. Combine pasta and water in the Instant Pot. Place the steamer basket over the water and arrange zucchini, pepper, onion, garlic and tomato in the basket. Close lid and set cooking time for 4 minutes on *HIGH* pressure.
2. Use quick release to remove the steam. Drain the pasta. Pour the contents of the steamer basket into the pasta and toss with olive oil, basil and Parmesan. Season to taste with salt and pepper.

Nutrition Facts:
Calories: 283; Fat: 12.44 g; Carbohydrates: 33.15 g; Fiber: 3.9 g; Protein: 10.59 g

Mushroom Balls in Coconut Mushroom Gravy

(Prep + Cooking Time: 20 minutes | Serves: 4)

Ingredients:
- 2 cups chopped' mushroom
- 1/2 tablespoon chopped' onion
- 1/4 teaspoon sugar
- 2 tablespoons coconut milk
- 2 tablespoons soy sauce
- 1/2 teaspoon ginger
- 1 teaspoon minced' garlic
- 1/2 teaspoon rice wine
- 1/2 cup water
- 1 teaspoon olive oil

Directions:
1. Place a cup of chopped' mushrooms in a food processor then add rice wine, sugar, ginger and minced' garlic. Process until smooth
2. Shape the mushroom mixture into medium ball forms then set aside.
3. Pour water into an Instant Pot then place a trivet in it. Arrange mushroom balls on the trivet then cover and seal the Instant Pot properly
4. Select *Steam* setting and cook the mushroom balls for 10 minutes.
5. Once it is done; quick release the Instant Pot and open the lid.
6. Remove the mushroom balls from the Instant Pot and place on a plate. Clean and wipe the Instant Pot then pour olive oil into the Instant Pot
7. Select Sauté* setting then stir in the chopped' onion to the Instant Pot. Sauté until wilted and aromatic then press the *Cancel* button
8. Pour water into the Instant Pot together with coconut milk and soy sauce then stir well
9. Carefully put the mushroom balls in the Instant Pot and cook for 3 minutes.
10. Once it is done; transfer the mushroom balls and the gravy to a serving dish then serve

Nutrition Facts:
Calories: 88; Net Carbs: 4g; Total Fat: 6.2g; Protein: 2.7g; Carbs: 5.2g;

Eggplant and Olives Spread

(Prep + Cooking Time: 30 minutes | Serves: 2)

Ingredients:
- 2 eggplants; peeled from one side only, chopped
- 1 tablespoon tahini
- 1 cup water
- 2 tablespoons olive oil
- 1 tablespoon fresh thyme leaves
- 1/4 cup black olives; pitted
- 2 garlic cloves
- 2 tablespoons freshly squeezed lemon juice
- 1 teaspoon salt

Directions:
1. Add oil to Instant Pot and press "Sauté" button (*Normal* preset), wait till you see Hot on the display.
2. Add eggplant, fry and caramelize from all sides, for about 5 minutes with the lid open. Press *Cancel* button.
3. Add garlic, water and salt. Close the lid and turn the vent to "Sealed".
4. Press *Pressure Cook* (Manual) button, use *+* or *-* button to set the timer for 3 minutes. Use *Pressure level* button to set Pressure to *HIGH*.

5. Once the timer is up; press "Cancel" button and allow the pressure to be released naturally; until the float valve drops down. Open the lid.
6. Discard most of the liquid from the pot. Get garlic cloves and remove the skin. Put them back to the pot, add lemon juice, black olives and tahini.
7. Use an immersion blender to make a puree. Transfer to a bowl. Sprinkle with a dash of olive oil and thyme before serving.

Nutrition Facts:
Calories: 175 g; Total Fat: 14 g; Total Carbohydrate: 13.1 g; Protein: 12.7

Eggplant Tomato Curry Stew

(Prep + Cooking Time: 8 minutes | Serves: 4)

Ingredients:
- 1½ cups chopped' eggplants
- 1/2 teaspoon cumin
- 1/2 teaspoon turmeric
- 1/2 teaspoon chopped' green chili
- 1 cup chopped' onion
- 1/4 cup chopped' bell peppers
- 2 teaspoons minced' garlic
- 1/2 teaspoon ginger
- 1/4 cup chopped' tomatoes
- 1/4 cup water
- 1 teaspoon cayenne pepper
- 1/2 teaspoon coriander
- 1/2 teaspoon garam masala
- 1 tablespoon olive oil
- 1/4 teaspoon salt

Directions:
1. Pour olive oil into the inner pot of an Instant Pot then select *Sauté* setting. Stir in chopped' onion and minced' garlic then sauté until wilted and aromatic
2. Add chopped' bell pepper, green chili, ginger and garam masala then mix well. Press the *Cancel* button.
3. Now, add chopped' tomatoes and eggplants to the Instant pot then sprinkle cumin, turmeric, coriander, cayenne pepper and salt. Do not stir.
4. Pour water into the Instant Pot then cover and seal the Instant Pot properly
5. Select *Manual* setting and cook the eggplant on high for 3 minutes.
6. Once it is done; quick release the Instant Pot and open the lid. Stir the eggplant stew then transfer to a serving dish

Nutrition Facts:
Calories: 108; Net Carbs: 6.8g; Total Fat: 7.6g; Protein: 1.7g; Carbs: 10.5g;

Quick Mac and Cheese

(Prep + Cooking Time: 20 minutes | Serves: 3)

Ingredients:
- 1-pound uncooked macaroni
- 3 cups whole milk
- 4 cups water
- 1 cup shredded Cheddar cheese
- 1/2 teaspoon black pepper
- 2 tablespoons flour
- 2 tablespoons butter
- 1/2 teaspoon salt

Directions:
1. Combine the macaroni and water in the instant pot. Close the lid and set cooking time for 4 minutes on *HIGH* pressure.

2. After cooking time, use the quick release to remove the steam. Drain the pasta and wipe out the pot.
3. With pot set to *Sauté* mode, melt butter. Add flour and cook until bubbling subsides and the mixture is slightly browned.
4. Gradually add milk, stirring constantly and cook until thickened slightly. Stir in cheese until melted. Season to taste with salt and pepper. Stir in pasta. Heat through and serve.

Nutrition Facts:
Calories: 713; Fat: 23.06 g; Carbohydrates: 97.02 g; Fiber: 3.8 g; Protein: 27.85 g

Cheesy Zucchini Noodles

*(**Prep + Cooking Time:** 12 minutes | **Serves:** 4)*

Ingredients:
- 2 large zucchinis; spiralized
- 1/4 cup Parmesan cheese; grated
- 2 tablespoons olive oil
- 3 garlic cloves; diced
- zest of Half lemon
- juice of Half lemon
- 2 tablespoons water
- Salt and Pepper to taste

Directions:
1. Add oil to Instant Pot and press "Sauté" button (*Normal* preset), wait till you see Hot on the display.
2. Add garlic and lemon zest and cook for 30 seconds stirring constantly.
3. Add zucchini noodles, water and lemon juice, mix well to coat the noodles with oil. Cook for 30-45 seconds, up to 1 minute. Press *Cancel* button.
4. Season zoodles with salt and pepper and add Parmesan cheese, mix well and serve.

Nutrition Facts:
Calories: 273 g; Total Fat: 20.6 g; Total Carbohydrate: 14.7 g; Protein: 13.4

Veg Rigatoni Bolognese

*(**Prep + Cooking Time:** 25 minutes | **Serves:** 6)*

Ingredients:
- 1/2 cup chopped onion
- 1/2 cup chopped celery
- 3 tablespoons olive oil
- 4-ounce mascarpone cheese
- 3 tablespoon chopped parsley
- 1 can crushed tomatoes
- 1 teaspoon dried oregano
- 1 teaspoon salt
- 1 tablespoon balsamic vinegar
- 1 teaspoon sugar
- 1 tablespoon minced garlic
- 1/2 cup chopped carrots
- 1-ounce chopped porcini mushrooms
- 1/2 tablespoon black pepper
- 1/4 teaspoon dried thyme
- 2 cup chopped mushrooms
- 1 tablespoon tomato paste
- 12-ounce rigatoni pasta
- 1/2 teaspoon crushed red pepper flakes
- 1/4 cup grated parmesan cheese
- 1 teaspoon dried basil
- 1/2 cup chopped bell peppers
- 1 cup water
- 1 cup whole milk
- 1 cup red wine

Directions:
1. Turn on the Sauté function of the Mini Instant Pot. Add olive oil to the pot placed in the Instant Pot.
2. Start adding the carrots, celery, garlic; and bell peppers and sauté for about 3 minutes. Do not stop stirring the veggies.
3. Now you can add the fresh mushrooms and sauté for another 2 minutes.
4. Turn off the Mini Instant Pot, In case there is any food stuck in the bottom of the pot, you need to deglaze it with 2 tablespoons of water.
5. Now start adding the dried porcini mushrooms, black pepper, crushed tomatoes, thyme, salt, oregano, basil, balsamic vinegar, salt, sugar, crushed red pepper, tomato paste, milk, pasta, wine; and water.
6. Mix everything gently.
7. Close the lid of the Mini Instant Pot and turn on the steam release function to *Sealing* position.
8. You can either turn on the Manual or Pressure Cook mode for about 7 minutes.
9. Once the cooking is done, you should do a quick release of pressure
10. Put in the mascarpone cheese, The pasta should be allowed to rest for about a few minutes until it thickens.
11. Pour the pasta in a bowl and sprinkle the parmesan cheese and parsley; and it is ready to dig in.

Nutrition Facts:
Calories: 293, Fat: 14g, Carbs: 27g, Protein: 10g

Spinach in Cheese Gravy

(Prep + Cooking Time: 10 minutes | Serves: 4)

Ingredients:
- 1 cup chopped' spinach
- 1½ tablespoons lemon juice
- 1 tablespoon flour
- 1/2 teaspoon nutmeg
- 2 tablespoons grated cheddar cheese
- 2 tablespoons butter
- 1/4 cup diced' onion
- 1 teaspoon minced' garlic
- 1/4 cup half and half
- 1/2 cup water
- 1/4 teaspoon pepper
- 1/4 teaspoon salt

Directions:
1. Place butter in the inner pot of an Instant Pot then select *Sauté* setting
2. Once the butter is melted, stir in flour to the Instant Pot and mix until combined. Add diced' onion and minced' garlic then sauté until lightly golden brown
3. Pour half and half into the Instant Pot and cook for 2 minutes. Press the *Cancel* button*
4. Now, pour water into the Instant Pot then put chopped' spinach in the Instant Pot together with nutmeg, cheddar cheese, pepper and salt.
5. Cover the Instant Pot with the lid and seal it properly
6. Select *Manual* setting on the Instant Pot and cook the spinach on low for 3 minutes.
7. Once it is done; quick release the Instant Pot and open the lid
8. Pour lemon juice over the spinach and stir well. Transfer the spinach together with the gravy to a serving dish and serve

Nutrition Facts:
Calories: 201; Net Carbs: 6.4g; Total Fat: 17.8g; Protein: 4g; Carbs: 7.4g

Delightful Quinoa Mixed Vegetable

(Prep + Cooking Time: 7 minutes | Serves: 3)

Ingredients:
- 8-ounce bag mixed vegetables; frozen
- 2 cups quinoa
- 2 tablespoons soy sauce
- 2 tablespoons rice vinegar
- 1 thumb grated ginger
- 2 tablespoons of sugar
- 4 cups water

Directions:
1. Place your Instant Pot on a flat kitchen surface', plug it and turn it on.
2. Open the lid and one by one add the mentioned ingredients in the pot except for veggies. Carefully close its lid and firmly lock it. Then after, seal the valve too.
3. To start making the recipe, press *Manual* button. Now you have to set cooking time', set the timer for 1 minute. Allow the pot to cook the mixture until the timer goes off.
4. Turn off the pot and press *Cancel.* Allow the built up pressure to vent out naturally', it will take 8-10 minutes to completely release inside pressure. Open its lid and add in the vegetables; serve warm!

Nutrition Facts:
Calories: 456; Fat: 7g; Carbohydrates: 42.3g; Fiber: 9.2g; Protein 18g

Cabbage with Apple Sauce

(Prep + Cooking Time: 15 minutes | Serves: 4)

Ingredients:
- 3 cups red cabbage; chopped
- 1 teaspoon apple cider vinegar
- 1 cup water
- 1 onion; chopped
- 1 tablespoon honey
- 1 teaspoon olive oil
- 1/2 cup unsweetened apple sauce
- Salt and Pepper to taste

Directions:
1. Add oil to Instant Pot and press "Sauté" button (*Normal* preset), wait till you see Hot on the display.
2. Add onion and cook for 3-4 minutes until soft. Press *Cancel* button.
3. Add cabbage, apple sauce, vinegar, cider, water, salt and pepper. Close the lid and turn the vent to *Sealed*.
4. Press *Pressure Cook* (Manual) button, use *+* or *-* button to set the timer for 3 minutes. Use *Pressure level* button to set Pressure to *HIGH*.
5. Once the timer is up; press *Cancel* button and turn the steam release handle to *Venting* position for quick release, until the float valve drops down. Open the lid.

Nutrition Facts:
Calories: 85 g; Total Fat: 1.7 g; Total Carbohydrate: 17.9 g; Protein: 1.4

Lentil Curry Recipe

(Prep + Cooking Time: 10 minutes | Serves: 3)

Ingredients:
- 1/2 (14 oz) can coconut milk
- 1 tablespoon ginger; minced
- 1/2 tablespoon curry powder
- 1 teaspoon coconut oil
- 1/2 onion; chopped
- 1/2 teaspoon turmeric; ground
- 1 teaspoon brown sugar
- 1 cup water
- 1 tablespoon lemon juice
- a pinch of cayenne pepper
- 1 cup lentils
- 3 garlic cloves; minced
- Salt; to taste

Directions:
1. Add oil to Instant Pot and press "Sauté" button (*Normal* preset), wait till you see Hot on the display.
2. Add garlic, ginger and onion, cook for 2 to 3 minutes until onion is soft. Add curry powder, brown sugar, turmeric, cayenne pepper and salt, stir well. Press *Cancel* button.
3. Rinse and drain lentils. Add coconut milk, water and lentils to the Instant pot. Close the lid and turn the vent to "Sealed".
4. Press *Pressure Cook* (Manual) button, use *+* or *-* button to set the timer for 15 minutes. Use *Pressure level* button to set Pressure to *HIGH*.
5. Once the timer is up; press "Cancel" button and allow the pressure to be released naturally for 10 minutes, then turn the steam release handle to *Venting* position for quick release, until the float valve drops down.
6. Open the lid. Stir in lemon juice and serve.

Nutrition Facts:
Calories: 538 g; Total Fat: 18.1 g; Total Carbohydrate: 39.9 g; Protein: 27.3

Healthy Black Beans

(Prep + Cooking Time: 45 minutes | Serves: 4)

Ingredients:
- 1 cup dry black beans
- 1/2 diced onion
- 1/4 teaspoon kosher salt
- 3 cup vegetable broth
- 1 ½ teaspoon oregano
- 1/2 teaspoon coriander powder
- 3 minced garlic cloves
- 1/2 teaspoon smoked paprika
- 2 teaspoon cumin
- 1 teaspoon chili powder
- 1 bay leaf
- Chopped mixed vegetables

For Garnishing
- Cilantro
- Hot sauce
- Cheese
- Sour cream
- Salsa

Directions:
1. Start the Sauté function in the Mini Instant Pot. Once the display shows as Hot, you can add the veggies and stir them. You should cook until they are almost done.
2. Now you can add the onions, stirring them occasionally.
3. Then; add the bay leaf, garlic, oregano, cumin, paprika, pepper, salt, coriander powder and chili powder.

4. Stir them frequently so that the garlic is not burnt.
5. Add the broth and the beans and keep on stirring.
6. Cover the pot with the lid and secure it safely. You should set the Steam Release knob in Sealing position.
7. Now you can stop the Sauté function.
8. Press the manual button of the Pressure Cooker and set the cooking time to 35 minutes.
9. Once the cooking ends, you should allow the pot to sit for about 15 minutes. allow the steam to be released naturally.
10. Turn on the Steam Release knob to Venting position and release the remaining steam or pressure.
11. Once the pin in the lid drops, you should open the lid and stir the beans. Adjust the salt according to your taste.
12. Garnish with cheese, salsa cilantro, or sour cream and enjoy a pot of beans, which is full of protein. Add some rice by the side and you will have a nice combo.

Nutrition Facts:
Calories: 232, Fat: 0.8g, Carbs: 35.7g, Protein: 13.3g

Sweet Potato Chili

*(**Prep + Cooking Time:** 14 minutes | **Serves:** 4)*

Ingredients:
- 1 chopped red pepper
- 1/2 teaspoon smoked paprika
- Crushed tortilla chips
- 2 teaspoon cumin
- 1 chopped carrot
- 1/2 cup corn
- 1 diced sweet potato
- 1 can diced tomatoes
- 1 can chili beans
- 1 chopped onion
- 2 chopped celery stalks
- 2 teaspoons olive oil
- 1 tablespoon chili powder
- Sliced jalapeño
- 1 cup vegetable broth
- 1/4 teaspoon cinnamon
- Salt and Pepper to taste

Directions:
1. Put the Mini Instant Pot in Pressure Cooker mode and add the olive oil and press the Sauté button.
2. Cook the veggies like peppers, celery, onions; and peppers until they soften.
3. Now add the beans and sweet potato along with the stock. Once the liquid starts to boil, add the drained tomatoes.
4. Place the lid and cook in Manual High for about 3 minutes, Once the cooking time ends, you will hear a beep. Use the Quick Release function to let out the steam.
5. Open the lid to check the corn; also check the seasoning and if required, add some salt and pepper.
6. Top the dish with crushed tortilla chips and jalapeño and enjoy the one-pot meal.

Nutrition Facts:
Calories: 199, Fat: 4g, Carbs: 34g, Protein: 8g

Chickpea Broccoli

(Prep + Cooking Time: 20 minutes | Serves: 3)

Ingredients:
- 1 (15 ounces) can chickpeas; drained
- 1/2 teaspoon olive oil
- 3 large cloves of garlic; chopped
- 1 bunch broccoli rabe; halved
- 1/4 cup vegetable broth
- Crushed red pepper as needed
- 1/8 teaspoon fennel seeds
- Salt to taste

Directions:
1. Place your Instant Pot on a flat kitchen surface', plug it and turn it on.
2. To start making the recipe, press *Sauté* button. Add the oil and garlic; cook for 2 minutes to brown the garlic.
3. Add the seeds and red pepper; cook for 30 seconds. Then after, add the broccoli, broth and chickpeas. Carefully close its lid and firmly lock it. Then after, seal the valve too.
4. To start making the recipe, press *Manual* button. Now you have to set cooking time', set the timer for 4 minutes. Allow the pot to cook the mixture until the timer goes off.
5. Turn off the pot and press *Cancel.* Allow the built up pressure to vent out naturally', it will take 8-10 minutes to completely release inside pressure.
6. Open its lid and transfer the cooked mixture into serving container/containers. Serve warm!

Nutrition Facts:
Calories: 506; Fat: 10g; Carbohydrates: 44.3g; Fiber: 12g; Protein 24.3g

Steamed Artichokes Recipe

(Prep + Cooking Time: 30 minutes | Serves: 2)

Ingredients:
- 2 medium-sized whole artichokes; rinsed, stem & top third removed
- 1 lemon wedge
- 2 cups water

Directions:
1. Use a lemon wedge to rub every cut top of the artichokes to stop browning.
2. Place a steam rack into Instant Pot. Put the artichokes on the steamer rack and add water. Close the lid and turn the vent to "Sealed".
3. Press *Pressure Cook* (Manual) button, use *+* or *-* button to set the timer for 20 minutes. Use *Pressure level* button to set Pressure to *HIGH*.
4. Once the timer is up; press "Cancel" button and allow pressure to be released naturally; until the float valve drops down.
5. Open the lid; Carefully take the artichokes out with tongs and serve with desired dipping sauce.

Nutrition Facts:
Calories: 64 g; Total Fat: 12.4 g; Total Carbohydrate: 13 g; Protein: 13.5

Tasty Baked Ziti

(Prep + Cooking Time: 20 minutes | Serves: 3)

Ingredients:
- 1-pound uncooked ziti pasta
- 1 onion; chopped
- 2 cloves garlic; minced
- 2 cups shredded mozzarella cheese
- 1 tablespoon olive oil
- 2 cups whole peeled tomatoes with juice; crushed

Directions:
1. Set the Instant Pot to *Sauté* and add the olive oil, followed by the onion and garlic. Cook until onion is translucent.
2. Add tomatoes and pasta. Add enough water to cover the pasta and stir. Close the lid and set cooking time for 5 minutes at low pressure. Use quick release to remove the steam, then open the lid.
3. Arrange cheese over the pasta. Close the lid and allow to sit on Keep Warm setting 5 minutes or until cheese melts.

Nutrition Facts:
Calories: 375; Fat: 17.11 g; Carbohydrates: 40.23 g; Fiber: 6.4 g; Protein: 16.83 g

Veg Stew Ratatouille

(Prep + Cooking Time: 20 minutes | Serves: 2)

Ingredients:
- 1 eggplant; cut into cubes, skin removed
- 1/2 can (14 oz) diced tomatoes; chopped
- 1 green pepper; cut into strips; seeded
- 1 tablespoon parsley; minced
- 1 tablespoon tomato paste
- 1/2 cup vegetable stock
- 1 onion; sliced
- 1 zucchini; sliced
- 2 tablespoons olive oil
- 2 cloves garlic; minced
- Salt and Pepper to taste

Directions:
1. Add oil to Instant Pot and press "Sauté" button (*Normal* preset), wait till you see Hot on the display.
2. Add garlic and onion, cook for 2 to 3 minutes. Add eggplant, pepper and zucchini. Cook until vegetables are soft. Add tomato paste, stir well. Press *Cancel* button.
3. Add parsley, vegetable stock and tomatoes, salt and pepper to taste. Close the lid and turn the vent to "Sealed".
4. Press *Pressure Cook* (Manual) button, use *+* or *-* button to set the timer for 6 minutes. Use *Pressure level* button to set Pressure to *HIGH*.
5. Once the timer is up; press "Cancel" button and allow pressure to be released naturally; until the float valve drops down. Open the lid.
6. Simmer the dish for 2 minutes. Serve warm.

Nutrition Facts:
Calories: 200 g; Total Fat: 14.3 g; Total Carbohydrate: 16.6 g; Protein: 3.9

Walnut Beets Bowl

(Prep + Cooking Time: 7 minutes | Serves: 3)

Ingredients:
- 1 ½-pounds beets; scrubbed, rinsed
- 2 teaspoons lemon juice
- 1 teaspoon Dijon mustard
- 2 teaspoons apple cider vinegar
- 1 ½ tablespoons olive oil; extra virgin
- 2 tablespoons walnuts; chopped
- 1 ½ teaspoons sugar
- 2 cups water
- Pepper and salt as needed

Directions:
1. Place your Instant Pot on a flat kitchen surface', plug it and turn it on.
2. Open the lid and one by one add the water and beets in the pot. Carefully close its lid and firmly lock it. Then after, seal the valve too.
3. To start making the recipe, press *Manual* button. Now you have to set cooking time', set the timer for 10 minutes. Allow the pot to cook the mixture until the timer goes off.
4. Turn off the pot and press *Cancel.* Allow the built up pressure to vent out naturally', it will take 8-10 minutes to completely release inside pressure.
5. Open its lid and transfer the cooked mixture into a bowl.
6. Drain the beets and chop into bite-sized pieces. In a mixing bowl; add all the ingredients for the dressing except oil and walnuts.
7. Whisk to combine thoroughly and add the olive oil slowly into the dressing; combine well. Add the dressing over the beets, toss and serve!

Nutrition Facts:
Calories 151; Fat: 10g; Carbohydrates: 15.2g; Fiber: 3g; Protein 2.7g

Zuppa Toscana Recipe

(Prep + Cooking Time: 35 minutes | Serves: 4)

Ingredients:
- 1/2 pounds Ground Italian Sausage (Mild)
- 3 - 4 cups chicken broth
- 2 - 3 slices bacon; chopped
- 1 teaspoon basil; dried
- 3 - 4 medium potatoes; cut into cubes
- 1 tablespoon oil
- 2 garlic cloves; minced
- 1 cup fresh kale; chopped
- 1 tablespoon red pepper; crushed
- 1/2 cup heavy cream or full fat coconut milk
- 1 small onion; chopped
- Salt and Pepper to taste

Directions:
1. Add oil to Instant Pot and press "Sauté" button (*Normal* preset), wait till you see Hot on the display. Add chopped bacon and cook for 2 to 3 minutes. Set aside.
2. Add sausage and cook until browned. Add onion and basil, cook until onion is translucent. Add garlic and cook for 1 to 2 more minutes.
3. Add potatoes, bacon, red pepper and broth, press *Cancel*. Close the lid and turn the vent to *Sealed*.
4. Press *Pressure Cook* (Manual) button, use *+* or *-* button to set the timer for 5 minutes. Use *Pressure level* button to set Pressure to *HIGH*.
5. Once the timer is up; press *Cancel* button and turn the steam release handle to *Venting* position for quick release, until the float valve drops down.

6. Open the lid.
7. Add kale to the Instant pot; close the lid for 5 minutes. Add heavy cream, stir until evenly mixed and then sprinkle with pepper, salt and crushed red pepper.

Nutrition Facts:
Calories: 410 g; Total Fat: 30 g; Total Carbohydrate: 6 g; Protein: 12

Classic Lentil Gumbo

*(**Prep + Cooking Time:** 17 minutes | **Serves:** 6)*

Ingredients:
- 1 cup chopped celery ribs
- 1 cup chopped okra
- 3 cup vegetable broth
- 1 can diced tomatoes
- 1 teaspoon minced garlic cloves
- 2 tablespoon apple cider vinegar
- 1/2 cup tomato sauce
- 1/2 teaspoon cayenne powder
- 1/2 tablespoon oregano
- 1 cup lentils
- Fresh cilantro
- 1 chopped cauliflower
- 1 tablespoon olive oil
- 1 ½ chopped onions
- 1 tablespoon dried thyme
- 1 chopped red bell pepper
- 1 teaspoon Cajun mix
- Sea salt and Pepper to taste

Directions:
1. Start the Sauté function in Mini Instant Pot and sauté the oil, garlic, celery; and bell peppers for about 5 minutes until they are softened.
2. Add the spices and keep on mixing them for about a minute, Mix all the other ingredients apart from salt and pepper. Mix everything well.
3. Place the lid on the pressure cooker and switch on the High–Pressure function and cook for about 12 minutes.
4. After you are done with cooking, you can add ½-1 teaspoon of salt or kosher salt along with black pepper. Adjust the seasonings as per your taste.
5. Stir the entire thing and keep them warm, It is best not to add extra salt in the lentil gumbo while cooking as the extra salt may ruin the texture of the lentils.
6. Prepare the serving bowls, pour the gumbo; and garnish them with your favorite toppings like red pepper flakes, fresh cilantro, or jalapeño. Enjoy your meal.

Nutrition Facts:
Calories: 173, Fat: 3.3g, Carbs: 25g, Protein: 8g

Green Beans Stew

*(**Prep + Cooking Time:** 40 minutes | **Serves:** 4)*

Ingredients:
- 1/2 cup dry green beans
- 1 teaspoon ground coriander
- 1/2 teaspoon garam masala
- 1/2 teaspoon cumin seeds
- 1/2 cup red onion; chopped
- 2 large tomatoes; chopped
- 4 garlic cloves
- 1/2 teaspoon cayenne pepper
- 1/4 teaspoon black pepper
- 5 cups water
- 1 teaspoon lemon juice
- 1 teaspoon oil
- 1-inch ginger root; grated
- 1 teaspoon turmeric
- 1 teaspoon salt

Directions:
1. Soak beans for about 15 minutes. Blend onions, garlic, tomato, ginger and spices with 3 teaspoons of water to make a smooth puree and set aside.
2. Add oil to Instant Pot and press "Sauté" button (*Normal* preset), wait till you see Hot on the display. Add cumin seeds. Roast the seeds until fragrant, for 30 seconds.
3. Add the puree, stir and cook until it thickens, for up to 10 minutes. Press *Cancel* button.
4. Drain beans and add to the Instant Pot. Add water, lemon juice and salt, mix well.
5. Close the lid and turn the vent to *Sealed*. Press *Pressure Cook* (Manual) button, use *+* or *-* button to set the timer for 15 minutes. Use *Pressure level* button to set Pressure to *HIGH*.
6. Once the timer is up; press *Cancel* button and allow the pressure to be released naturally; until the float valve drops down. Open the lid and serve.

Nutrition Facts:
Calories: 45 g; Total Fat: 1.5 g; Total Carbohydrate: 7.6 g; Protein: 1.6

Cheesy Asparagus Garlic

*(**Prep + Cooking Time:** 7 minutes | **Serves:** 4)*

Ingredients:
- 1 handful asparagus
- 3 teaspoons minced' garlic
- 3 tablespoons grated cheddar cheese
- 1/4 cup butter

Directions:
1. Trim the ends of the asparagus then place in a disposable aluminum pan
2. Sprinkle minced' garlic over the asparagus then drop butter at several places on top. Pour water into the Instant Pot and place a trivet in it
3. Place the aluminum pan with asparagus on the trivet then cover and seal the Instant Pot properly.
4. Select *Steam* setting on the Instant Pot and cook the asparagus for 4 minutes.
5. Once it is done; naturally release the Instant Pot and open the lid
6. Take the aluminum pan out of the Instant Pot and transfer the cooked asparagus to a serving dish.

Nutrition Facts:
Calories: 265; Net Carbs: 2.6g; Total Fat: 26.6g; Protein: 4.6g; Carbs: 4g;

Green Beans Stir Fry

*(**Prep + Cooking Time:** 9 minutes | **Serves:** 4)*

Ingredients:
- 1/2 lb. chopped' green beans
- 3/4 tablespoon olive oil
- 2 teaspoons minced' garlic
- 1 teaspoon fish sauce
- 1/4 teaspoon salt

Directions:
1. Pour water into the Instant Pot then place a trivet in it.
2. Put the chopped' green beans on the trivet then cover and seal the Instant Pot properly
3. Select *Manual* setting on the Instant Pot and cook the green beans on low for 2 minutes.
4. Once it is done; quick release the Instant Pot and open the lid

5. Remove the cooked green beans from the Instant Pot and transfer to a plate. Wipe and clean the Instant Pot.
6. Pour olive oil into the Instant Pot and select *Sauté* setting. Stir in minced' garlic then sauté until lightly golden brown and aromatic
7. Add green beans to the Instant Pot and season with salt and fish sauce
8. Stir well and press the *Cancel* button. Transfer the cooked green beans to a serving dish then serve.

Nutrition Facts:
Calories: 85; Net Carbs: 5.2g; Total Fat: 5.4g; Protein: 2.4g; Carbs: 9.1g;

Quinoa Burrito Bowls Recipe

(Prep + Cooking Time: 25 minutes | Serves: 4)

Ingredients:
- 1/2 diced red onion
- 1 ½ cup cooked black beans
- 1 diced bell pepper
- 1 teaspoon extra-virgin olive oil
- 1 teaspoon ground cumin
- 1 cup water
- 1 cup quinoa
- 1 cup salsa
- 1/2 teaspoon Salt

Directions:
1. Heat the olive oil in the Mini Instant Pot. Turn on the Sauté function. Start to sauté the peppers and onions until they soften properly.
2. It will take about 5-8 minutes for the entire process. Add the salt and cumin and sauté for about a minute until you smell beautiful flavors.
3. You should turn off the Mini Instant Pot for a moment, then; start adding the salsa, water; and quinoa along with the beans and seal the lid in a secured manner. Switch on the Sealing function.
4. Cook everything at low pressure for about 12 minutes. The pressure should release naturally once the cooking is done.
5. By the end of cooking time, the quinoa should absorb every bit of the liquid. It will take about 10-15 minutes.
6. Remove the lid now and be careful about the hot steam. Fluff the quinoa with a fork.
7. Serve the dish warm with your favorite toppings. You can also add some shredded lettuce in case you love some additional veggies.

Nutrition Facts:
Calories: 163, Fat: 7g, Carbs: 50g, Protein: 13g

Quick Peas Risotto

(Prep + Cooking Time: 20 minutes | Serves: 2)

Ingredients:
- 1 cup baby green peas
- 2 celery sticks; make small cubes
- 2 cups vegetable stock
- 1 cup Arborio rice
- 2 cloves garlic; diced
- 3 tablespoons olive oil
- 1 brown onion; diced
- 2 tablespoons lemon juice
- 1/2 teaspoon salt
- 1/2 teaspoon pepper

Directions:
1. Take your Instant Pot and place it on a clean kitchen platform. Turn it on after plugging it into a power socket.
2. Put the pot on *Sauté* mode. In the pot; add the oil, celery, onions, pepper and salt; cook for 4-5 minutes until the ingredients become soft.
3. Mix in the zest, stock, garlic, peas and rice. Stir the ingredients. Close the lid and lock. Ensure that you have sealed the valve to avoid leakage.
4. Press *Manual* mode and set timer for 5 minutes. It will take a few minutes for the pot to build inside pressure and start cooking.
5. After the timer reads zero, press *Cancel* and quick release pressure. Carefully remove the lid, add the lemon juice and serve warm!

Nutrition Facts: Calories: 362; Fat: 13g; Carbohydrates: 52.5g; Fiber: 3g; Protein 8g

Mushroom Soup Recipe

(Prep + Cooking Time: 25 minutes | Serves: 4)

Ingredients:
- 1 cup fresh Baby Bella mushrooms; chopped
- 2 teaspoons olive oil
- 1 tablespoon garlic; minced
- 1 teaspoon dried thyme; crushed
- 2 cups cauliflower; chopped
- 4 cups homemade vegetable broth
- 1 yellow onion; chopped
- Salt and Pepper to taste

Directions:
1. Add oil to Instant Pot and press "Sauté" button (*Normal* preset), wait till you see Hot on the display. Add onion and garlic and cook for about 2 to 3 minutes.
2. Add mushrooms and cook for 4 to 5 more minutes. Press *Cancel* and mix in cauliflower and broth. Season with salt, pepper and thyme.
3. Close the lid and turn the vent to *Sealed*.
4. Press *Pressure Cook* (Manual) button, use *+* or *-* button to set the timer for 5 minutes. Use *Pressure level* button to set Pressure to *HIGH*.
5. Once the timer is up; press *Cancel* button and allow the pressure to be released naturally; until the float valve drops down.
6. Open the lid.
7. Puree the soup with an immerse blender.

Nutrition Facts: Calories: 86 g; Total Fat: 12.2 g; Total Carbohydrate: 7.5 g; Protein: 4.1

butternut Squash and Mushroom Meal

(Prep + Cooking Time: 23 minutes | Serves: 2)

Ingredients:
- 1-pound butternut squash; cubed
- 1 cup mushroom
- 1/2 cup almond slivers; toasted
- 1/4 cup minced white onion
- 1-pound beans; sliced into 2-inch long slivers
- 1/8 cup minced chives
- 1 tablespoon olive oil
- 1 cup vegetable broth; unsalted
- A pinch of white pepper
- 1/4 teaspoon kosher salt

Directions:
1. Place your Instant Pot on a flat kitchen surface', plug it and turn it on.
2. To start making the recipe, press *Sauté* button. Add the oil and onions; cook for 4 minutes to soften the ingredients.
3. One by one add the mentioned ingredients in the pot (do not add the almonds, chives and beans). Carefully close its lid and firmly lock it. Then after, seal the valve too.
4. To start making the recipe, press *Manual* button. Now you have to set cooking time', set the timer for 10 minutes. Allow the pot to cook the mixture until the timer goes off.
5. Turn off the pot and press *Cancel.* Allow the built up pressure to vent out naturally', it will take 8-10 minutes to completely release inside pressure.
6. Open its lid and add in the beans. Close lid and warm for 2 minutes to warm the beans. Adjust seasoning if needed. Top with almond slivers and chives; serve warm!

Nutrition Facts:
Calories 406; Fat: 17g; Carbohydrates: 43g; Fiber: 18.3g; Protein 28g

Garbanzo Beans and Potato

(Prep + Cooking Time: 15 minutes | Serves: 3)

Ingredients:
- 1 cup garbanzo beans; cooked
- 2 potatoes; peeled & cubed
- 1 cup diced tomatoes
- 1/2 tablespoon whole cumin seeds
- 1 teaspoon turmeric
- 1 large onion; chopped
- 1/4 teaspoon ginger
- 1 teaspoon coriander
- 1/2 teaspoon salt

Directions:
1. Place your Instant Pot on a flat kitchen surface', plug it and turn it on.
2. To start making the recipe, press *Sauté* button. Add the 1/2 cup of water, cumin seeds and onions; cook for 2-3 minutes to soften the ingredients.
3. Add the potatoes, turmeric, tomatoes, ginger, coriander, bean, salt and 1/4 cup water. Carefully close its lid and firmly lock it. Then after, seal the valve too.
4. To start making the recipe, press *Manual* button. Now you have to set cooking time', set the timer for 5 minutes. Allow the pot to cook the mixture until the timer goes off.
5. Turn off the pot and press *Cancel.* Allow the built up pressure to vent out naturally', it will take 8-10 minutes to completely release inside pressure.
6. Open its lid and transfer the cooked mixture into serving container/containers. Serve the potatoes with your favorite bread or rice.

Nutrition Facts:
Calories: 236; Fat: 2g; Carbohydrates: 42g; Fiber: 7.2g; Protein 7g

Glazed Cinnamon Honey Carrots

(Prep + Cooking Time: 4 minutes | Serves: 4)

Ingredients:
- 1/4 lb. carrots
- 1/2 tablespoon butter
- 1 tablespoon honey
- 1/4 cup vegetable broth
- 1/2 teaspoon cinnamon
- 1/4 teaspoon salt

Directions:
1. Pell the carrots then set aside. Pour vegetable broth into the Instant Pot then place a trivet in it. Rub the carrots with salt then put on the trivet
2. Cover the Instant Pot with the lid and seal it properly. Select *Manual* setting on the Instant Pot and cook the carrots for 2 minutes.
3. Once it is done; naturally release the Instant Pot then open the lid
4. Take the cooked carrots out of the Instant Pot then place on a plate. Clean and wipe the Instant Pot then put butter in it
5. Return the carrots back to the Instant Pot then drizzle honey and sprinkle cinnamon on top
6. Select *Sauté* setting and cook the carrots for 1 minute. Stir well. Transfer the carrots to a serving dish then serve

Nutrition Facts:
Calories: 50; Net Carbs: 6.2g; Total Fat: 0.4g; Protein: 3.9g; Carbs: 10.5g;

Spinach and Fusilli Pasta

(Prep + Cooking Time: 20 minutes | Serves: 3)

Ingredients:
- 1-pound spinach
- 1-pound fusilli pasta
- 2 garlic cloves; crushed
- 1/4 cup pine nuts; chopped
- A drizzle of olive oil
- Black pepper and salt to taste

Directions:
1. Take your Instant Pot and place it on a clean kitchen platform. Turn it on after plugging it into a power socket.
2. Put the pot on *Sauté* mode. In the pot; add the oil, garlic and spinach; cook for 6-7 minutes until the ingredients become soft.
3. Add the pasta, salt and pepper; add water to cover the pasta. Close the lid and lock. Ensure that you have sealed the valve to avoid leakage.
4. Press *Manual* mode and set timer for 6 minutes. It will take a few minutes for the pot to build inside pressure and start cooking.
5. After the timer reads zero, press *Cancel* and quick release pressure. Carefully remove the lid; mix the chopped garlic and pine nuts. Serve warm!

Nutrition Facts:
Calories: 198; Fat: 1g; Carbohydrates: 6.5g; Fiber: 1g; Protein 7g

Mushroom Risotto

(Prep + Cooking Time: 20 minutes | Serves: 4)

Ingredients:
- 1 tablespoon olive oil
- 2 cups vegetable broth
- 1/2 onion; diced
- 2 garlic cloves; minced
- 3 ½-ounce button mushrooms; sliced
- 1 cup risotto rice
- 1/2 tablespoon white wine
- parmesan cheese; grated, for serving
- Salt and Pepper to taste

Directions:
1. Add oil to Instant Pot and press "Sauté" button (*Normal* preset), wait till you see Hot on the display.
2. Add garlic and onion. Sauté for 1 to 2 minutes. Add mushrooms and cook for 3-4 more minutes. Press *Cancel* button.
3. Add rice, broth and white wine, salt and pepper. Close the lid and turn the vent to "Sealed".
4. Press *Pressure Cook* (Manual) button, use *+* or *-* button to set the timer for 6 minutes. Use *Pressure level* button to set Pressure to *HIGH*.
5. Once the timer is up; press *Cancel* button and turn the steam release handle to "Venting" position for quick release, until the float valve drops down.
6. Open the lid; serve topped with parmesan.

Nutrition Facts:
Calories: 428 g; Total Fat: 8.6 g; Total Carbohydrate: 20.2 g; Protein: 12.9

Buttery Green Beans Recipe

(Prep + Cooking Time: 15 minutes | Serves: 4)

Ingredients:
- 1-pound. fresh green beans
- 2 tablespoons butter
- 1 garlic clove; minced
- 2 cups water
- Salt to taste

Directions:
1. Add water, beans, garlic and salt to the Instant pot. Close the lid and turn the vent to *Sealed*.
2. Press *Pressure Cook* (Manual) button, use *+* or *-* button to set the timer for 5 minutes. Use *Pressure level* button to set pressure to low.
3. Once the timer is up; press *Cancel* button and turn the steam release handle to *Venting* position for quick release, until the float valve drops down.
4. Open the lid; Add butter and stir a bit, drain excess liquid and serve.

Nutrition Facts:
Calories: 86 g; Total Fat: 14.7 g; Total Carbohydrate: 6.7 g; Protein: 11.7

Carrots with Dill

(Prep + Cooking Time: 7 minutes | Serves: 4)

Ingredients:
- 1/4 lb. baby carrots
- 1 teaspoon thyme
- 1 teaspoon dill
- 1/4 cup vegetable broth
- 1 tablespoon olive oil

Directions:
1. Peel the carrots then place in a bowl. Drizzle olive oil over the carrots then sprinkle thyme and dill on top.
2. Toss to combine. Pour vegetable broth into the Instant Pot then place a trivet in it
3. Arrange the carrots on the trivet then cover and seal the Instant Pot properly. Select *Manual* setting and cook the carrots on high for 3 minutes
4. Once it is done; naturally release the Instant Pot and open the lid. Transfer the carrots to a serving dish then enjoy

Nutrition Facts: Calories: 30; Net Carbs: 5g; Total Fat: 0.2g; Protein: 0.7g; Carbs: 1.8g;

Cauliflower Florets

(Prep + Cooking Time: 6 minutes | Serves: 4)

Ingredients:
- 1½ cups cauliflower florets
- 1 teaspoon cornstarch
- 2 teaspoons sesame seeds
- 1/2 teaspoon ginger
- 1 teaspoon sesame oil
- 1 teaspoon minced' garlic
- 1/4 cup water
- 2 tablespoons soy sauce

Directions:
1. Combine water with soy sauce, sesame oil, minced' garlic, ginger and cornstarch then stir until incorporated.
2. Place the cauliflower florets in the inner pot of an Instant Pot then drizzle the liquid over the cauliflower florets
3. Cover the Instant Pot with the lid and seal it properly. Select *Manual* setting and cook the cauliflower florets on high for 4 minutes
4. Once it is done; naturally release the Instant Pot and open the lid. Transfer the cauliflower florets to a serving dish then sprinkle sesame seeds on top

Nutrition Facts:
Calories: 65; Net Carbs: 5.2g; Total Fat: 3.2g; Protein: 2.9g; Carbs: 7.5g;

Brussels sprouts Tender

(Prep + Cooking Time: 3 minutes | Serves: 4)

Ingredients:
- 1/2 lb. Brussels sprouts
- 1/4 teaspoon pepper
- 1/2 cup water
- 1/4 teaspoon salt

Directions:
1. Cut each Brussels sprouts into half then place in the inner pot of an Instant Pot. Pour water over the Brussels sprouts then cover and seal the Instant Pot properly
2. Select *Manual* setting on the Instant Pot and cook the Brussels sprouts on high for 1 minute.
3. Once it is done; quick release the Instant Pot and open the lid
4. Strain the cooked Brussels sprouts and place on a serving dish. Sprinkle salt and pepper over the Brussels sprouts then toss to combine

Nutrition Facts:
Calories: 50; Net Carbs: 6.2g; Total Fat: 0.4g; Protein: 3.9g; Carbs: 10.5g;

Mushroom and Navy Bean

(Prep + Cooking Time: 40 minutes | Serves: 3)

Ingredients:
- 3 cups mushrooms; chopped
- 1 cup navy beans; dried
- 2 tablespoons onion powder
- 1 tablespoon shallot powder
- 2 tablespoons barley
- 1 tablespoon red curry paste
- 1/2 cup farro
- 9 garlic cloves; minced
- 2 tomatoes; diced
- 1 seeded jalapeno pepper; chopped
- Pepper and salt as needed

Directions:
1. Take your Instant Pot and place it on a clean kitchen platform. Turn it on after plugging it into a power socket.
2. Open the lid from the top and put it aside; start adding the beans, faro, barley, mushrooms, garlic, jalapeno, curry paste, shallot and onion powder, pepper and salt.
3. Add water to cover all the ingredients', gently stir them.
4. Close the lid and lock. Ensure that you have sealed the valve to avoid leakage.
5. Press *Manual* mode and set timer for 30 minutes. It will take a few minutes for the pot to build inside pressure and start cooking.
6. After the timer reads zero, press *Cancel* and naturally release pressure. It takes about 8-10 minutes to naturally release pressure.
7. Carefully remove the lid and add the tomatoes. Sprinkle cilantro and scallions; serve warm!

Nutrition Facts: Calories: 238; Fat: 6.5g; Carbohydrates: 38g; Fiber: 1.5g; Protein 11g

Tuscan Pasta Recipe

(Prep + Cooking Time: 20 minutes | Serves: 3)

Ingredients:
- 8-ounce penne pasta (any other pasta will also work well)
- 1 bell pepper; chopped
- 1 cup fresh spinach; chopped
- 1/2 onion; chopped
- 1 cup broccoli florets
- 2 cups water
- 1/2 cup mozzarella; grated
- 1/2 cup tomato sauce
- 1 tablespoon olive oil
- 3 ½-ounce cremini mushrooms
- 1 tablespoon parmesan cheese; grated
- Salt and Pepper to taste

Directions:
1. Add oil to Instant Pot and press "Sauté" button (*Normal* preset), wait till you see Hot on the display.
2. Add onion, mushrooms and bell pepper, cook for 3-4 minutes until soft.
3. Add pasta, broccoli, spinach, tomato sauce, water, salt and pepper, press *Cancel* button. Close the lid and turn the vent to "Sealed".
4. Press *Pressure Cook* (Manual) button, use *+* or *-* button to set the timer for 5 minutes. Use *Pressure level* button to set pressure to low.
5. Once the timer is up; press *Cancel* button and turn the steam release handle to *Venting* position for quick release, until the float valve drops down.
6. Open the lid.

7. Add mozzarella, stir well until melted. Serve topped with parmesan cheese.

Nutrition Facts: Calories: 322 g; Total Fat: 7.6 g; Total Carbohydrate: 52.29 g; Protein: 13

Spicy Cabbage Wedges

*(**Prep + Cooking Time:** 10 minutes | **Serves:** 4)*

Ingredients:
- 3/4 lb. cabbage
- 1/2 cup water
- 1/2 teaspoon sugar
- 1/4 cup grated carrots
- 1 teaspoon sesame oil
- 1/2 teaspoon cayenne pepper

Directions:
1. Cut the cabbage into wedges then set aside. Pour sesame oil into the inner pot of an Instant Pot then select *Sauté* setting
2. Put the cabbage wedges in the Instant Pot then cook for about 3 minutes until brown on one side. Press the *Cancel* button
3. Sprinkle grated carrots, sugar and cayenne pepper over the cabbage then pour water into the Instant Pot.
4. Cover the Instant Pot with the lid and seal it properly
5. Select *Pressure cook* setting and cook the cabbage on high for 5 minutes
6. Once it is done; naturally release the Instant Pot and open the lid. Transfer the cooked cabbage to a serving dish then serve

Nutrition Facts: Calories: 70; Net Carbs: 7g; Total Fat: 2.5g; Protein: 2.3g; Carbs: 11.6g;

Tomato Eggplant and Cheese Lasagna

*(**Prep + Cooking Time:** 8 minutes | **Serves:** 4)*

Ingredients:
- 1½ cup chopped' eggplant
- 3/4 cup diced' tomatoes
- 1/2 cup grated Mozzarella cheese
- 1/2 teaspoon salt
- 1/4 cup tomato sauce
- 1/4 cup diced' onion
- 1/4 cup white wine
- 1/2 teaspoon garlic powder
- 3/4 teaspoon oregano
- 2 tablespoons chopped' parsley
- 1/4 teaspoon pepper

Directions:
1. Place diced' tomatoes in a bowl then add tomato sauce and onion. Season with garlic powder, oregano, salt and pepper then pour white wine over the tomatoes. Stir until combined.
2. Place half of the eggplant on the bottom of a disposable aluminum pan then put half of the tomato mixture over the eggplant. Spread evenly
3. Layer with the remaining eggplant and tomatoes then sprinkle grated Mozzarella cheese on top.
4. Pour water into an Instant Pot and place a trivet in it. Place the aluminum pan with eggplant on the trivet then cover and seal the Instant Pot properly
5. Select *Steam* setting on the Instant Pot and cook the eggplant lasagna for 3 minutes.
6. Once it is done; naturally release the Instant Pot and open the lid
7. Remove the eggplant lasagna from the Instant Pot and serve warm

Nutrition Facts: Calories: 134; Net Carbs: 6.9g; Total Fat: 6.6g; Protein: 7.9g; Carbs: 11.1g;

Desserts

Tasty Tapioca Pudding

(Prep + Cooking Time: 16 minutes | Serves: 2)

Ingredients:
- 1/2 cup tapioca pearls; rinsed and drained
- 1 tablespoon lemon zest
- 1/2 lemon; sliced (for serving)
- 1/2 teaspoon sweetener Stevia
- 1 ¼ cup milk
- 1 ½ cup water

Directions:
1. Pour 1 cup water into the inner pot of the Instant pot and set a trivet inside.
2. Prepare a baking dish that fits into the Instant pot; mix tapioca pearls, milk, sweetener, remaining water and lemon zest in a baking dish.
3. Mix well until sweetener dissolves. Put the baking dish on the trivet, close the lid and turn the vent to *Sealed*.
4. Press *Pressure Cook* (Manual) button, use *+* or *-* button to set the timer for 6 minutes. Use *Pressure level* button to set Pressure to *HIGH*.
5. Once the timer is up; press *Cancel* button and turn the steam release handle to *Venting* position for quick release, until the float valve drops down.
6. Open the lid; Pour the pudding into 4 to 5 cups and serve with lemon slices.

Nutrition Facts:
Calories: 214 g; Total Fat: 3.2 g; Total Carbohydrate: 41.8 g; Protein: 5.1

Honey Yogurt Panna Cotta

(Prep + Cooking Time: 26 minutes | Serves: 2)

Ingredients:
- 1 cup Basic Yogurt
- 1 teaspoon vanilla
- 1 tablespoon hot water
- 1/4 cup sugar
- Juice of 1 orange with pulp
- 1 teaspoon unflavored gelatin
- 1/4 teaspoon cardamom
- 1/4 cup honey

Directions:
1. Whisk together yogurt, sugar and vanilla.
2. Sprinkle gelatin over water and allow to soften. Whisk together until gelatin dissolves. Whisk gelatin mixture into yogurt mixture.
3. Pour yogurt mixture into two small ramekins or one large ramekin. Chill 2 hours. Meanwhile; make a sauce. Combine honey, orange and cardamom in the Instant Pot.
4. Close lid and set cooking time to 1 minute. Chill completely.
5. When panna cotta is set, run a knife around the inside of the ramekin and invert onto a plate. Top with sauce.

Nutrition Facts:
Calories: 343; Fat: 4.1 g; Carbohydrates: 75.25 g; Fiber: 1.7 g; Protein: 5.08 g

Plain Banana Bread Recipe

(Prep + Cooking Time: 40 minutes | Serves: 4)

Ingredients:
- 2 bananas; mashed
- 3 teaspoons lemon juice or white vinegar
- 3/4 cup sugar
- 1/3 cup butter
- 2 cups flour
- 1/3 cup milk
- 1 egg
- 1 teaspoon baking soda
- 1/2 teaspoon baking powder
- 2 cups water
- a pinch of salt

Directions:
1. Mix milk and lemon juice or white vinegar in a bowl. Mix butter and sugar, add egg and mashed bananas, mix well.
2. Mix flour, baking soda, baking powder and salt in a separate bowl.
3. Add to the ghee mixture, mixing constantly. Slowly add milk mixture.
4. Pour the dough into the greased cake pan, make sure it will fit your Instant pot. Cover the pan with aluminum foil, make sure to create a tight seal.
5. Add water to the Instant pot. Place a trivet into the Instant pot; put the cake pan on the trivet. Close the lid and turn the vent to "Sealed".
6. Press *Pressure Cook* (Manual) button, use *+* or *-* button to set the timer for 30 minutes. Use *Pressure level* button to set Pressure to *HIGH*.
7. Once the timer is up; press *Cancel* button and allow the pressure to be released naturally; until the float valve drops down.
8. Open the lid; Remove the pan and pour off excess moisture if any. Let cool and serve.

Nutrition Facts:
Calories: 267 g; Total Fat: 20.4 g; Total Carbohydrate: 6.6 g; Protein: 13.7

Chocolate Ramekins

(Prep + Cooking Time: 18 minutes | Serves: 2)

Ingredients:
- 2 ounces' semi-sweet chocolate; chopped
- 1/2 tablespoon sugar
- 3 tablespoons all-purpose flour
- 1 egg yolk
- 1 egg
- 1/4 cup butter
- 1/2 cup confectioner's sugar
- 1/2 teaspoon instant coffee
- 1/2 teaspoon vanilla extract
- 1/8 teaspoon salt

Directions:
1. Grease two ramekins and coat them with the sugar.
2. In a mixing bowl, mix the butter and chocolate. Add the confectioners' sugar and combine well.
3. Whisk in the egg yolk, egg, vanilla and coffee. Add the salt and flour; combine again. Divide into the ramekins.
4. Switch on the pot after placing it on a clean and dry platform.
5. Pour 2 cups water into the pot. Arrange the trivet inside it*, arrange the ramekins over the trivet.
6. Close the pot by closing the top lid. Also, ensure to seal the valve. Press *Manual* cooking function and set cooking time to 9 minutes.

7. It will start cooking after a few minutes. Let the pot mix cook under pressure until the timer reads zero.
8. Press *Cancel* cooking function and press *Quick release* setting.
9. Open the instant pot; take out the ramekins and top with some powdered sugar.

Nutrition Facts:
Calories: 561; Fat: 32.5g; Carbohydrates: 58g; Fiber: 2.5g; Protein 7g

Pumpkin Pie

*(**Prep + Cooking Time:** 45 minutes | **Serves:** 3)*

Ingredients:
- 1 can pumpkin
- 1 prepared graham cracker pie crust in aluminum pan
- 1/2 teaspoon nutmeg
- 1/2 cup milk
- 1/2 cup brown sugar
- 1 teaspoon cinnamon
- 1 egg

Directions:
1. Blend together pumpkin, milk, egg, sugar, cinnamon and nutmeg. Pour into prepared graham cracker crust.
2. Place the trivet in the pot and pour in enough water to reach just the top of the trivet.
3. Place the pie over the trivet. Close the lid and set cooking time for 35 minutes on *HIGH* pressure. Chill pie before serving.

Nutrition Facts:
Calories: 413; Fat: 13.85 g; Carbohydrates: 68.5 g; Fiber: 4.8 g; Protein: 6.1 g

Delightful Brownies

*(**Prep + Cooking Time:** 30 minutes | **Serves:** 2)*

Ingredients:
- 2/3 cup flour
- 1 cup sugar
- 2 eggs
- 1 teaspoon vanilla
- 1/3 cup cocoa powder
- 1/2 teaspoon baking powder
- 1/2 cup butter
- 1/2 teaspoon salt

Directions:
1. Cream butter and sugar, then beat in eggs one at a time. Add vanilla last. In a separate bowl, whisk together flour, cocoa, baking powder and salt.
2. Fold dry ingredients into wet ingredients. Pour batter into a baking pan that fits into the Instant Pot.
3. Place a trivet in the Instant Pot. Add enough water to just reach the top of the trivet. Place the baking pan over the trivet.
4. Close the lid and set the cooking time to 20 minutes. Serve brownies warm or room temperature.

Nutrition Facts:
Calories: 524; Fat: 26.25 g; Carbohydrates: 70.72 g; Fiber: 2.7 g; Protein: 6.45 g

Pumpkin Cake

***(Prep + Cooking Time:** 45 minutes | **Serves:** 4)*

Ingredients:
- 2 cups pumpkin puree
- 2 tablespoon pumpkin pie spice
- 1/2 cup honey
- 1 cup water
- 3 eggs
- 1/2 cup milk
- a pinch of salt

Directions:
1. Mix puree and eggs in a bowl or in a blender. Add milk, honey, spice and salt.
2. Grease a 6-inch round cake pan with a coconut-oil based spray. Pour in the cake batter and cover tightly with foil. Pour water into your pressure cooker and insert a trivet.
3. Place the cake pan on the trivet, close the lid and turn the vent to *Sealed*. Press *Pressure Cook* (Manual) button, use *+* or *-* button to set the timer for 35 minutes. Use *Pressure level* button to set Pressure to *HIGH*.
4. Once the timer is up; press *Cancel* button and allow the pressure to be released naturally; until the float valve drops down.
5. Open the lid; Let it cool and refrigerate for couple of hours.

Nutrition Facts:
Calories: 237 g; Total Fat: 18.9 g; Total Carbohydrate: 28.9 g; Protein: 15.2

Mix Berry Cheesecake

***(Prep + Cooking Time:** 30 minutes | **Serves:** 4)*

Ingredients:
- 1/2 cup strawberries; chopped
- 1/2 cup blackberries
- 1 teaspoon vanilla extract
- 6 tablespoons sugar
- 2 eggs
- 1 ½ pack 8-ounce cream cheese
- 1 teaspoon butter
- 1 cup water

Directions:
1. Grease your spring form pan with butter. Make sure the pan fits into the Instant Pot.
2. Blend cream cheese until smooth and creamy. Add vanilla extract and sugar, mix well. Add eggs, one at a time, mix until incorporated. Add strawberries and blackberries to the batter and mix well.
3. Pour cheesecake batter into your pan. Cover the pan with a foil tightly, make sure it is covered from all sides.
4. Place a trivet into the Instant pot; pour water into the pot and place the pan on the trivet. Close the lid and turn the vent to *Sealed*.
5. Press *Pressure Cook* (Manual) button, use *+* or *-* button to set the timer for 20 minutes. Use *Pressure level* button to set Pressure to *HIGH*.
6. Once the timer is up; press *Cancel* button and allow the pressure to be released naturally; until the float valve drops down.
7. Open the lid; Take out the cheesecake pan and unwrap. Run a knife around the edges, but don't try to take it out.
8. Cover the pan with a foil or a plastic wrap and refrigerate for an hour. Serve topped with mixed berries.

Nutrition Facts: Calories: 254 g; Total Fat: 23.9 g; Total Carbohydrate: 3.7 g; Protein: 16.7

New Cheese-cake

(Prep + Cooking Time: 35 minutes | Serves: 2)

Ingredients:
- 1 package cream cheese; softened
- 1 prepared graham cracker crust in aluminum pan
- 1/2 cup sour cream
- 2 eggs
- 2/3 cup sugar
- 2 teaspoons vanilla
- 2 tablespoons cornstarch

Directions:
1. Beat together cream cheese, sour cream, eggs, sugar, cornstarch and vanilla. Pour into pie crust.
2. Place a trivet in the Instant Pot. Add enough water to reach the top of the trivet.
3. Place the pie pan on the trivet. Close lid and set cooking time for 25 minutes on *HIGH* pressure. Chill before serving.

Nutrition Facts:
Calories: 523; Fat: 23.78 g; Carbohydrates: 69.89 g; Fiber: 0.9 g; Protein: 7.37 g

Nutty Chocolate Fudge Balls

(Prep + Cooking Time: 10 minutes | Serves: 2)

Ingredients:
- 1 (12-ounce) package chocolate chips; semi-sweet
- 1 (14-ounce) can of condensed milk
- 1/2 cup almonds
- 1 teaspoon vanilla
- 1/2 cup walnuts
- 2 cups water

Directions:
1. Combine the milk and chocolate chips in a medium bowl. Cover it with aluminum foil.
2. Switch on the pot after placing it on a clean and dry platform.
3. Pour the water into the pot. Arrange the trivet inside it*, arrange the bowl over the trivet. Close the pot by closing the top lid. Also, ensure to seal the valve.
4. Press *Manual* cooking function and set cooking time to 5 minutes. It will start cooking after a few minutes. Let the pot mix cook under pressure until the timer reads zero.
5. Press *Cancel* cooking function and press *Quick release* setting.
6. Remove the bowl and mix in the nuts and vanilla. Prepare unformed balls and arrange onto wax paper and allow to cool. Enjoy!

Nutrition Facts:
Calories: 156; Fat: 8g; Carbohydrates: 18g; Fiber: 0.5g; Protein 3.5g

Raisin Apples

(Prep + Cooking Time: 15 minutes | Serves: 2)

Ingredients:
- 2 apples; cored
- 3 tablespoons raisins
- 1/4 cup sugar
- 1/2 teaspoon cinnamon
- 1/4 cup red wine

Directions:
1. Switch on the pot after placing it on a clean and dry platform.
2. Open the pot lid and place the above-mentioned ingredients in the cooking pot area.
3. Give the ingredients a little stir. Close the pot by closing the top lid. Also, ensure to seal the valve.
4. Press *Manual* cooking function and set cooking time to 10 minutes. It will start cooking after a few minutes. Let the pot mix cook under pressure until the timer reads zero.
5. Press *Cancel* cooking function and press *Natural release* setting.
6. It will take 8-10 minutes for natural pressure release. Open the pot and serve warm.

Nutrition Facts:
Calories: 377; Fat: 0g; Carbohydrates: 62g; Fiber: 11.5g; Protein 3.5g

Fruit Bowl

(Prep + Cooking Time: 20 minutes | Serves: 2)

Ingredients:
- 1/4 cup coconut; shredded
- 1/4 cup pecans; chopped
- 3 tablespoons coconut oil
- 1 apple; chopped
- 2 tablespoons granular stevia or sugar
- 1 plum; chopped
- 1 pear; chopped
- 1/2 teaspoon cinnamon
- 1 cup water

Directions:
1. In a bowl (heatproof) of medium size, thoroughly mix the plum, apple, pear, coconut oil, coconut, cinnamon and stevia/sugar.
2. Take your instant pot and place it on a clean kitchen platform. Turn it on after plugging it into a power socket.
3. In the pot; slowly pour the water. Take the trivet and arrange inside it*, place the bowl over it. Close the lid and lock. Ensure that you have sealed the valve to avoid leakage.
4. Press *Manual* mode and set timer for 10 minutes. It will take a few minutes for the pot to build inside pressure and start cooking.
5. After the timer reads zero, press *Cancel* and quick release pressure.
6. Carefully remove the lid; divide into bowls and serve with pecans on top.

Nutrition Facts:
Calories: 150; Fat: 4g; Carbohydrates: 13.5g; Fiber: 4g; Protein 6.5g

Oreo Crust Cheese-cake

(Prep + Cooking Time: 30 minutes | Serves: 3)

Ingredients:
- 1 ½ pack 8-ounce cream cheese
- 3 tablespoons butter (unsalted)
- 1 teaspoon vanilla
- 1 cup water
- 3/4 cup Oreo cookies
- 2 eggs
- 1/3 cup sour cream
- 6 tablespoons sugar

Directions:
1. Grease your springform pan with butter. Make sure the pan fits into the Instant Pot.
2. Preheat the oven to 350 F. Crush Oreo cookies and melt butter.
3. Mix cookies with butter and press the crumbs into the bottom of the springform pan. Bake in the oven for 10 minutes.
4. Blend cream cheese until creamy and smooth. Add sugar and vanilla, then sour cream, mix to combine.
5. Add egg, one at a time, keep mixing to combine. Pour the cheesecake mixture on top of crust. Cover the pan with a foil tightly, make sure it is covered from all sides.
6. Place a trivet into the Instant pot; pour water into the pot and place the pan on the trivet. Close the lid and turn the vent to *Sealed*.
7. Press *Pressure Cook* (Manual) button, use *+* or *-* button to set the timer for 20 minutes. Use *Pressure level* button to set Pressure to *HIGH*.
8. Once the timer is up; press *Cancel* button and allow the pressure to be released naturally; until the float valve drops down.
9. Open the lid; Take out the cheesecake pan and unwrap. Run a knife around the edges, but don't try to take it out.
10. Cover the pan with a foil or a plastic wrap and refrigerate for an hour.

Nutrition Facts: Calories: 677 g; Total Fat: 53 g; Total Carbohydrate: 41.3 g; Protein: 12.1

Wine Pears

(Prep + Cooking Time: 17 minutes | Serves: 2)

Ingredients:
- 1/4 bottle of your choice of red wine
- 1 cinnamon stick
- 1 piece of ginger
- 2 pears; peeled
- 1/2 cup sugar
- 1 clove

Directions:
1. Switch on the pot after placing it on a clean and dry platform.
2. Open the pot lid and place the above-mentioned ingredients in the cooking pot area. Give the ingredients a little stir.
3. Close the pot by closing the top lid. Also, ensure to seal the valve.
4. Press *Manual* cooking function and set cooking time to 6 minutes. It will start cooking after a few minutes. Let the pot mix cook under pressure until the timer reads zero.
5. Press *Cancel* cooking function and press *Quick release* setting. Open the pot and carefully take out the pears, setting them aside.
6. Switch the pot to sauté and let the liquid cook until it reduces by half quantity. Drizzle the hot juice over the pears; serve warm!

Nutrition Facts: Calories: 328; Fat: 3g; Carbohydrates: 38.5g; Fiber: 6g; Protein 2g

Made in the USA
Middletown, DE
03 January 2019